The Communicating Company

Contributions to Management Science

www.springer.com/series/1505

Hartmut Hübner

The Communicating Company

Towards an Alternative Theory of Corporate Communication

With 19 Figures and 18 Tables

Physica-Verlag

A Springer Company

Series Editors

Werner A. Müller
Martina Bihn

Author

Dr. Hartmut Hübner
Eduard-Schmid-Straße 19
81541 München
Germany
h_huebner@web.de

Library of Congress Control Number: 2006939789

ISSN 1431-1941

ISBN 978-3-7908-1928-1 Physica-Verlag Heidelberg New York

Physica-Verlag is part of Springer Science+Business Media

springer.com

© Physica-Verlag Heidelberg 2007

Production: LE-TEX Jelonek, Schmidt & Vöckler GbR, Leipzig
Cover-design: WMX Design GmbH, Heidelberg

SPIN 11948346   134/3100YL - 5 4 3 2 1 0   Printed on acid-free paper

Preface

Corporate communication has developed as a domain of management theory, embracing fields like public relations, marketing and management communication. Most research on the topic has so far concentrated on positivist approaches, leading to a limited view of corporate communication as a set of communication tools and instruments.

It is now common knowledge how communication programs can be effectively planned and executed. The challenge for communication managers, however, remains to explain and deliver proof of how successful their work supported the company's strategy. Extant theory, however, delivers little insight into how corporate communication activities unfold their performative capacity in this sense.

The purpose of this study is to review extant corporate communication theory from strategy-as-practice and discourse perspectives. This makes it possible to expand the existing picture of corporate communication theory by more 'communicational' aspects. The review takes an interdisciplinary approach and particularly draws on social constructionist research in strategic management and organisational communication fields.

Following an ethnographic case study approach, the study is based on an extensive pool of discourse fragments (naturally occurring talk, text and interviews), collected over a period of 15 months. These fragments represent corporate communication discourse at Intech, a major international conglomerate, based in Germany. Data was structured and analysed, supported by ATLAS.ti computer-aided qualitative data analysis software. Additionally, methods of discourse analysis were applied in order to identify and explain concrete communication practices.

An integrative framework – allowing insight into key practices driving the performative capacity of corporate communication – is proposed as a key contribution to and extension of extant corporate communication theory. This framework incorporates seven propositions which are developed on the basis of the key findings.

As part of these, corporate communication is re-defined as a set of participatory and context-sensitive practices. A strong focus is put on the local lens through which corporate communication needs to be managed. It is argued that legitimising processes, involving peer-to-peer communication, should be implemented throughout the company in order to increase the performative capacity of corporate communication. Overall, it is suggested to move in emphasis from communication tools and instruments to managing corporate communication in the form of strategic practices enacted in specific genres.

This book makes the case for an alternative theory of corporate communication. The value of its contribution, however, will emerge and gain in its actual use and refinement. Researchers may adopt the alternative view of corporate communication proposed in the integrative framework and test or apply it in further case studies or in more large-scale, perhaps quantitative research projects across companies or even cultural boundaries. Gradually, this will lead to an increased sophistication of the integrated framework of alternative corporate communication.

Additionally, practitioners can benefit from knowledge about the effects and effectiveness of corporate communication which is created throughout this study. The book explores in detail how individual projects reached relevance at Intech, describing the emergence of intended as well as unintended outcomes. This way, it helps corporate communication managers to reflect on their own strategies. Additionally, the integrative framework can be applied as a strategic tool or grid, for example, when it comes to prioritizing practices and processes that need to be considered when launching a new communication programme. As such, it can be used by managers as a reference point for making decisions in a concrete organizational setting.

Munich,   H. Hübner
October 2006

Acknowledgements

I have a great deal of people to thank for helpful discussions and comments throughout the process of completing my Ph.D.

First of all, I would like to thank my Supervisor Professor Laurie Wood at the University of Salford for stimulating my academic interests and reasoning towards completing this Ph.D. Her comments and help have been very important for my progress. Laurie was always accessible in case there was need for discussion. This way, I was able to come to conclusions and finish my thesis in an efficient way, despite the part-time situation I worked in.

I would also like to thank Professor Richard Varey who was my Supervisor during the initial stages of this project – before he moved from Salford to the University of Waikato, New Zealand. Conversations with Richard were always very stimulating.

Of high importance for the success of this project was all the support which I got from my employer Intech during the last three years. I would like to thank my colleagues who participated directly – e.g. by giving interviews and feedback – or indirectly – e.g. by allowing me access to information which I would otherwise not have been able to gain. Unfortunately, these people remain anonymous at this point, because I decided to use Intech as a pseudonym in order to ensure confidentiality throughout the research process.

I send very heartfelt thanks to my wife and my daughter – who has grown from a baby to a little princess during the three years of research – along with my parents for support during this demanding time.

You all contributed considerably to this exciting project.

Munich,   H. Hübner
October 2006

Contents

I. Theoretical context

For clarity, the 12 Chapters of this study have been clustered into three Parts, following the logic of Chapters, Sections and Subsections.

Part I clusters Chapters 1 to 5, outlining the theoretical context. Following a general introduction, Chapter 2 defines the purpose of the study, Chapter 3 explains methodological considerations, Chapter 4 decides on a framework which is used as a reference point, and Chapter 5 presents the case on which the study is based.

Part II comprises all Chapters focusing on the analysis of data, and Part III deals with the key findings and conclusions.

1 Introduction

In striving for acceptance as a management discipline, a whole stream of theory and research on corporate communication[1] has been engaged in analysing corporate communication management in various settings. In consequence, corporate communication is now widely recognized as a management function and set of instruments responsible for handling managed communication with internal and external audiences (e.g. Cornelissen 2004).

However, an increasing number of academics have become critical of the dominant positivist research tradition in a broad field of management disciplines, also touching upon issues of managed communication (Rühli 2000; Varey and White 2000; Tsoukas 2001; Easton 2002). They make the point that it is rather fruitless to search for universal, general and timeless principles and instrumental solutions for management challenges. Instead, detailed empirical descriptions of how companies are organized and how they work are demanded (Brunsson and Olsen 1998).

Literature focusing on corporate communication from a management viewpoint is critically examined. This finds a predominantly outmoded concept of communication underlying most recent corporate communication research. A different perspective might be to review corporate communication as organisational discourse to explain and unfold the full performative capacity of corporate communication. This leads to the consideration of corporate communication not as a management instrument in a functional sense, but as an ongoing strategic practice.

The purpose of this research project is to contribute to and make the case for an alternative corporate communication theory following such a discursive and practice-oriented approach. This is advanced through a lon-

---

[1] In literature the term corporate communication can be found with an 's' at the end and without the 's'. In line with Jackson (1987), in this thesis the version without the 's' is used. Jackson (1987) denoted: 'Incidentally, note that it is corporate communication – without a final 's'. Tired of being called on to fix the company switchboard, recommend an answering machine or meet a computer salesman, I long ago adopted this form as being more accurate and left communications to the telecommunications specialists. It's a small point but another attempt to bring clarity out of confusion.'

gitudinal case study of corporate communication discourse at Intech[2], a major multinational conglomerate, based in Germany.

1.1 Corporate communication as a management instrument

Cornelissen, in a recent textbook on corporate communication, summarises that scholars following a management approach to corporate communication are primarily concerned 'with the management processes that professionals engage in to build relationships with stakeholders' (2004, 17). Generally, a focus in corporate communication management theory and research is put on structures, instruments and effective procedures to manage this process (van Riel 1992).

Van Riel proposes a rather typical definition of corporate communication from this viewpoint:

> 'Corporate communication is an instrument of management by means of which all consciously used forms of internal and external communication are harmonised as effectively and efficiently as possible, so as to create a favourable basis for relationships with groups upon which the company is dependent.' (van Riel 1992, 26)

Similar definitions can be found in most recent mainstream management literature on corporate communication (e.g. Jackson 1987; Grunig and Dozier 1992; Dozier, Grunig et al. 1995; Horton 1995; Argenti 1997; Grunig, Grunig et al. 2002; Steyn 2003). Corporate communication, according to this view, embraces a set of instruments which are managed to support relationships the company holds with stakeholders. To apply the communication instruments purposefully, the communication manager is required 'to link the communications strategy to the corporate strategy and to corporate objectives' (Cornelissen 2004, 22). In that, communication is seen as widely focusing on the mediated transmission of information and the reproduction of intended meanings in the application of a specific set of techniques (Hunt and Grunig 1994). A favourable reputation is often considered as the end to which corporate communication works (Davies, Chun et al. 2003).

By focusing heavily on cause-effect argumentations and reducing the role of corporate communication to a means for supporting the achievement of a company's goals, a positivist paradigm (Johnson and Duberley

---

[2] The term 'Innovation Technology' (abbreviated 'Intech') is a pseudonym. The decision to use a pseudonym was made to ensure confidentiality with regards to all information displayed in this thesis.

2000) can be assumed behind most extant corporate communication theories. This research approach is regularly criticized by researchers following alternative paradigms – primarily for leading to 'black box models that provide little in the way of explanation' (Easton 2002, 106). The predominant positivist approach leaves corporate communication research challenged with questions like how corporate communication can work more effectively, or even, how it can concretely increase company performance (van Riel 1997).

1.2 The knowledge gap – corporate communication reviewed

It is argued that the mainstream[3] approach to corporate communication has not yet delivered convincing answers to exactly that kind of questions, i.e. "how"-questions, explaining in depth the management processes and mechanisms configured through communication. It needs an approach to communication which moves beyond viewing communication as merely sending messages and moving information.

This request, as such, is not new. The need to review corporate communication theory has been put forward several times during the last decades until very recently.

Some of these critiques are summarised chronologically.

Drucker (1974) was among the very first who pointed out that communication is not the means of conducting business, but the mode. Communication should not be seen as a relatively peripheral support process, but as a principal constitutive element in the process of organising.

Buttle (1995), in his review of the treatment of marketing communication, which is one aspect of the overall corporate communication frame, in marketing textbooks confirmed that most of these texts are based on the 'container' metaphor (Krippendorf 1994, 86) of communication[4]. These

---

[3] Following the argumentations of Weick (1995), also the term 'orthodox' is used to identify and frame mainstream management literature.

[4] Shannon and Weaver (1949), mathematicians and telephone engineers, had worked on the physical problems of transmitting data through telephone lines, when they developed their model of data transmittance. According to this model, a source produces a piece of information which is received by a recipient. In order to get there it needs to be encoded. Another central element of the model are noise-sources which means that while being transported, there may be unintended elements added to the original information, e.g. interferences in the telephone line. The core challenge, therefore, is to transmit the information as exactly as possible.

theories go back to authors like Schramm (1948) and Shannon and Weaver (1949), viewing communication as a means of transporting information.

Within Buttle's (1995) analysis of 101 marketing communication texts, Schramm alone was cited 27 times explicitly as a theoretical source and foundation. Over 70 texts did not quote any theoretical sources, but made claims similar to the ideas of Schramm or Shannon and Weaver. Buttle concluded that contemporary literature 'has failed to take account of recent advances made in communication theory more generally... What we have is outdated, ill-informed and in need of revision' (1995, 308).

Also Tsoukas criticized the predominance of the container metaphor in the information society and holds it responsible for creating 'paradoxes that prevent it from satisfying the temptations it creates (1997, 827). He concludes, 'what the conduit metaphor ignores is precisely what makes human communication a distinctly *human* activity, namely that the presence of an information item presupposes an act of *human interpretation*' (1997, 830).

Langer's (1999, 76) conclusion from his 'stocktaking' work matches these assessments when he advances that a state of 'wretchedness' prevails in communication research. The same conclusion drew Cheney and Christensen (2001). In working towards an explanation why exactly corporate communication theory does not make use of recent extant communication theory, they state that corporate communication 'grew out of a highly practical context and subsequently developed a theoretical apparatus to support the analysis and legitimisation of its professional practice' (2001, 167). Their argument is that a sort of complacency is inherent in the existing orthodoxy of corporate communication, public relations and marketing communication theory that hinders theory development. In other words, it looks like corporate communication theory is caught in 'a self-absorbed form of auto-communication' (2001, 169).

Another critique of extant corporate communication is related to the thesis that the market is too complex to be responded to with a functional management approach to corporate communication (Christensen, Torp et al. 2005). These authors criticize that mainstream approaches instil 'the desire to control and order the world in order to complete a project' (2005, 157). The approach of integrated marketing communication is mentioned as one example for such control-based concepts. Instead of imposing control through one-way managerial approaches, Christensen, Torp et al. argue, engagement in 'co-construction of communicated meanings' (2005, 165) is necessary to gain shared understanding and collective ownership through communication.

Cheney and Christensen made the point that is the right time for a 're-construction' of corporate communication theory (2001, 175). This study will follow up on this. The researcher proposes that two notions provide particularly fruitful perspectives for such a reconstruction or review of corporate communication in order to advance towards an alternative theory: First, viewing communication, including corporate communication, as *discourse* makes it possible to explain many of the prevalent corporate communication processes at a deeper level than the container model is able to. Second, it is argued that viewing corporate communication as a *strategic practice* rather than a management instrument will make it possible to understand the performative capacity of corporate communication much more fully than the current definition as a support process can provide.

1.2.1 Communication as discourse

In recent years, the field of organisational discourse has emerged as a new way to conceptualize company life (e.g. Grant, Keenoy et al. 1998; Schiffrin, Tannen et al. 2001). Similar to Drucker's (1974) proposal to view communication as a mode of management, these theorists view communication as the core process of organizing.

This notion was first advanced by Karl Weick (1979). Weick's theory of organisation examines the actual behaviours in the dynamic process of organising. He moves the perspective from the entity to processes[5]. Weick sees the company context as the information to which people react, and not the physical surroundings (e.g. buildings and equipment). The view is that of action and process as people perceive messages and create meanings in response. Organisation arises through the interlocked behaviours of company members. In this theory, Weick stresses human interactions, information processing and communication as central activities of organising. Organising becomes the assembling of ongoing interdependent actions into sensible sequences in order to create sensible outcomes. Indeed, Iedema and Wodak (1999, 7) stated that companies do not exist independently of

---

[5] Organisations are viewed as processes throughout this thesis. Therefore, a more specific term to identify a process-defined organisation focusing on the production of goods and provision of services needed to be found. According to Brunsson (1994), from a process viewpoint, there are three basic types of organisations, namely the 'political organisation' (used for governmental organizations), the 'company' ('the most important prototype for organizing the production of goods' (1994:324)), and the 'association' (used for special-interest groups). From the framework of these definitions, the term 'company' was chosen which is applied consistently throughout this thesis, because this term fits best to the character and structure of the Intech case.

their members, but are 'created and recreated in the acts of communication between members.'

Weick's more recent work (1995) has developed the notion of 'sense-making' as the creation of a frame for meaning, which has a cue and a connection. The amount of sensemaking activities increases as processes of change occur (Weick and Quinn 1999). Jones, Watson et al. (2004, 723) made the point that also communication is changing 'both to create and to reflect the new structures, processes, and relationships.'

Most recently, Weick (2004) refers to the contrast between crystal and smoke to explain how communication becomes a core process of organizing:

'Crystal is a perfectly structured material, in its repeated symmetry of pattern, but because its structure is perfect, it never evolves: It is fixed for eternity. It is not life. But it is order. Smoke is just randomness, a chaos of interacting molecules that dissolves as fast as it is produced. It is not life either. But it is dynamic. Life appears when some order emerges in the dynamic of chaos and finds a way to perpetuate itself, so that the orderliness begins to grow, although never to the point of fixity (because that would mean the loss of the essential elasticity that is the ultimate characteristic of life).' (Taylor and Van Every 2000, 31)

According to Weick (2004, 406), organisation emerges through communication 'when portions of smoke-like conversation are preserved in crystal-like texts that are then articulated by agents speaking on behalf of an emerging collectivity. Repetitive cycles of texts, conversations and agents define and modify one another and jointly organize everyday life.'

These cycles of talking and writing and their various representations are generally referred to as 'discourse' (Grant, Hardy et al. 2004, 3)[6]. Even viewed from the above orthodox definition, all products of corporate communication activities come under this definition. However, they are not viewed as containers, means or instruments any more. Instead, corporate communication discourse becomes an instance of the company's social practice (Grant, Hardy et al. 2004), constitutive of social reality (Phillips and Hardy 2002) and, as such, contributes to the 'social becoming' of the company (Sztompka 1991).

---

[6] Whereas communication and discourse are similar terms, an alternative term for discursive is 'communicational' (Taylor, Cooren et al. 1996). Communicational and discursive are used interchangeably throughout this thesis.

1.2.2 Communication as strategic practice

Whereas corporate communication, according to the orthodox theory, was defined as a mere support process, taking this revised perspective, it now gets a much more active, constitutive role in shaping the 'becoming' of the company.

Managing the 'becoming' of the company, e.g. through processes of forming the business policy, planning and leading the company to achieve its goals are generally referred to as part of strategy or strategic management (Mintzberg and Lampel 1999; Müller-Stewens and Lechner 2001). The assumption is that, if corporate communication discourse constitutes the becoming of the company, it also needs to be viewed as a strategic process. In practice, 'this will require that managers recognize the corporate communication managing system as central to the work of the enterprise community' (Varey and White 2000, 6).

Interestingly, there is a strand in strategy research which views strategy as discourse (Barrett, Thomas et al. 1995; Barry and Elmes 1997; Vaara, Kleymann et al. 2004). Banerjee, Browne et al. (2004, 532) go as far as to define strategy as 'a story, or narrative, which attempts to 'write' or account for a whole series of disconnected and emergent elements as though they were a unified whole – but more than one such story is possible. These stories then act as guides to action.'

The orthodox, functionalist view of strategy had assumed that social phenomena have a concrete, solid reality, based on a systemic order (Morgan 1980). The management task was 'to understand the machine-like interactions of variables within this reality, so that one can ultimately control and predict them' (Heracleous 2003, 23).

Experience shows that this theory is flawed in practice, i.e. that members of a company act not always in the way they are supposed to. In response, an activity-based, practice-oriented approach to strategy has emerged focusing 'on the detailed processes and practices which constitute the day-to-day activities of organisational life and which relate to strategic outcomes' (Johnson, Melin et al. 2003).

Practices, according to de Certeau (1984, ix) are defined as 'ways of operating or doing things'. In the context of a company, practices are 'established procedures that actors carry with them from the previous experience of their community and apply to the exigencies of particular situations' (Whittington 2002, 129). This moves the focus to practitioners and leads Jarzabkowski (2004, 529) to the conclusion that strategy should be studied 'not as something a firm has, but something a firm does'.

This process of doing, again, has been identified as highly socially constructed in practices, 'those traditions, norms, rules, and routines through which the work of strategy is constructed' (Jarzabkowski 2004, 545). There is an increasing body of research analysing the role of discourse in this process (e.g. Barry and Elmes 1997; Heracleous and Barrett 2001). This literature points to the importance of context and the role of discourse in forming strategic practices. Sztompka (1991, 96), for example, highlighted the critical importance of discourse and interaction upon 'what people are doing'.

Viewing corporate communication as strategic practice in the sense of Jarzabkowski (2004), also, draws attention to another important aspect of communication as part of the management system: corporate communication does not obviously or does not automatically support strategy by sending out messages in containers. Instead, the mere distribution of information can both facilitate or constrain the intention to transform strategy into action. Therefore, simply 'communicating more', as the orthodox model would have suggested, is obviously not the solution (Tsoukas 1997).

2 Purpose of the study

Having broadly outlined the field of study, Chapter 2 provides a more in-depth analysis of literature. This includes a review of theory and research covering extant concepts of corporate communication, discourse and strategic practices.

2.1 Extant corporate communication theories

Kirchner (2001) and, more recently, Cornelissen (2004) provided analyses and stocktaking with regards to the management strand of theory and research on corporate communication. According to Cornelissen (2004, 17-18), in this strand of research a double focus is put on corporate communication, i.e. it is viewed both as the execution of communication activities and as the set of analysis, planning, execution and evaluation processes associated with these activities. In summary, it is common for all these theories to view corporate communication as a management instrument from a functional perspective.

Five theories were selected as a basis for the literature review in this study. The first is Grunig and Hunt's (1984) concept of communication management. This concept has continuously been refined throughout the last two decades (Grunig and Dozier 1992; Hunt and Grunig 1994; Dozier, Grunig et al. 1995; Grunig, Grunig et al. 2002), with an ongoing focus on public relations within the overall corporate communication framework. The second is Argenti's theory of corporate communication. This was selected, because it is one of the most frequently quoted works on corporate communication and ranks amongst the theories most prominently defending 'the notion of [corporate communication] as a functional area of management equal in importance to finance, marketing, and production' (Argenti 2003, vi). These two theories represent the American view of corporate communication.

The other three theories selected have their origins in European scholarship and are more frequently quoted in the context of European research, namely van Riel's (1992) principles of corporate communication, Bruhn's

(2003) notion of integrated corporate communication and Cornelissen's (2004) strategic management perspective of corporate communication.

The major notions and themes prevailing in these five works are summarised in the following subsections. This produces an overview table, summarising and displaying the core themes dominating the orthodox view of corporate communication management.

2.1.1 Grunig's concept of communication management

Grunig's basic notion was presented in 1984 as a theory of public relations management. This theory was continuously refined in several empirical studies and textbooks (Grunig and Dozier 1992; Hunt and Grunig 1994; Dozier, Grunig et al. 1995; Grunig, Grunig et al. 2002), resulting in a broad definition of public relations as communication management: 'Public relations / communication management is broader than communication technique and broader than specialized public relations programs such as media relations or publicity. Public relations and communication management describe the overall planning, execution, and evaluation of an organization's communication[7] with both external and internal publics – groups that affect the ability of an organization to meet its goals' (Grunig 1992, 4-5). Corporate communication, according to this definition follows the purpose of mediating between top management, in Grunig's terms the 'dominant coalition', and external as well as internal publics. In this process, all publics should be treated equally, but it is assumed that there are differences of opinion between company and audiences.

The refinements of Grunig's original model follow the maxim of 'excellence'. Grunig, Grunig et al. (2002, 11) conclude that 'for public relations to be excellent, public relations must be viewed as symmetrical, idealistic and critical, and managerial.' 'Symmetrical' means that corporate communication managers serve the interests of both parties – company and audiences – 'while still advocating the interests of the organizations that employ them' (2002, 11). 'Idealistic and critical' refers to the demand that corporate communication managers should be granted the right to propose opinions of the audiences to management in a critical manner. The 'managerial' aspect refers to the role of corporate communication as the manager

---

[7] Two ways of spelling the term of organisation are used throughout this thesis: (1) the British English spelling with an 's' which was preferred by the researcher, and (2) the American English spelling with a 'z' which was kept in quotations when also used in the original text.

of relationships in the negotiation process between company and audiences.

This generic model of communication, according to Grunig, Grunig et al. should be applied to both internal and external communication in order to have 'value both to organizations and to society' (2002, 11).

2.1.2 Argenti's functional definition of corporate communication

Argenti's (2003, x) model has also developed over an extended period of time. He advances, however, that corporate communication only recently can be ranked among 'the newest and most important' management functions, due to developments like the internet and the increased speed of information, growing scepticism of the public towards company intentions, 'glossy' packaging of information and the general increase in complexity of the company.

In a changing business environment, Argenti argues, it is crucial for a company to communicate 'strategically' (2003, 21). The understanding of communication theory which underlies this notion, again, follows a container approach. The loop described by Argenti (2003, 22) is the following: 'Communication through *messages* ... To its *constituencies* ... Who then *respond* to ... The *organization* ...' A communication strategy is developed in a step-by-step process, starting with analysing the company strategy and deriving communication objectives, resources and existing reputation. In a next step, constituencies are analyzed, including their attitude towards and knowledge about the company. Deciding 'how' (i.e. through which channel) and by 'what approach' the messages are 'delivered' are the next steps in the strategy development process (2003, 31). After having delivered the message, a process of measuring constituency responses follows in order to measure success.

The channels available to corporate communication for delivering these messages, in Argenti's (2003) terms, are corporate advertising, media relations, internal communication, investor relations, government relations and crisis communication. Key to all message-delivery through these channels is the concept of identity which Argenti (2003, 58) defines as 'the visual manifestation of the company's reality as conveyed through the organization's name, logo, motto, products, services, buildings, stationery, uniforms, and all other tangible pieces of evidence *created by the organization* and communicated to a variety of constituencies.' This visual identity conveys an image of the company which the target groups hold. If identity and image are aligned, it is argued, this is the foundation of a solid reputation. '*Reputation* differs from *image* because it is built up over time and is not simply a perception at a given point in time. It differs from *identity* because it is a product of both internal and external constituencies, whereas identity is constructed by internal constituencies (the company itself)' (2003, 71). To create a strong reputation is viewed as an overarching aim for corporate communication, the value of which, in the end, is also measured like an intangible asset (Lev 2001).

Strategic communication, according to Argenti, Howell et al. (2005, 83), is defined as 'communication aligned with the company's overall strategy, to enhance its strategic positioning'. Top management involvement, clarity and consistency of messages which are elements of the overall strategy, the selection of suitable and integrated channels and a long-term orientation of communication activities are seen as key components of this alignment process.

2.1.3 Van Riel's principles of corporate communication

Similar to Argenti, van Riel (1992) holds a functional view of corporate communication. 'Communication is increasingly gaining the status of a valuable, if not indispensable management tool, together with the obligations that such a status carries' (1992, 1).

While Argenti puts a strong focus on the strategic planning process, van Riel (1992) approached the corporate communication function from what he called 'basic forms of communication', i.e. management communication, marketing communication and organisational communication, which are encompassed by corporate communication.

Among these three forms, management communication – communication between managers and the company's target groups – takes up a key role, because management communication is necessary 'not only to transmit authority, but also to achieve cooperation' (1992). In this model, developing a common vision, creating an atmosphere of trust, accompanying change processes and motivating employees become core internal tasks of corporate communication, while externally selling the vision to target groups is a key function.

Marketing communication is viewed as comprising communication activities which 'support sales of particular goods and services' (1992, 10-11). Most of these activities are persuasive in character, stressing product benefits in order to 'create favourable impressions.' According to van Riel, also the major proportions of overall communication budgets are spent in this domain.

The term 'organisational communication' was used by van Riel in order to collect all other forms of managed communication, i.e. 'public relations, public affairs, investor relations, labour market communication, corporate advertising, environmental communication and internal communication' (1992, 12).

In order to align all three domains, van Riel (1992, 19) proposes to develop 'common starting points', derived from the company's strategy. Similar to Argenti, van Riel views image and identity as core concepts, whereas he does not refer to reputation. Also, he views identity more comprehensively than Argenti. Van Riel (1992, 28) defines identity as going beyond the visual world, indicating 'the way in which a company presents itself by the use of symbols, communication and behaviour.'

2.1.4 Bruhn's concept of integrated corporate communication

Also arguing from a functional perspective, Bruhn (2003) acknowledges the notion that most corporate communication theories argue for an integrated view of various communication activities. He criticises, however, a lack of focus on how to structure corporate communication work in a concrete way.

Bruhn (2003) defines integrated corporate communication as a planning and organisation process which follows the aim of creating a single unit out of various differentiated sources of internal and external communication provided by a company. Only this way, he argues, is it possible to create a consistent appearance of the company towards all target groups.

Integration, in Bruhn's (2003) model, affects the use of all communication instruments, and contains three aspects: (1) content, (2) formal aspects, and (3) timing. The integration of content means an alignment of the messages and issues used in all means of communication towards concrete key objectives of corporate communication. Even if different target groups are approached, the instruments need to follow a consistent set of rules. Bruhn argues for formal integration of communication – a far-reaching standardization of all design rules applied to the various communication instruments, i.e. of corporate design, logos, slogans, and so on. An alignment of timings is viewed as necessary in order to ensure that all communication activities support each other.

All these alignments need to be laid down in a strategy document, which includes properly formulated and written aims, target groups and core instruments, as well as the rules that apply for these instruments.

Bruhn's (2003) model draws on aspects of both traditional business administration and orthodox management theories, resulting in concrete instructions for communication managers.

2.1.5 Cornelissen's approach to the organisation of corporate communication

Cornelissen (2004) advanced an approach to corporate communication following a functional management theory. His definition of corporate communication:

'Corporate communications is a management function that offers a framework and vocabulary for the effective coordination of all means of communications with the overall purpose of establishing and maintaining favourable reputations with stakeholder groups upon which the organization is dependent.' (Cornelissen 2004, 23).

While this definition summarises many of the elements presented in earlier definitions and theories, and, broadly speaking reinforces the functional view of corporate communication, it newly launches the notion of 'stakeholders'. Cornelissen (2004, 24) explains this as 'a shift towards a more inclusive view in which the organization recognizes a larger number of groups upon which it is dependent (and that literally hold a 'stake' in the organization).' The stakeholder concept, for the first time in an approach to corporate communication management, launches the notion that there is a kind of mutual dependency between company and stakeholders, and 'in particular the need for an organization to be found legitimate by all [stakeholders]' (Cornelissen 2004, 67).

Also with regards to the issues of identity and reputation, Cornelissen points to the relevance of social construction. Corporate and organisational identity is seen as closely related together, as 'two sides of a coin' (2004, 71): the former is concerned with differentiating the company in the interaction with stakeholders, whereas the latter is based on processes of meaning-creation and sense-making in the company itself. A company's reputation, according to Cornelissen, is based on three key elements (2004, 83-84): (1) it is a perceptual construct, i.e. it refers to what different stakeholders perceive of the company, (2) it is formed by several stakeholder groups, resulting in the existence of more than one reputation of a company, and (3) it includes an evaluation by the stakeholders so that it can differ from what the company projected as its corporate identity.

Cornelissen (2004) concludes that, in order to gain such a status of legitimisation, the company should actively project its identity to all stakeholder groups. According to Cornelissen, corporate communication provides the right instruments to fulfil this aspect of stakeholder management. In recognizing that corporate communication, from this stakeholder perspective, gets involved in processes of identity formation, Cornelissen (2004, 71), therefore, proposes that the concepts of corporate identity – how the company presents itself – and organisational identity – how company members perceive the company – should be viewed together. His conclusion is that organisational identity needs to be analysed first, before elements of the corporate identity can be defined.

Another area of Cornelissen's work focuses on the organisation of communication functions (Cornelissen and Lock 2000; Cornelissen 2001; Cornelissen, Lock et al. 2001; Cornelissen and Thorpe 2001; Cornelissen 2003). One of the critical issues raised in this work is that management fashions like integrated marketing communication have made their arrival in the debate of corporate communication and the notion of aligning and coordinating all communication activities have gradually become shared currency – although the increased managerial endorsement of integrated marketing communication does not reflect the actual implementation of the idea in practice. Instead of automatically following one of the management fashions, Cornelissen (2004, 152) proposes to aim for 'consolidated departments placed at a high location in the organization's hierarchy'.

Cornelissen (2004, 178-181) concludes that there are three challenges that corporate communication theory and practice face: (1) the strategy-related challenge is that corporate communication should get closely linked to a company's overall objectives in order to make its contribution measurable; (2) in terms of organisational structure, the challenge is to make corporate communication visible as a function in its own right; and (3) the people-related challenge is to heave more corporate communication practitioners into a manager role.

The summary of extant corporate communication theories gained so far, does not claim completeness in terms of covering every detailed aspect of all corporate communication theories available. It is claimed, however, that this stocktaking is a sufficient basis for defining the need for an explicitly discourse and strategy-related turn in corporate communication theory.

Table 1 provides a summary of this stocktaking of extant corporate communication theories. The picture gained reveals a high degree of consistency among the themes covered across the corporate communication theories which were analysed.

Table 1. Overview of prevailing themes in corporate communication theories

Themes	Grunig (1984-2002)	Argenti (2003)	Van Riel (1992)	Bruhn (2003)	Cornelissen (2004)
Concept of communica- tion man- agement	Four models of public relations/ communica- tion; twoway symmetrical model nor- mative	Corporate communica- tion as func- tional area of management	Corporate communica- tion as a valuable management tool	Corporate communica- tion as a planning and organisation process to in- tegrate vari- ous commu- nication activities	Corporate communica- tion as managerial framework for managing communica- tion activi- ties, as well as a set of techniques
Audiences	External and internal publics	Constituen- cies	Internal and external tar- get groups	Internal and external tar- get groups	Stakeholders
Corporate identity	n/a	Identity (vis- ual), image (held by con- stituencies) and reputa- tion (intang- ible asset) as the funda- mental func- tion of corporate communi- cation	Self- portrayal of the company conveyed through be- haviour, communica- tion and symbolism	Identity cre- ated through consistent appearance of the com- pany in all communica- tion channels	Corporate and organ- isational identity seen as con- structed and closely related to each other
Reputation	n/a		Reputation as an intan- gible asset		Perceptual construct involving stakeholders
Internal communica- tion	Symmetrical model to be applied	Connected with senior management and strategy	Motivating employees, creating trust	n/a	Company members as internal stakeholders
Communica- tion function	Manager / technician dichotomy Concept of integrated communica- tion	Middle ground between centralized and decentralised structure; reporting line to CEO	Embraces marketing communica- tion, organ- isational communica- tion and management communica- tion	Integration of corporate communica- tion activi- ties in terms of content, formal as- pects and timing	Alignment through suitable management processes rather than integration in organisa- tional structures

First of all, corporate communication in all five theories is seen as a management function, applying a certain set of communication instruments, mainly focusing on the areas of management communication, marketing communication, public relations and other forms of organisational communication. Following this functional definition, all five models implicitly, or explicitly, like in the case of Argenti (2003), based their theory on a container theory of communication, i.e. corporate communication was assigned the purpose of transporting information from the company to diverse target groups and back, mostly in the form of a mediator between the company and its audiences. Terms like target groups, constituencies or publics that were used in four of the five theories to identify these audiences point to the fact that these audiences were designated as recipients rather than active participants. Only recently, Cornelissen (2004) introduced the concept of stakeholders to corporate communication theory, granting audiences a more active role in the game. Even Cornelissen's overall approach to corporate communication, however, focused on a functional conception of corporate communication.

Identity and reputation were mostly mentioned directly as key concepts within the respective corporate communication theories. Identity was equated with corporate identity, i.e. a visual or verbal identity that is created by the company, manifested in various corporate communication tools. If this identity matches the image held by the target groups, a strong reputation in the sense of an intangible asset emerges.

Three of the five theories also referred to internal communication as a key part of corporate communication. This focus, however, was seen as closely connected to management communication, i.e. internal corporate communication was widely seen as transferring information from management to employees and back, in the hope that by facilitating this process employees get motivated and trust is created.

In all theories, a lot of space was conceded to explaining the need for an integrated approach to corporate communication, generally leading to a discussion of organisational structures, or even – as the example of Bruhn (2003) showed – to proposals for aligning the organisation as well as all corporate communication activities.

In the following Sections the argument will be concluded that a review of corporate communication from the perspectives of discourse and strategic practices can provide a deeper insight into what is happening in the business reality of corporate communication, and, therefore, is a sound approach to advance the theory of corporate communication.

2.2 Implications of the discourse perspective

It has been argued that the field of organisational discourse[8] has become a widely accepted concept to study companies. Karl Weick (1979) was quoted as one of the ancestral theorists.

The original notions of this 'linguistic turn' in social sciences reach even further back to Wittgenstein (1967) and Winch (1958). These early theories were also informed by social constructionist sociology (see e.g. Berger and Luckmann 1966; Gergen 1994; Parker 1998; Gergen 2001) which will be summarised in some more detail in Chapter 3 which covers methodological issues. As Grant, Keenoy et al. (2001) stated, also social theorists like Foucault, Courtine, Gramsci and Habermas were informed by this approach.

2.2.1 Constitutive capacity of communication

According to the discursive paradigm, communication is viewed as '*constitutive* of social reality' (Phillips and Hardy 2002, 12) and 'central to the social construction of reality' (Grant, Keenoy et al. 2001, 7). Other authors used the term 'performative' instead of constitutive (Watson 1997, 215; Feldman 2000). All these terms express that communication takes an active stance in management processes, rather than purely supporting management processes. In other words, the attention shifts from the motto 'who works produces' to the motto 'who works communicates' (Baecker 2003, 18).

This view of communication goes further than the application of the container metaphor utilized in orthodox corporate communication theory. Corporate communication, then, is not viewed as a means for transporting information from one place to another, but it is viewed as a process in which the company itself is constructed. Indeed, the company then can be defined as 'a social collective, produced, reproduced and transformed through the ongoing, interdependent, and goal-oriented communication practices of its members' (Mumby and Clair 1997, 181). This does not mean that companies only exist in discourse, but communication, as Weick

---

[8] According to Grant, Hardy et al. (2004:3) organisational discourse refers to 'practices of talking and writing ... that bring organizationally related objects into being as these texts are produced, disseminated and consumed'. Based on the above analysis of existing corporate communication theory, it is assumed that corporate communication practices significantly contribute to this organizational discourse.

(1995) had argued, is the major means by which members of a company make sense of the company and themselves.

Corporate communication, through members of the corporate communication department and through the content and symbols communicated in communication tools, actively participates in this organisational discourse. In Boden's (1994, 8) words, 'it is through the telephone calls, meetings, planning sessions, sales talks, and corridor conversations that people inform, amuse, update, gossip, review, reassess, reason, instruct, revise, argue, debate, contest, and actually *constitute* the moments, myths and, through time, the very *structuring* of the organization.'

This leads right to the core purpose of this study. Throughout this study the notion is advanced that corporate communication is constitutive of a company's structure and reality, and that, therefore, it is through corporate communication discourse that the constitutive capacity of corporate communication can best be understood.

While Mumby and Clair (1997) list a variety of specific communication problems which have been analysed this way, ironically corporate communication discourse itself has not yet been submitted to such a procedure. Insofar, approaching corporate communication on this route involves a lot of exploration, and the task clearly becomes one of gaining deeper understanding of corporate communication rather than evaluating the concept.

Even before entering an analysis, the discursive view of the company draws attention to some issues which have been addressed differently in orthodox corporate communication theory. In the following paragraphs two of the most obvious examples are referred to, namely processes of sensemaking and identity formation.

2.2.2 Sensemaking

Weick's (1995) approach to sensemaking was mentioned in the introduction already. The discursive perspective suggests that meaning is generally negotiated in companies (Grant, Hardy et al. 2004) – rather than created in a transfer or exchange of information as had been advanced in orthodox corporate communication theory. Companies, therefore, do not 'possess' meaning, instead meanings are created and contested through communicational interactions among stakeholders (Mumby and Clair 1997).

According to Weick (2004, 407), viewing sensemaking as discourse 'moves away from the prevailing view of organization as computational and thought-driven, towards an image of organisations as ocular and perception-driven.' This means that communication produces meaning not purely by sending information to recipients. Instead, meaning is created in discursive interaction – and this also means that 'more communication' does not necessarily enforce sensemaking in the intended direction, but can also lead to phenomena like information overflow (Tsoukas 1997).

2.2.3 Identity

Corporate identity formed one of the key concepts in orthodox corporate communication theory. A strong identity, the authors had argued (Argenti 2003; Bruhn 2003), can be achieved through a consistent application of corporate design, a uniform messaging, and so on. Recent discursive research has shown that identities, in fact, are constructed in 'overlapping and interwoven influences of language, interactions, stories and discourses; the struggles that underpin the negotiations among actors; the basis of broader institutional forms in locally situated talk; the way in which identity is a resource in and outcome of these processes' (Ainsworth and Hardy 2004, 167-168). Identities emerge in complex relationships, these authors conclude. Orthodox corporate communication theory has not addressed these aspects of complexity in identity formation.

These are two examples of themes that had appeared in the analysis of orthodox corporate communication theory and applied to which an alternative communicational perspective can provide additional depth of insight.

2.3 Implications of the strategy-as-practice perspective

While strategies and strategy processes – in contrast to corporate communication – have already been reviewed from discursive perspectives (Barrett, Thomas et al. 1995; Barry and Elmes 1997; Vaara, Kleymann et al. 2004), it was argued in Chapter 1 that, by acknowledging the constitutive role of discourse, corporate communication also becomes more strategically relevant for companies. Rather than limiting the strategy aspect in corporate communication theory to the strategic planning of communication programmes (Argenti 2003; Steyn 2003), corporate communication is viewed as contributing to the company's 'becoming' (Sztompka 1991), i.e. its emergence in a series of practical processes. In the context of companies, these processes have been referred to as strategic practices (Jarzabkowski 2003; Jarzabkowski 2004). Based on this view, several authors have proposed a 'practice turn' as necessary for management research – in addition to the 'linguistic turn' referred to earlier on – as a second conclusion emerging from a social constructionist worldview (Whittington 2002).

Whittington (2004) sets out the following definitions:

'Praxis refers to the actual work of organising, all the meeting, consulting, writing, presenting, communicating and so on that is required in order to get reorganisations done. The concept of practices includes all the tools, techniques and technologies of organising, whether conceptual tools such as those of organisation design, process tools such as project management, or physical tools such as computers and documents.'(Whittington 2004, F2)

Following this definition, corporate communication – even in orthodox terms – can be viewed as a practice applying certain techniques – regularly referred to as communication instruments. All five orthodox theories had positioned corporate communication that way. Considering the 'practice turn' towards these instruments, however, suggests viewing these instruments through a different lens. Rather than concentrating on their standardisation (Bruhn 2003), now the 'deep interconnectedness of everyday activity to the structural properties' (Whittington 2002, C2) of companies is recognized.

2.3.1 Corporate communication in context

Viewing strategy from a practice perspective moves the focus of concern towards how managers perform the work of strategy, both through their social interactions with other company members or stakeholders and with recourse to the specific practices present within a specific context (Hendry 2000). In the sense of Baecker's motto 'who works communicates' (2003, 18), then, also corporate communication becomes part of these strategy or strategic practices[9].

Jarzabkowski (2003), drawing on activity theory, developed a framework for interpreting and analysing strategy practices which is also useful for understanding corporate communication as practice.

Central to this framework is the acknowledgement of interaction as 'an interpretive basis from which individuals attribute meaning to their own and others actions and, so, are able to engage in shared activity' (2003, 24). Drawing on Blackler (1993), Jarzabkowski develops the notion of the company as an activity system based on actors, collective social structures, and the practical activities in which they engage.

Strategic practices emerge as shared activity between these three components of the system. Transferred to viewing corporate communication as

---

[9] In literature the terms 'strategy practice' (Whittington 2002) and 'strategic practice' (Jarzabkowski 2003) occur interchangeably. They are used interchangeably throughout this study, too.

a strategic practice, this means: Actors, e.g top management or communication managers, interact with collective structures, i.e. stakeholders, history, culture, and engage in 'a form of shared endeavour' in strategic activity (Jarzabkowski 2003, 25). Communication is one of these strategic activities (Baecker 2003) in which interaction occurs. This draws the attention to several aspects: (1) Corporate communication not only mediates the relation between management and stakeholders (Cornelissen 2004), but this mediation happens in a practical activity which is embedded in a concrete context. (2) Corporate communication tools have a practical purpose in this interaction in that they 'generate meaning from and impose meaning upon the context' (Jarzabkowski 2003, 26) in which corporate communication is conducted, i.e. context and practice become part of the meaning creation process. In orthodox corporate communication theory, in contrast, communication tools had been reduced to passive and functional instruments. (3) Also in line with Jarzabkowski (2003), first conclusions can be drawn with regards to methods: corporate communication needs to be analysed in a practical environment which embraces actors, structures and activities in order to reveal the full interplay between these constituents in strategic, i.e. communicational practice.

2.3.2 Organisational paradigm

An activity-based practice view of corporate communication draws attention to another aspect of company life which has not occurred at all in the analysed orthodox corporate communication theories – the concept of 'organizational paradigm' which Heracleous (2003) has launched in the context of defining his organisational action view, and which Johnson (1988, 84-85) has framed as 'the set of beliefs and assumptions, held relatively common through the organization, taken for granted, and discernible in the stories and explanation of environmental stimuli and configuration of organizationally relevant strategic processes.' This concept is similar to that of corporate culture and identity – in Jarzabkowski's (2003) model covered by 'collective structures'. Heracleous (2003, 29) views this paradigm as a reason why the functional approach cannot explain 'that the same environmental stimulus can be interpreted differentially by different dominant coalitions, and consequently leads to different strategic choices and actions.' Similarly, the same core message put forward in a corporate communication practice can produce different choices of different stakeholders. The functional view may acknowledge this, but it does not provide answers – whereas a practice-oriented, activity-based, i.e. context- and culture-sensitive approach to corporate communication can.

2.4 Purpose

In this Chapter, it has been argued that reviewing corporate communication theory from a discursive, i.e. communicational, perspective as well as following the strategic practices approach can be fruitful in order to gain a deeper understanding of corporate communication than the reduced, functional definition advanced in orthodox theory has allowed so far. Several indications were given with regards to aspects of extant corporate communication theories that can particularly gain from such a review.

Two more terms need to be defined, before the actual purpose of this research project can be formulated, namely the terms of theory and understanding.

The term theory, according to Weick (1987, 102), is defined as 'an inference from data that is offered as a formula to explain the abstract and general principle that lies behind them as their cause, their method of operation, or their relation to other phenomena.' Theories, therefore, describe 'dimensions along which ideas can vary' (Weick 2003, 455) rather than definite categories. Weick, therefore, views the process of theory-building as highly iterative:

'As ideas become elaborated more fully into abstract variables, underlying principles, interrelations, and conditions for relatedness, their resulting content moves away from mere speculations and becomes more deserving of the label theory. As the ideas become more abstract they also move away from the phenomenology of practice.' (Weick 2003, 455)

This notion also informs the theorising approach in this study. The level of abstraction increases throughout the study, ending with one of the highest levels of abstraction which are available – a re-definition of corporate communication (see Chapter 12).

Understanding, on the other hand, according to Weick (2003, 457), 'is to make sense of, to be conversant with, to apprehend, and to know thoroughly by close contact and long experience.' Also understanding is developed step by step rather than imparted suddenly. Understanding, in this definition, is based on past experiences, gained in practice, i.e. a backward-oriented process. Understanding unfolds over time, 'as learning rather than reading' (Schwandt 1999, 451). In consequence, discursive research intending to gain understanding focuses on the 'how and why the social world comes to have the meanings that it does' (2002, 13).

The process of theory-building, according to Weick (2003), then can be seen as an iterative process of moving forward (theorizing) and backward (understanding) in a world constructed in complexity.

This study is intended to provide an example of such a process of moving forward and backward between theories and practices. In consequence, the purpose of this study is defined from a theory-building perspective:

- *Purpose in terms of theory-building:*
  The purpose of the study is to explore the gap between orthodox corporate communication theory and management theories considering the linguistic and practice turns in social theory, i.e. to make the case for an 'alternative' theory of corporate communication.

According to Gergen and Thatchenkery (2001, 164-167), however, a pure focus on theory-building is not sufficient in order to close an identified gap from a social constructionist viewpoint. In addition, these authors propose to (1) mirror results back into practice, i.e. to create theories of 'use-value' which can be 'absorbed into ongoing relationships', and (2) to explore the applicability of the theories for activation in company settings. Based on this proposition, two further aspects of purpose are added.

- *Purpose in terms of understanding:*
  The purpose of this study is to gain a deeper understanding of how corporate communication discourse unfolds its performative capacity in the form of strategic practices.

Following Weick's (2003) approach, the two dimensions of purpose covered so far will be treated as mutually enforcing throughout the study, and, therefore, be followed up in parallel in processes of theorizing (forward) and understanding (backward). This notion is also reflected in the dualities of research questions which are defined in detail in Chapter 4.

Combining an approach of theorising and understanding will also allow a contribution to the practical side of corporate communication. Understanding, according to Weick (2003), is gained in practice. If theory-building and understanding are treated in an iterative process throughout this study, then also practical implications can be drawn. This matches Gergen and Thatchenkery's (2001, 164-167) proposition of the need to explore the applicability of the theories for activation in company settings – and it leads to the third aspect of purpose:

- *Purpose in terms of practical implications:*
  The purpose of this study is to draw practical lessons from both theory-building and understanding in terms of developing an effective corporate communication strategy.

These practical implications are drawn together at the very end of this study in Chapter 12.

3 Methodological considerations

This study presents the results of an interpretive research project (Denzin 1994; Deetz 2001) conducted between October 2003 and December 2004 at 'Intech', a large international industrial conglomerate based in Germany. The study is termed interpretive following the approach of Schwandt (1994, 118) defining this type of research as fundamentally concerned with meaning and seeking to understand social members' definition of a situation. At the same time, it puts a focus on the ways in which organization members' discursive practices contribute to the development of shared meaning' (Mumby and Clair 1997, 182). Interpretive research involves building a second order theory or theory of members' theories (Schutz 1973) in contrast to positivism which is concerned with objective reality and meanings thought to be independent of people. This means, interpretivists assume that knowledge and meaning are acts of interpretation.

The researcher collected data while he worked full-time for Intech. The aim was to make sense of 'the thick of what is going on' (Stake 2003, 149) at Intech through an 'iterative process of interaction and integration of theory and empirical data' (Brown 1998, 39).

Results are presented as a single case study (Yin 1994; Stake 2003), following an ethnographic process (Tedlock 2003), which was conducted from a social constructionist worldview (Berger and Luckmann 1966; Gergen 1994; Shotter and Gergen 1994; Gergen 2001).

First, a more detailed account of the epistemology and ontology of social constructionism is proposed. Second, methodological choices are explained and defences made. Third, the overall research process is described, and fourth, ethical issues regarding the research process are considered.

It is noted here that the intention of this Chapter is not to explain in depth how the data would be analysed (Gubrium and Holstein 2003). That account will be made in Chapter 6, after some further theoretical foundations have been laid.

3.1 Social constructionism

It has been argued in the literature review that, according to the alternative view on communication, language is not only seen as a medium of communication (as is the case in orthodox corporate communication), but that communication is fundamental to and constitutive of organisations (Westwood and Linstead 2001). In other words, 'discourse is the principal means by which organization members create a coherent social reality that frames their sense of who they are' (Mumby and Clair 1997, 181).

In parallel, alternative strands of strategy literature have emerged which take the impact of communication and narratives on strategy in general (Barry and Elmes 1997; Hardy, Palmer et al. 2000), and, more specifically, on strategy processes (Pettigrew 1992; Pettigrew 2003) and strategy practices (Jarzabkowski 2004) into consideration.

Within these discursive approaches to organisation, Keenoy, Oswick et al. (1997) identified two dominant epistemologies, one modernist and one social-constructionist, 'reflecting an understanding of organizations as monologic and dialogic entities, respectively' (Bargiela-Chiappini 2004, 3). The alternative view of corporate communication on which this study is based, i.e. viewing communicative action and practice as constructive of social and organisational reality (Heracleous and Barrett 2001; Heracleous 2003), follows the social constructionist paradigm.

3.1.1 Epistemological considerations

The core interest of social constructionists is in understanding how humans create knowledge, i.e. 'anything a society holds to be true, real and meaningful' (Hruby 2001, 52). Allen (2005, 37-38) acknowledges differences in social constructionist approaches, but identified four key assumptions which can be viewed as common to a social constructionist worldview: (1) it encourages to be critical and 'suspicious of how we understand the world and ourselves', (2) knowledge is viewed as 'historically and culturally specific, (3) language and communication are seen as a fundamental process sustaining knowledge, and (4) knowledge and social action are viewed as interconnected.

Gergen (1994; 2001), one of the generic contributors to a social constructionist worldview, stresses the importance of meaning in the processes of knowledge creation. He advances that, taking a social constructionist stance, 'the traditional view that meaning originates within the individual mind, is expressed within words (and other actions), and is deciphered within the minds of other agents is deeply problematic' (Gergen 1994,

262). Instead he proposes to put human interaction into focus 'as it generates both language and understanding' (1994, 263). This leads to the conclusion that 'social realities are constructed between us in our conversations' (Cunliffe 2003, 986).

3.1.2 Ontological considerations

Nightingale and Cromby (2002) as well as Bargiela-Chiappini (2004) point to differences in social constructionist approaches according to their ontological assumptions. A key issue in this debate relates to referentiality, i.e. 'the extent to which language can be said to refer to a world beyond or 'before' language' (Nightingale and Cromby 2002, 702).

Bargiela-Chiappini (2004, 8) clustered extant views in this debate into a five-step 'engagement continuum' spanning the function of discourse from purely 'descriptive', via 'interpretative', 'constitutive' and 'transformative' to 'generative'.

Possible assumptions regarding the function of language, according to this continuum, range from a purely descriptive function of language – common in much positivist research – to a generative function where discourse is granted absolute 'ontological primacy' (2004, 7). Social constructionism assumes that language not only passively describes reality, but it also shapes and frames it (Oswick, Keenoy et al. 1997, 6). In theory, therefore, social constructionism can cover constitutive, transformative and/or generative discourse.

The stance taken in this study fits into the range between acknowledging the constitutive and transformative capacitities of communication, which in the following discussions will also be referred to as 'performative' capacity (Watson 1997; Feldman 2000). Communication is seen as an engine of the social world as acknowledged in constitutive discourse (Mumby and Clair 1997), as well as shaping practices as suggested by the transformative discourse perspective (Deetz 2001). A generative discourse view, however, is not assumed because the implication would be to oppose the existence of a material world which is not the position taken by the researcher – it can, for example, not be denied that financial resources play an important role in business, although they are not normally constructed in communication, but in figures and currencies.

There is agreement, however, with Shotter and Gergen (1994) who make the point that social constructionism, with its focus on the productive capacities of communication, provides a blueprint for theorizing organisational communication, accentuating the centrality of language, and stressing the significance of social interaction processes.

3.2 Towards a general research design

It is now moved on towards the consideration of research design which is 'concerned with turning research questions into projects' (Robson 2002, 79). Robson (2002) distinguishes two generic types of research designs which can also be combined: (1) fixed research design incorporating primarily quantitative methods, and (2) flexible research design incorporating primarily qualitative methods.

A fixed design is feasible if the interest is in quantitative outcome measures and some degree of control can be exerted over the situation. This is not the case for the research issues to be explored in this study, a purpose of which is to contribute to an alternative theory of corporate communication. A theory will be proposed, but not evaluated at the same time. Therefore, a flexible research design is required.

3.2.1 Selecting suitable methods

One of the generic points in terms of researching companies which are continuously and differently enacted in different locations and context was recently made by John Law (2004). He argues that methods do not just describe social realities, but also help to create them. In this sense, realities need to be seen as vague and 'messy'. This raises the question of what methodology is appropriate to research such a fluid world. 'The answer, of course, is that there is *no* single answer' (Law 2004, 151). Focus on practice, commitment to symmetry, multiplicity and reflexivity are some of the recommendations he gives.

Allen (2005) proposed that social constructionism is not limited to one narrow methodology, but that the range of qualitative methods may be most appropriate to pursue the questions raised by social constructionism.

Cunliffe (2003, 988) provided an alternative entry point for defining a research method by pointing out that constructionist research 'explores how meaning is created between research participants' – and that research methods should be able to inform this approach. Therefore, a suitable method needs to make it possible to dismantle companies in their discursive constructions and to reveal performative aspects of ongoing practices, like communication, in these companies.

Robson (2002), in his flexible research paradigm proposed three options for methods: case study, ethnography and grounded theory. Balogun, Huff et al (2003) narrowed the debate further down by advancing a combination of case study and ethnographic approach. The researcher identified this combined view as a suitable approach to meet the purpose of this study.

Single case studies, conducted in an ethnographic process, have been carried out several times before in management research. Some of these case studies have become frequently quoted examples of social constructionist management literature over a considerable period of time, like the examples provided by Mintzberg (1973), Jackall (1988), Watson (1994), and recently Weeks (2004) show.

Strictly speaking, case-based research is less a method 'but a choice what is to be studied' (Stake 2003, 134), whereas ethnography can be understood as 'an ongoing attempt to place specific encounters, events, and understandings into a fuller, more meaningful context' (Tedlock 2003, 165). The case study approach stresses the need to analyze mechanisms in their real life context, whereas ethnographers illuminate the idea that people construct the world both through their interpretations of it and through the actions based upon those interpretations (Hammersley and Atkinson 1995).

A combination of both, therefore, might reasonably provide an approach to meet the social constructionist demands for methods which make it possible to challenge taken-for-granted ways of viewing corporate communication, to analyse processes in a concrete context and to assess performative capacities of social processes (Allen 2005).

3.2.2 Elements of case study research

Stake (2003, 140) found that 'case study methodology [is] written largely by people who presume that the research should contribute to scientific generalization.' According to the social constructionist paradigm mentioned above (Gergen 2001), however, this scientific generalization is hardly possible. 'Thick description' (Stake 2003) of ongoing social construction processes in a local context is what this paradigm demands.

Yin (1994) proposed that the decision for or against a case method should also be made in accordance with the purpose of the study. As has been laid out above, key aspects of this study's purpose are to theorize and to understand interrelations between strategy and communication practices. This involves moving into new terrain, exploring social construction in business reality, and finally, theorising. Several authors have stressed that case study work is a legitimate approach to produce theory in highly constructed research settings (Hammersley, Gomm et al. 2000).

A key advantage over other methods, for example put forward by Eisenhardt (1989) and Yin (1994), is that the case study allows the researcher to understand the problem investigated in its natural environment and focus on the actual dynamics related to the setting. This permits the discovery of social processes in the case studied (Hammersley, Gomm et al. 2000) – rather than simply testing whether these processes occur elsewhere which would have been an aim according to a positivist research design.

Similarly, 'learning' rather than generalising in the orthodox sense is the insight readers of case study reports can gain. 'Naturalistic, ethnographic case materials, to some extent parallel actual experience, feeding into the most fundamental processes of awareness and understanding' (Stake 2003, 145). Passing on experience in this sense clearly is one of the aims the researcher connects with case study research.

Based on these assumptions, a first decision in terms of methodology in favour of a case study approach was taken. This, at the same time, was a decision for a single and against multiple cases. In line with Dyer and Wilkins (1991) it is argued that a focus on context is more important than the number of cases analyzed, particularly if the overall research purpose is to generate theory. According to Dyer and Wilkins (1991, 614) it is 'the careful study of a single case that leads researchers to see new theoretical relationships and question old ones' and that, therefore 'the classical case study researchers tend to focus on comparisons within the same organizational context.'

In order to remain sensitive to context, the focus of this project is to conduct explanatory research in one particular case. The case selected was Intech, since this consists of several organisational units, hierarchical levels, projects, committees, departments, individuals, etc. These entities are not cases in an attempt to control variations across units and variables, distinguishable in space and time. Instead, they are viewed as components of the system and individual elements to one 'thick description' (Stake 2003). Intech was also a suitable case for practical reasons, because it was the researcher's workplace, providing the researcher with access to relevant networks.

3.2.3 Elements of an ethnographic approach

Whilst the decision to pursue a case study approach arose from an analysis of research needs (see Subsection 3.2.5), a decision on how to conduct the research project remains. It is argued now that ethnography is a suitable way to produce research data in the context of this study (Tedlock 2003)[10].

---

[10] Ethnography, at the same time, is a 'way in which such information or data are transformed into a written or visual form' (Tedlock 2003: 165). This aspect of ethnography is not meant in the above argument. Instead, the challenges to transform the data generated from the case study are dealt with separately in Chapter 6 of this thesis.

Brewer goes even further in that he states that 'while not all cases are qualitative, all ethnographic research involves case study' (2000, 77).

An advantage of ethnography, it has been argued, is that it helps to provide insight into, and interpretive depth of processes of knowledge creation and how objects and events are shaped (Alvesson and Deetz 2000). This conclusion was drawn because ethnography is particularly sensitive to issues of context and culture. In addition to this, Watson (1994) positioned ethnographic research as a profound method for researching management issues:

'Ethnographic research involves feeling one's way in confusing circumstances, struggling to make sense of ambiguous messages, reading signals, looking around, listening all the time, coping with conflicts and struggling to achieve tasks through establishing and maintaining a network of relationships. But this is what we do all the time as human beings. And it is what managers do in their more formalised 'managing' roles.' (Watson 1994, 8)

Ethnographic research, however, is often seen as difficult to conduct because its practice is 'replete with the unexpected' (Hammersley and Atkinson 1995, 2). Critiques generally arise from two viewpoints: on the one hand, the 'natural science critique' that ethnography does not fulfil the standard requirements for positivist science, and on the other, the 'postmodern critique' which 'deconstructs ethnography into its constituent processes, and accuses ethnography of melting into air and dissolving into nothingness' (Brewer 2000, 19).

Similarly, significant concerns with regards to the feasibility and presentation of ethnography have been brought up (Fetterman 1989; van Maanen 1995; Alvesson and Deetz 2000). Most of this critique relates to difficulties of handling the large amount of empirical data collected during the observation and issues of selectivity when producing an ethnographic report.

Alvesson and Deetz (2000, 201-207) proposed a 'situational focus' for ethnographic studies as a solution to this research problem. Situational focus means not only to locate ethnography in a concrete case, but also to focus research on a concrete situation rather than the totality of behavioural patterns.

This is the approach to ethnography applied in this study. The situation selected for the Intech case was the launch of the Intech management system throughout the observation period (see Chapter 5). This selectivity allowed 'actors as well as institutional context' to be present (Alvesson and Deetz 2000, 201) – meaning that the researcher had the opportunity to participate in all relevant events associated with this situation, and that all observations happened in the specific context of the launch of this new management system. Focusing on events associated with the launch of this project also made it possible to specifically focus on associated organisational processes, i.e. strategy and communication practices, which brought ethnography even closer to the study's purpose.

A second approach to reduce and manage complexities remaining within the focused definition of ethnography was to actively use extant theory in the iterative process between data and theorising (Eisenhardt 1989). This will be discussed in the next Subsection.

3.2.4 Using extant theory

These considerations challenge Robson's (2002) view that a flexible research design needs to incorporate a grounded theory approach, i.e. that theory should be developed just from collected data. Instead, the proposition is advanced that extant theory should play an important role in addition to empirical data, particularly if the research purpose is to advance an alternative corporate communication theory.

Pragmatist pluralist approach to incorporating extant theory

Eisenhardt (1989), for example, proposed an iterative process moving back and forth between primary data and existing theory. Gergen and Thatchenkery (2001) indirectly supported this notion by inviting a variety of theoretical perspectives to be included in generative theorizing processes.

Watson (1997), however, had warned that this should not occur indiscriminately and instead suggested a 'pragmatist pluralist approach' for including existing theory in management research:

'The pragmatic pluralism being advocated is, effectively, an approach whereby a researcher, in producing an analysis of some aspect of social life, draws elements from various disciplines or perspectives to produce what amounts to their personal paradigm – with its own ontological, epistemological and methodological integrity – to stand as the conceptual foundation of that particular piece of research.' (Watson 1997, 6)

The notion of such a pragmatist pluralist approach was felt as particularly important due to the variety of extant strategy and communication research, but also to be able to clearly differentiate between orthodox and alternative corporate communication theory in the end. The basis for such a pragmatist pluralist approach was laid in Chapters 1 and 2, when the orthodox approach was reviewed, and elements of an alternative approach based on extant theory were developed.

As part of this process, it was important to clearly define the alternative theory as based on discourse and practice approaches, and to associate this theory with social constructionist epistemology and ontology. Following the pragmatist pluralist approach, only extant theories following these intellectual strands were used to inform the explanation of what was going on at Intech in the later stages of analysis.

Use of a framework

Related to the question of which extant theory to include was the question of how to define clear boundaries for which aspects of strategy and communication practices to include in the study and which to leave out.

The mere definition and description of the alternative view of corporate communication had not narrowed down the field as such. On the contrary, viewing communication discursively soon led to the conclusion that also discourse as empirical raw materials would have to be collected and analysed (Brunsson 1982; 1990).

As suggested by Miles and Huberman (1994, 17) and Stake (2003, 142), the decision was taken to use a conceptual framework as a reference point in order to narrow down and structure data collection, preparation and analysis. A conceptual framework explains, either graphically or in narrative form, the main themes to be studied – the key factors, constructs or variables, and the presumed relationships among them (Miles and Huberman 1994, 18). An initial framework (see Chapter 4) was developed according to Watson's (1997) pragmatist pluralist approach, based on extant theory. In specifying what will and what will not be studied, the framework also revealed the concrete research questions that were defined in order to fulfil the purpose of the study.

In summary, a case study approach was selected which would be researched in an ethnographic process and informed by a pragmatist pluralist approach to incorporate extant theory in the actual theorizing stages.

3.2.5 Selecting the Intech case

According to Stake (1995), it is fairly usual that, for researchers aiming to conduct case study research, there is not even such a thing as "choice" in selecting the case:

'The case is given. We are interested in it, not because studying it we learn about other cases or about some general problem, but because we need to learn about that particular case, and we may call our work intrinsic case study.' (Stake 1995, 3)

This was true for the Intech case. The researcher took a straightforward decision between doing case study or ethnographic research at the place the researcher works in order not to discard the desire to conduct the research at all (Hammersley and Atkinson 1995, 37). The simple reason is that the researcher worked full-time for Intech during the observation period.

Intech, similar to Watson's (1994) 'ZTC Ryland' or Weeks' (2004) 'British Armstrong Bank', provided a very sound research site for the subject under study during the observation period. First of all, Intech is a large and highly diversified conglomerate with comparably large corporate communication and strategy units. Therefore, the researcher was confident to experience strategy and communication practices to a very broad extent in terms of both scale and scope. Second, Intech had entered into a long-term phase of continuous change, initiated by the launch of a new Intech management system. This launch made it necessary for communication and strategy functions to collaborate closely during the implementation phase.

The researcher's assumption was that this, on the one hand, would produce a sufficient amount of corporate communication discourse[11], and, on the other, it would also produce discourse covering various aspects of 'performative capacity' of corporate communication, because demands at Intech that corporate communication should accompany the processes regularly and professionally were high.

In addition, the researcher had already known Intech as a manager for roughly five years at the beginning of the observation period, providing him with a long-term experience as one of the presumptions for taking a reflexive ethnographer's stance (Cunliffe 2003) throughout the research process.

It is at this stage referred to Chapter 5 in which the Intech case is presented in more detail.

3.2.6 Overview of analytical strategy

Chapter 6 is going to cover issues of data collection, preparation and analysis in-depth. In order to allow readers easier orientation through the ensuing Chapters and Sections, a quick overview of these processes is given in note form at this stage.

---

[11] Corporate communication discourse, as defined in this study, covers the perspectives of two groups of company members, namely strategy and communication managers (senior and middle levels). This point will be explained in more detail in Section 5.4.

A structure for evaluation was developed which is closely adjusted to the purpose of the study. The overall focus on theory-building made it necessary to lead the analysis process towards exploring the gap between orthodox and alternative corporate communication to define the gap in concrete terms. This was achieved by developing a complete stocktaking and taxonomy of themes (McCurdy, Spradley et al. 2005) covered in corporate communication discourse[12] at Intech. Thematic analysis (Owen 1984) was chosen as a method for achieving this level of analysis.

At the same time, it was necessary to add more interpretive and reflective methods in order to be able to deal with aspects of gaining a deeper understanding of how corporate communication discourse unfolds its performative capacity at Intech. Discourse analysis (Fairclough 2003) emerged as the most suitable method in supporting exactly this part of the study's purpose.

Two more aspects appeared as important throughout the analysis process: (1) the extensive use of a computer-assisted data analysis software package (Diaz-Bone and Schneider 2003), name ATLAS.ti, and (2) the repeated use of extant theories (Weick 2003) to increase the depth of interpretation throughout the analysis process. The ATLAS.ti software package supported the analysis process from data collection, via sorting and coding, to conducting the actual thematic analysis. Using computer-assistance allowed the efficient management of large amounts of primary data, but did not replace an in-depth discourse analysis which was conducted conventionally. Extant theories were used at several selective points during the analysis: In cases, where the analysis of codes in ATLAS.ti had not revealed a clear set of themes, extant theories were used to make sense of and structure the respective discourse fragments; in addition, extant theories were regularly applied as part of the discourse analysis in order to gain a deeper insight into each of the themes which were analysed.

Overall, the analysis process can be structured into eight steps, which are summarised in Table 2.

---

[12] Based on naturally occurring talk, text and interviews (Silverman 2001) collected throughout the observation period. For exact definition see Chapter 6.2.

Table 2. Overview of analytical process

Steps	Steps in analysis process	Methods applied	Computer-aided [ATLAS.ti]	Use of extant theories
1	Data collection: Corporate communication discourse at Intech from October 2003 to December 2004	Participation as active member (Adler and Adler 1994)	X	
2	Identifying relevant quotations	Sorting	X	
3	Assigning generic codes (according to reference points in conceptual framework)	Sorting	X	
4	Developing taxonomies for each of the reference points	Thematic analysis	X	(X)[13]
5	Analysis of each of the themes as identified in the taxonomy	Thematic analysis		
6	Gaining deeper insight into each of the themes from discourse and strategic practices perspectives	Discourse analysis		X
7	Analysing discourse fragments assigned to each of the themes in order to identify and explain underlying communication practices	Discourse analysis	(X)[14]	X
8	Analysing interrelationships between the underlying communication practices	Intertextuality analysis		

3.3 Quality and ethical considerations

Stacey made the point that 'research projects may well produce more interesting results if they utilise people who are actually engaged in the work and management of an organisation' (Stacey 1996, 261-262). Social constructionism with its focus on context and ongoing processes even demands a research process embedded into company reality.

This gives rise to questions regarding "how" to practically conduct such research, primarily focusing on two issues: (1) how qualitative research

---

[13] Where necessary in order to structure the data; each of these cases is indicated in Chapters 7 to 11.

[14] ATLAS.ti software package used in order to retrieve relevant documents; actual discourse analysis of each of the fragments was conducted manually.

should be conducted in order to maintain a high standard of quality (Seale 1999), and (2) how the researcher's obligation to protect participants in the research process can be maintained, i.e. how ethical challenges can be managed throughout the research process (Kimmel 1988). These two aspects are covered with regards to the case study/situational ethnography approach chosen for the Intech case in the following Subsections.

3.3.1 Issues in case study research

Quality issues

It had been argued that single case studies are a useful approach when theory-building and gaining understanding are the purpose of the study (Yin 1994; Gill and Johnson 2002, 157). In consequence, the case study was selected as a suitable method for this research project.

Concerns with regards to the quality of case study research have been the lack of rigor of case study research and that they provide little basis for scientific generalization.

Measures taken to ensure rigor are discussed in detail in Chapter 6 focusing on the analysis of the case study.

Generalizations from statistical samples, as proposed by positivists, are just one type of generalization. It is argued that generalization is also possible from case studies, but that it has to be approached differently (Gummesson 2000). The possibility to generalize depends on how far it is possible to reach a fundamental understanding of structure, process and driving forces rather than a superficial establishment of correlation or cause-effect relationships. In contrast to theory testing (the primary concern of positivist researchers), case studies may be applied for theory generation – the attempt to find new ways of approaching reality in a local, historical context (Gummesson 2000, 94). This is where the focus was in the Intech case. The case for an 'alternative' corporate communication theory was explored in a very concrete Intech context.

Also the use of extant theory (Yin 1994), based on a reference framework (Miles and Huberman 1994) can contribute to generalization of case study research. Both these techniques were also applied for this study (see above).

The iterative approach to theory development was supplemented by peer group reflections as suggested by Mutch (1999). He had tested this approach to obtaining written reflections from managers as a means of improving the reliability of his research. This approach was applied in two ways in the Intech case: (1) the reference framework was applied in open-ended interviews which were conducted in order to obtain reflections from strategy and communication managers with regards to completeness and ongoing processes (see Chapter 6), and (2) draft versions of this study were circulated to the managers who had participated in interview rounds at Intech. Feedback was not intended to influence the results of the analysis, but to sound out results against the practicing managers and in order to check to what extent the results produced were also of relevance to them (Watson 1994).

Ethical issues

When it comes to ethical issues of case study research, two additional areas need to be considered – taboos and anonymity (Gummesson 2000). There are taboos of the research process as such, e.g. concerning prejudices among members of the organisation researched. 'Those whose lives and expressions are portrayed, risk exposure and embarrassment, as well as a loss of standing, employment and self-esteem' (Stake 2003). The ethical stance taken by the researcher towards this kind of taboo was to strictly apply rules of confidentiality (Weiss 1994), i.e. the company name was changed into the Intech pseudonym and, for this report, the names of all participants were anonymized and assigned to general role categories such as 'strategy manager' and 'communication manager'.

3.3.2 Issues with regards to an ethnographic approach

In addition to the case study issues considered above, ethical and quality issues in ethnographic research tend to focus around the researcher's role.

Quality issues

Specifics of the ethnographer's role become clearer when comparing this role with an action researcher's role. Action research (Aguinis 1993; Coghlan and Brannick 2001; Altrichter, Kemmis et al. 2002) could have been used as an alternative to the ethnographic approach chosen for this study, particularly given the researcher's position as a full-time employee of Intech.

Action research involves a planned intervention by a researcher into some natural social setting, similar to a consultant. The general problem with action research is that the researcher, even if working full-time in the organisation, is probably stereotyped as an academic. Ethical dilemmas as well as problems of role ambiguity may arise at all phases of action research projects and can be summarised as follows (Gill and Johnson 2002): (1) problems of independence and confidentiality of the work, because meaningful data often can only be collected with the consent and support of the contractors, (2) collaboration between researcher and client in defining the goals might be at the expense of neutrality, (3) pressure of time can arise due to the temporary nature of the project.

The distinction between action research and ethnography is that the action researcher is always asked to do the research. In contrast, the ethnographer selects an organisation as a research site on the basis of specific research interests. While action researchers are supposed to change the system as part of the research process, ethnographers assume they are not in the 'change business' but that their endeavour is to draw interferences from how the system works (Gill and Johnson 2002, 89).

Also the position of the researcher throughout the process of data collection differs in an important point, although both include participation in the research site: a client would normally pay the action researcher fees to get his challenge fixed. The situational ethnographer, in contrast, only needs to have local knowledge of the respective company and needs to have access 'to a number of situations in order to find out one (or more) to concentrate on' (Alvesson and Deetz 2000, 202). The aim is always to get uncensored access to uncensored organisational settings (Gill and Johnson 2002, 147). The ethnographer decides when there is sufficient research data to fulfil the research goals, whereas, in the action research context, the client decides when sufficient help has been provided.

Due to the above-mentioned concerns with respect to action research, the researcher decided to take an ethnographic position in the research process. Rather than advising Intech in how to possibly improve their corporate communication efforts, the focus of the research project would be on contributing to an alternative corporate communication theory reflecting the original purpose of the study. In addition to the employment contract, a research contract was concluded between Intech and the researcher, which ensured access for the researcher to company events and data, and obligating the researcher to strict confidentiality.

According to the research contract, the researcher was also granted a two-month offsite period for writing up the dissertation, and Intech funded fees and costs associated with the PhD programme at Salford University.

Therefore, the ethnographic role adopted by the researcher can best be described as one of 'active membership' (Adler and Adler 1994). The researcher disclosed his dual position (corporate communication manager at Intech business unit and researcher) to all participants in the Intech setting which made it possible to step in and out of the researcher role which Nandhakumar and Jones (1997, 126) describe as demanding for the 'engaged' researcher who as 'participant observer on the one hand, [wishes] to experience the taken-for-granted world of the social actors and, on the other, they seek to be the continuously questioning researcher exposing its hidden assumptions.'

Ethical issues

Hammersley and Atkinson (1995, 264-275) give a fairly detailed account of ethical considerations necessary when conducting ethnographic research. In their terms, the key issues are: (1) informed consent, (2) privacy, (3) harm, and (4) exploitation.

Informed consent

'Informed consent' (Hammersley and Atkinson 1995, 264) was partly an issue in the research which was conducted at Intech. Although all participants were informed about the ongoing project of the researcher beforehand and had the opportunity, for example, to agree whether a situation was recorded or not, the researcher is not fully sure whether all participants at all points in the research process were aware that information discussed could become relevant for evaluation in the research process as such. This has to do with the dual role of the researcher which made it possible for him to participate in many situations relevant for conducting the study not purely as researcher, but also due to his function as corporate communication manager at Intech. Additionally, the researcher has the impression that due to the longitudinal observation period of 15 months (see Chapter 5) an increasing number of participants had simply forgotten about the researcher's role as researcher towards the end of the observation period. Peer group reflections (Mutch 1999) which had been conducted with draft version of this dissertation were part of the process to balance this effect.

Privacy

'Privacy' (Hammersley and Atkinson 1995, 267) covers the issue that ethnography can make things public that were done for private consumption. This was less of a problem in the Intech case because the situations that were considered for ethnographic review were at least 'public' within Intech. Privacy was secured, in addition, by applying confidentiality precautions (see above).

Harm and exploitation

The researcher did not observe any occasions of 'harm' (1995, 268), i.e. ethical issues arising from the problem that research can have important consequences for the people researched. Also, 'exploitation' (1995, 273) was not observed, particularly, because all issues regarding return from the research and also other issues, such as copyrights, had been agreed on in the research contract between Intech and researcher in advance, and Intech had not demanded the researcher to take a specific action researcher's stance.

4 Reference points for theory development

As explained above, an iterative process between moving forward (theorizing) and backward (understanding) was seen as necessary in order to fill the gap between extant corporate communication theory and management theories considering the linguistic and practice turns.

In this Chapter a first step towards closing this gap is made by moving forward in theorizing. The aim is to develop and propose a complete set of reference points according to which, in later stages of the study, corporate communication discourse and practices as they occurred at Intech will be structured.

4.1 From practices to processes

A framework of reference points which helps to advance this study towards its purposes should, first of all, conform with the theory-building approach, i.e. it should be based on – or at least be supportive of – discursive and practice-oriented theory. Additionally, however, the framework should also provide a suitable structure for the later stages of gaining understanding by analysing corporate communication discourse in practice.

It has become clear from the literature review and development of the purpose of the study that a framework which can be used without further amendments does not exist. Also starting the development of a framework from one of the orthodox models of corporate communication did not seem as a sensible approach, since these models do not fulfil the theory-building purpose of the study, i.e. they are not supportive of discursive and practice-oriented management theories.

Therefore, the approach was turned towards strategy theory where discursive approaches had been probed several times (e.g. Barrett, Thomas et al. 1995; Barry and Elmes 1997; Vaara, Kleymann et al. 2004). Whereas also this discursive work has not revealed a concrete framework, several indications were given that looking at strategy from a process perspective might be fruitful. Hendry (2000) argued that both discourse and action perspectives meet in strategy processes. And also Whittington proposed that process studies provide a useful starting point when 'real work of strategy practitioners' (2002, C4) is under scrutiny.

These traces were followed, but, first of all, the term 'strategy process' requires closer examination. Van de Ven and Poole (1995, 512) defined process 'as the progression (i.e. the order and sequence) of events in an organizational entity's existence over time'. Pettigrew (1997, 338) similarly defined process as 'a sequence of individual and collective events, actions, and activities unfolding over time in context.' This should not be confused with other uses of process in management literature, e.g. as the underlying logic explaining a causal relationship or a category of concepts of organisational action in terms of work flows, as applied in orthodox theories. Instead, Pettigrew – drawing on Sztompka (1991) – proposes that 'the driving assumption behind process thinking is that social reality is not a steady state. It is a dynamic process. It occurs rather than it merely exists' (1997, 338).

With regards to strategy processes, Mintzberg and Lampel (1999) pointed to the fact that processes are a far from homogeneous field of study. Indeed, each of the ten strategy schools identified in that study provided a different view of how strategy is formed. Among these are some schools, however, which incorporate the dynamic view of strategy processes advanced by Pettigrew. As Lechner and Müller-Stewens (2000) argued, this is particularly the case in strategy research which explicitly focuses on aspects of language and communication (e.g. Knights and Morgan 1991; von Krogh and Roos 1995). This literature, however, does not provide a stocktaking of strategy processes that occur in a company and which can be considered for further analysis.

For Mintzberg and Lampel (1999), crafting strategy is a continuous and adaptive process. As Whittington (2001, 23) puts it: 'This view of strategy is an unglamorous one: hands get dirty, steps are small and there are few bold lunges into the unknown long term.' This leads back to the idea that strategy processes are closely related to ongoing practices in daily business.

4.2 An integrative framework of strategy processes

This short review of strategy processes has shown that some, but by far not all approaches to strategy processes can serve as a reference point for pursuing the purpose of this study. Instead, following the concept of Mintzberg and Lampel (1999), several of the ten schools of thought on strategy processes would have to be examined in combination in order to give a full account of strategy processes, including both discourse and practice perspectives.

The development of such a 'unifying theory that can reconcile and connect these multiple perspectives' was forwarded first by Chakravarthy and White (2002, 182), and then, in a refined version by Chakravarthy, Müller-Stewens et al. (2003).

Among the limitations of extant theories of strategy processes identified by Chakravarthy and White (2002) were explicitly the lack of focus on concrete situations, e.g. in decision-making processes and subsequent actions and an inadequate simplification of the complexity and layered structure of processes. Apart from bridging these limitations, the authors also, in line with Kirsch (1997; 1997), determined strategy process as a collective process, legitimised by members of the company, rather than purely based on individual decisions, as a functional view would have suggested.

It is denoted at this point that Chakravarthy, Müller-Stewens et al.'s (2003) framework itself was not created from a discursive research process, but displayed a rather functional approach. In treating strategy as a social process and by providing a complete stocktaking of recurrent strategic processes in companies, however, the researcher assumed that Chakravarthy and his colleagues developed a framework which could serve as a reference point for further steps in the research process of this project. The framework is clearly not used as an epistemological basis throughout this study, but purely to match it with further communicational and practice-based aspects in the following Sections.

The integrative framework of strategy processes which Chakravarthy, Müller-Stewens et al. (2003) presented defines four key strands of strategy processes:

The framework is a composite of four distinct relationships: (1) the dynamic equilibrium that top management keeps a firm in through its continuous redefinition of the relevant strategic dynamics for the firm, (2) the influence of organizational context on the core elements of the strategy process, (3) the impact of decisions and actions on a firm's competitive position and distinctive competencies, and (4) the relations between competitive position, distinctive competencies, business context, firm performance and financial market evaluation.' (Chakravarthy, Müller-Stewens et al. 2003, 4)[15]

---

[15] This quote represents the original wording, but the order of the relationships was turned around in order to improve the 'top-down' readability of the figure. In the course of this thesis, the four distinctive relationships mentioned in the quote will also be referred to as 'Strands' in order to do justice to the layered structure of strategy processes.

It is argued that this framework of strategy processes provides an adequate stocktaking and structuring of strategy processes for the purpose of this study[16]. Major elements of an alternative view of strategy are referred to: The concept assumes a dynamic view of strategy (Markides 1999), i.e. the purpose of the company is formed in dynamic interaction. In the second Strand[17] of relationships it is explicitly referred to sensibility with regards to context. The third Strand of relationships contains the performative element of action, and, as part of Strand 4, competitive position, distinctive competencies, business concept are put into relation, i.e. are viewed as informed by communication processes.

4.3 Matching strategy and communication processes

Before being able to apply the framework in order to, first, derive concrete research questions, and, second, use it as a point of reference for the case study as such, it needs to be extended by the dimension of communication processes.

It has to be acknowledged at this point that an in-depth understanding of precisely these corporate communication processes is one of the overall purposes of the study. Therefore this next move of matching the four distinctive strands of strategy processes with respective communication processes needs to be seen as a one of the creative steps in theory-building – informed, though, by the alternative view of corporate communication which had been proposed earlier. In order to leave space for interpretation in the actual analysis Chapters, the associated communication processes are not formulated as facts, but rather as intended outcomes of the constitutive or performative capacity of communication. This will be achieved by reviewing each of the four strategy strands from a communication perspective, and then proposing the performative capacity which corporate communication can add to the respective strategy process. This will result in a reformulated explanation of the process in the form of four descriptors.

---

[16] For a more detailed examination of each of the components of this framework at this stage of the thesis refer to the original works of Chakravarthy and White (2002) and Chakravarthy, Müller-Stewens et al. (2003). An in-depth analysis of the individual components, assembled to the four distinctive relationships will be undertaken with regards to their relevance for corporate communication theory in Chapters 7 to 11.

[17] The term 'Strand' is used consistently throughout this thesis in order to identify interrelations between strategy and communication processes.

Strand 1: The dynamic equilibrium that top management keeps a firm in through its continuous redefinition of the relevant strategic dynamics for the firm

This process relates to the need to continuously adapt the purpose of the company in order to remain competitive in the long run (Markides 1999). In Chakravarthy, Müller-Stewens et al.'s (2003, 6) words: 'Firm performance, strategy, competencies, decisions, actions, business, and organizational contexts, all change over time and influence each other dynamically.' In orthodox corporate communication, the concept used to transport the company's purpose to various audiences was that of corporate identity. According to a communicational perspective, it is argued that identity is created (and changed) in communication. This involves processes of 'co-orientation' (Taylor 2004) towards one common purpose of the company. The perspectives stakeholders hold, 'are not dictated by managers but negotiated by the players inside and outside of the company' (Heath 1994, 32). Heath termed the constitutive capacity of communication in this process as 'coordination' – not understood in a direct and functional sense, but by 'creating the understanding members need to coordinate their efforts with one another and with external audiences' (1994, 59). In adopting this notion, the original strategy process is re-framed, considering the interrelation between strategy and communication processes:

- **Strand 1 Descriptor:** Coordinating the company around dynamic purposes.

Strand 2: The influence of organizational context on the core elements of the strategy process

This strand of strategy processes covers aspects of how company context 'shapes the premises for both decisions and actions within the firm (Chakravarthy, Müller-Stewens et al. 2003, 6). A concrete question in the Intech case, for example, was how a management system should be configured in order to enable the process of turning decisions into actions. This can be viewed as a core task of organising a company.

The point that had been made in Chapter 1 was that communication is one of the core organising processes. According to Weick (1979), the communication aspect is that, through discursive practices, company members continuously create meanings, i.e. make and remake organisation. In considering communication as a mode of organising, the revised interrelated strand of strategy and communication processes is described the following way:

- **Strand 2 Descriptor:** Organising by linking decisions and actions

Strand 3: The impact of decisions and actions on a firm's competitive position and distinctive competencies

This strand of strategy processes draws the focus towards outcomes of decisions and actions. Chakravarthy, Müller-Stewens et al. (2003, 6) write that they 'accept that strategy is realized through both emergent and planned actions that implement prior decisions. In turn, these decisions and actions are continuously revised based on feedback and feed-forward learning.' A communication perspective suggests that discourse plays a crucial role in such implementation and change processes by pointing out that 'organizations change when there is an alteration in the way members conceive of themselves, in the stories, accounts, and versions a community tells about itself and thereby enables in its members' practices' (Barrett, Thomas et al. 1995, 367). Implementation and change, therefore, happen in communication. Barrett, Thomas et al. (1995, 370) propose that managers, in order to facilitate implementation and change, should act as 'choreographers of discourse scenarios'. The revised and interrelated strand of strategy and communication processes, therefore, is termed:

- **Strand 3 Descriptor:** Facilitating implementation and change processes

Strand 4: The relations between competitive position, distinctive competencies, business context, firm performance and financial market evaluation

Competitive position and distinctive competencies are key concepts for this strand of strategy processes. The key task for process managers is to continuously adapt positioning and competencies to changes in the business context in order to achieve best possible financial performance (Chakravarthy, Müller-Stewens et al. 2003). Positioning and competencies are also crucial in communication processes, e.g. in processes of differentiating the company from others in processes of communicating with stakeholders. While, from a communicational viewpoint, these processes again are highly negotiative (Deetz 1995), Aberg (1990) had argued that these conversations still follow the primary aim of 'profiling' in a process of striving for justification and acceptance. The basic nature of strategy processes (i.e. achieving financial performance) and communication processes (i.e. gaining profile) can be viewed as similar – it is one of leveraging the competitive position and distinctive competencies. The Strand 4 Descriptor is framed in applying exactly this term:

- **Strand 4 Descriptor:** Leveraging the competitive position and distinctive competencies

Applying the mode of communicating to the original framework also changes the original model's structure as such in two aspects: (1) All strategy processes are no longer seen as one-way routes but as two-way and dialogic by definition (Ruigrok, Achtenhagen et al. 2000; Varey 2001; Achtenhagen, Melin et al. 2003), and (2) the strategy process should not only focus on financial performance but on all 'outcomes' based on the involvement of all stakeholders in the processes of communicating and strategizing (Schwaninger 2001).

The result of both applying the mode of communicating and implementing the revised descriptors of interrelated strategy and communication processes is displayed in Figure 1.

This revised framework provides a structure for deriving a set of research questions: the communicational perspective has been incorporated and strategy and communication processes are treated as interrelated. The four Strands of interrelationships between strategy and communication processes displayed above will be used as a reference point throughout this study. In particular, they inform and structure the evaluation process.

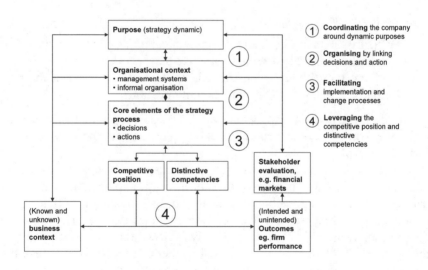

Fig. 1. Framework for analysing interrelated strategy and communication processes

4.4 Concluding concrete research questions

As stated in Chapter 2, the purpose of this study is threefold: (1) to explore the gap between orthodox theories and theories considering a discourse and practice approach. It has been argued that this purpose is fulfilled throughout the course of this study by moving forward and backward between processes of theorising and understanding; (2) to gain a deeper understanding of how corporate communication discourse unfolds its performative capacity in the Intech case; and (3) to draw practical lessons from both theory-building and understanding.

It is the second aspect of the purpose which is now considered with respect to specific research questions.

Gaining understanding in discursive studies often involves two steps: (1) producing a stocktaking of themes in the sense of identifying 'the main parts of the world' (Fairclough 2003, 129); and (2) to analyse how the discourse associated with these themes influences organisational processes (Heracleous and Barrett 2001).

Applied to the topic studied, the following two generic research questions can be formulated:

Generic research questions

1. What are the themes corporate communication discourse covers when approached from the discourse/practice perspective?
2. How are these themes constructed, i.e. how did they enact the performative capacity of corporate communication?

Based on the revised framework which was developed and summarised in Figure 1 above, these generic research questions can be broken down further, as displayed in Table 3.

With regards to the above research questions, it is at this point referred to Chapter 6. In that Chapter follows an in-depth explanation of how the data collected for the Intech case is analysed. In anticipation of this explanation, it is pointed out that data analysis includes two generic steps: (1) thematic analysis, and (2) discourse analysis. Research questions related to the stocktaking of themes are analysed in thematic analysis, whereas the questions focusing on the construction of themes are analysed in discourse analysis. In Chapters 8 to 11 the analysis of data related to all four Strands of interrelations identified in the revised framework takes place, including individual Sections which are explicitly framed as 'thematic analysis' and 'discourse analysis'.

Table 3. Sub-set of research questions based on revised framework

Descriptors of Strands of interrelation between strategy and communi-cation processes	Research questions related to the stocktaking of themes [Thematic analysis]	Research questions related to the construction of themes [Discourse analysis]
Strand 1: Coordinating the company around dynamic purposes	Which purpose-related themes did corporate communication discourse cover?	How did the performative capacity of corporate communication emerge with regards to coordinat-ing the company around dynamic purposes?
Strand 2: Organising by linking decisions and ac-tions	Which themes with regards to organising processes did corporate communication discourse reveal?	How did corporate com-munication discourse con-stitute organisation in the concrete case? How was it constituted by other modes of organising?
Strand 3: Facilitating im-plementation and change processes	Which themes covered discourse focusing on implementation and change processes?	How did corporate com-munication discourse un-fold its performative ca-pacity in these processes?
Strand 4: Leveraging the competitive position and distinctive competencies	Which themes were cov-ered by corporate commu-nication discourse relating to competitive position and distinctive competencies?	How did corporate com-munication discourse con-tribute to the constitution of competitive position and distinctive competen-cies? How was it formed by these?

5 Presentation of case study

Having proposed a framework for examining interrelations between strategy and communication practices and after having concluded a set of concrete research questions, the empirical field of the Intech case is now introduced.

This case study is based on corporate communication discourse happening at Intech, one of the major industrial conglomerates based in Germany.

As explained above, the ethnographic stance taken by the researcher focuses on a specific situation, namely the launch of the Intech management system which took place during the observation period. Much of the discourse was deeply embedded in the company's history, its overall structure and the specifics of the communication and strategy departments at Intech, as will become apparent in the subsequent Chapters. These three facets play a major role in the following presentation of the case.

Due to its framework as a diversified company (Mintzberg 1999), it was also important to observe corporate communication discourse at several hierarchical levels within Intech, including the interplay between these hierarchical levels. Again, considering the situational focus of the case study, two core hierarchical levels were concentrated on – corporate level ('Intech corporation') and business unit level ('Intech business unit').

Apart from presenting the company, this Chapter will give further information on scope and timing of this case study.

5.1 Intech corporation (IC)

With its history reaching back to the mid of the 19th century and with over 400,000 employees worldwide, Intech nowadays represents one of the large companies, spanning products, solutions and services in the broad field of electronics and electrical engineering.

According to Mintzberg (1999, 343-346), age and size of a company, apart from its management system and its external context, are major 'situational factors' influencing the structure of the company. Mintzberg (1999, 346-353) classifies companies into seven 'configurations', namely entrepreneurial, machine, professional, diversified, innovative, missionary and political companies. Among these, diversified structures are regularly found at large and mature organisations. Not surprisingly, Intech can also be classified as a diversified company.

Diversified companies typically combine a range of factors including high levels of education, job mobility, professional affiliation, a focus on middle management and continuous acts of balancing of power between head-offices and divisions. Authors like Kunda (1992) and Kärreman and Alvesson (2004) have argued that this makes it a good site in which to study company practices, because members of such companies are seen to be particularly susceptible to communication and participation.

5.1.1 History

The origins of Intech go back to the middle of the 19th century when it started as a small ten man workshop in Germany. Beginning with advances in telegraph technology, the company expanded its product line and geographical scope. It was already a multi-national presence by the end of the 19th century, when it also became listed on the stock exchange. Power and electricity, from that time on, were highly regulated markets so that socio-political factors continuously and significantly influenced the company's development – expansions as well as contractions – throughout most parts of its history. Having been increasingly integrated into the Nationalist Socialist war economy, it took the company two decades after World War II to regain its former position.

It was not until the early 1990s that markets gradually began to open and deregulate and a process of privatization began. Following Germany's reunification, restructuring measures (verticalisation) set the stage for operating units to take on global entrepreneurial responsibilities. 'One man – one business' started to become the motto for this trend. The challenge also entailed closing the productivity gap on competitors who had been quicker to realign their processes. In order to react to issues like price pressure and agility of response, the company introduced measures designed to boost productivity, innovation and growth in the format of a precursor to company-wide strategy programmes. The productivity gap, however, remained static.

At the end of the 20th century, the company for the first time released so-called corporate principles, i.e. official company values, at a major corporate anniversary event. As part of this, issues like customer- and employee-focus, innovation, commitment to value-creation and corporate responsibility were communicated as key elements of corporate culture.

Only shortly after that, a drop in earnings, basically due to changes in the market, prompted corporate strategists to develop a ten-point programme to achieve a comprehensive turnaround in terms of earnings performance. This programme included items like the launch of portfolio policies, a business excellence programme and the reorganisation of financial reporting. The concept of economic value-added was introduced in order to develop the company towards the creation of shareholder value (Rappaport 1986).

The collapse of the New Economy in 2001 and the difficult economic and political environment following the terrorist attacks on September 11, 2001, again disrupted plans to turn the conglomerate discount into a conglomerate bonus. As a response, in October 2003 the Intech management system was launched in order to implement strategies and achieve strategic goals in the long run.

5.1.2 Structure

Like many other companies, Intech emerged from the 1990s as a fairly decentralised company (Whittington, Pettigrew et al. 1999; Pettigrew and Massini 2003). 'Decentralised' is a term generally associated with a diversified company, although decentralisation from the corporate viewpoint can, in many cases, be equated with centralization of power in the divisions (Mintzberg 1999, 648).

In order to explain Intech's diversified structure as part of this case study, Mintzberg's (1999) six basic parts of company structures are drawn upon. These six components are defined as follows (1999, 333): (1) the 'operating core', i.e. parts of the company which produce the products and deliver services, (2) the 'strategic apex' overseeing the company, (3) a 'middle line' as additional hierarchies between strategic apex and operating core, (4) the 'technostructure', detached from line hierarchies, established in order 'to plan and control formally the work of others', (5) 'support staff' providing internal services to the other units, and (6) a company ideology or culture.

Mintzberg (1999, 349) defined the diversified company as an enterprise which 'is not so much an integrated organization as a set of rather independent entities coupled together by a loose administrative structure'. The headquarters in this type of company heavily relies on performance control mechanisms to supervise the fairly autonomous business units.

The term 'Intech corporation (IC)' is used in order to identify the whole Intech conglomerate. Within IC, the six components of the company structure were categorised as follows (see Figure 2): (1) The operating core consisted of 14 business units active in seven different business areas. One of these business units, subsequently referred to as 'Intech business unit', also forms part of this case study. Each of these bodies was managed as an entrepreneurial unit, carrying global responsibilities for its business, including delivery of financial performance. (2) The strategic apex was represented by general managers forming the management board of Intech corporation. Within this board, separate sponsors had been defined for overseeing activities within individual business units. (3) Business unit heads acted as the 'middle line' i.e. the linking pins between business units and management board. The term 'middle management', as used later on in the analysis, is understood in a broader sense than this 'middle line'. The term middle management unites managers on first, second and third levels of hierarchy at Intech business unit. (4) A corporate strategy department formed part of Intech corporation's technostructure. (5) The corporate communication department, in Mintzberg's (1999) terminology would form part of the 'support staff' alongside other support units, e.g. human resources and information technology. (6) Instead of 'ideology' or 'culture' for the purpose of this study the term 'identity' is used, a detailed definition and explanation of which follows in Chapter 8.

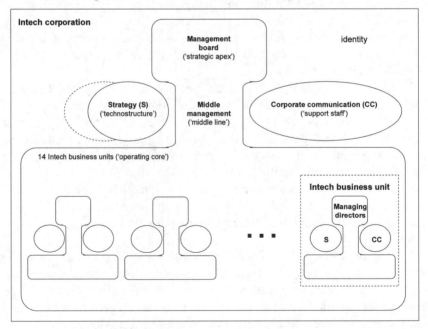

Fig. 2. Basic components of the Intech structure (adapted from Mintzberg 1999b: 350)

In addition, Intech's business units were supported by regional units. These included sales units in each region to complement sales efforts of the individual business units, also taking advantage of cross-marketing opportunities.

5.1.3 Strategy and communication functions

Business processes at Intech were defined in accordance with a hierarchical process framework which had been derived from Porter's (1985) value chain concept. Apart from business processes like customer relationship management, supply chain management and product lifecycle management, the Intech process framework also defined (1) management processes, i.e. 'processes to define, affect, analyse, manage and control the business processes'[18], and (2) support processes assisting the business and management processes.

Two separate functions, each staffed with over 100 employees, managed the strategy and communication processes at Intech corporation. While strategy processes, according to the Intech process framework, were viewed as management processes – part of the technostructure in Mintzberg's (1999) terminology –, corporate communication was defined as a support process – i.e. support staff (Mintzberg 1999).

The corporate strategy department's major units focused on developing corporate strategies, supporting business unit and region strategies, and a business intelligence and portfolio analysis unit drawing up recommendations for the management board. Part of the tasks was to implement company-wide strategy projects like the Intech management system, and to manage internal reporting processes.

The corporate communication department was equipped with a diversified, functional structure covering department units like a press office, internal communication, corporate marketing communication and public relations as well as specialized teams for corporate messages, corporate brand and design, global sponsoring and further communication functions.

5.2 Intech business unit (IBU)

The Intech business unit was configured similarly to a profit centre within the corporation, covering similar functions, based on concrete business processes in terms of the Intech process framework.

---

[18] As defined by Intech corporation.

5.2.1 History

Intech business unit's history covers only a very short period of Intech's history, starting with the founding of Intech business unit in 1997. One of the founding reasons for IBU was to separate operating and financing activities within Intech to make the financial sphere visible for external investors in Intech shares. The second motivation was to expand sales financing activities for the other operating core units and provide financial services also to third-party customers. Hopes were high in 1997 that the new business unit would grow fast, driven by the excitement surrounding the new economy and soaring share prices. Indeed, during the first years of operations several units were acquired and annexed so that volumes increased.

From 2000 onwards, Intech business unit pursued a strategy to stabilize business and maintain competitiveness by introducing process improvements in areas such as risk management, cost management and IT platforms. In addition, new operations were founded in new regional markets, such as Asia and the Nordic countries.

5.2.2 Structure

Intech business unit was among the smaller business units within Intech corporation, covering about 1,500 employees worldwide. Intech business unit's operations covered roughly 30 countries out of the 200 in which Intech corporation was present.

Intech business unit was in charge of Intech corporation's financing business, providing a variety of financial services and products to third parties and, on arm's-length terms, to other Intech business units and their customers. Intech business unit was organized in six business divisions, two of which have significant dealings with third parties including customers of other Intech business units. The four other divisions mainly supported and advised Intech corporation and other business units, without significant external business.

In its captive businesses, Intech business unit makes an important contribution to Intech through financing arrangements and services in the context of financing of goods and services sold by Intech and financial services delivered to Intech as a whole. More than 50 percent of Intech business unit's assets were derived from other Intech business units through customer financing and equipment leasing services.

Further aspects need to be considered regarding Intech business unit's culture and identity. When IBU was founded as a business unit within Intech corporation in 1997, this, for management and employees equally, meant a change from a protected head-office environment to an entrepreneurially-driven profit centre. Additionally, particularly during the first years of IBU's existence as a business unit, many employees were recruited from outside Intech corporation in order to manage strong growth. This process included the major acquisition of a financing company in the UK. Finally, Intech business unit due to its focus on financing and service business can be viewed as a knowledge-intensive unit (Kärreman and Alvesson 2004) within a rather manufacturing-focused environment in wide parts of Intech corporation. This will particularly play a role in the analysis of identity-related discourse.

5.2.3 Strategy and communication functions

At Intech business unit, strategy and corporate communication were managed in one overall business unit function, but split into two departments, each staffed with six employees. The researcher was responsible for Intech business unit's corporate communication team during the observation period.

Both departments covered similar tasks to their counterparts at Intech corporation level, but focusing on the execution for Intech business unit. The strategy team focused on tasks like the strategic planning process and steering business unit-wide strategic projects, e.g. the implementation of the Intech management system within IBU. Also divisional strategy projects within Intech business unit were set up and managed. The corporate communication team developed the internal and external communication strategy and implemented IBU-wide communication activities. These focused on the positioning of Intech business unit, media relations, branding and corporate design, internet, intranet and internal communication.

5.3 Situational focus

In Chapter 3, it was argued that a situational focus (Alvesson and Deetz 2000, 201) of the case study was essential. This aspect will now be addressed by highlighting the Intech management system as one of the core projects during the observation period in which strategy and communication processes were closely interrelated on Intech corporation and business unit levels.

Interaction and communication, as well as control and incentive systems have been identified as important elements of the management system in extant studies (e.g. Chakravarthy and White 2002). 'Exploration' of new strategy frontiers and 'exploitation' of existing markets and competencies are two major orientations in management systems (2002, 196-197).

Also within Intech, the case for implementing the management system within Intech was to embark on a path of permanent optimization to become an industry leader. The new management system was launched in October 2003 on the occasion of the Intech business conference – an annual event assembling the global top 500 managers. In the management magazine reporting on the launch, the board member in charge of the management system, explained the approach as follows:

'The [Intech] management system is a vehicle for implementing our strategy. As the name says, it's about taking a systemic approach to things. All three components of the system are conceptually and chronologically coordinated as well as logically linked to each other.'
(Intech board member) [55:22]

The manager refers to three key components of the IMS. The IMS contains (1) three company programmes (focusing on the topics of innovation, customer focus and global competitiveness), (2) a corporate calendar in order to align planning, decision-making, reporting and communications in business units, regions and corporate units along a common schedule, (3) the liability of managers for implementation.

In the initial phases after the launch, the three company programmes particularly dominated the interplay between strategy and corporate communication and also the output from the corporate communication department.

In order to facilitate and support the implementation of the company programs, a committee and office structures were launched. Members of the management board, business unit presidents, heads of regional companies and corporate units became members of these structures. Additionally, management development programmes were adjusted to the contents of the company programmes. The managers' performance in terms of active contribution to the management system became part of the incentive structures in addition to existing incentivization on economic value-added.

Both on Intech corporation and business unit levels a whole range of communication measures and publications were implemented in order to support the goals of the IMS. Intech corporation launched a new semi-annual corporate magazine for managers with news and interviews on proceedings in terms of the IMS. An intranet website was introduced with detailed information regarding the status of company programs and initiatives. The corporate communication department also started a new "Communications Excellence Program", an IMS-focused training initiative. Conferences were held for knowledge exchange and discussions among communication managers, followed by online chats with the three company programme heads.

Intech business unit corporate communication supported these corporate processes by reporting on the business conference and the relevance of the IMS for Intech business unit in their quarterly employee newsletter. Additionally, the IMS was presented and discussed by IBU top management at quarterly employee events which were filmed and subsequently broadcasted over the intranet.

5.4 Definition of corporate communication discourse

As this explanation of the IMS has shown, the launch of this management system had stimulated an intensive interplay between strategy and communication practices.

In the course of this study several aspects have been identified that point to the vital role of discourse in organising processes: (1) A gap for reviewing corporate communication from a discourse and practice perspective was identified, (2) discourse was found as an 'important and intrinsic aspect of managing' (Oswick, Keenoy et al. 1997, 5), and (3) it has been argued that discourse and communication have performative capacity to enact management processes (Watson 1997; Feldman 2000).

Due to this central role of discourse the decision was made to concentrate on a situational case study (Alvesson and Deetz 2000) focused on aspects of discourse. In order to fulfil the purpose of this study, it is necessary to focus the case specifically around corporate communication discourse which is interlinked with all four Strands of the framework in the situation of the launch of the Intech management system.

The general approach taken was to collect corporate communication discourse related to this situational focus as completely as possible (for a more detailed account of data collection and preparation, see Chapter 6). On the one hand, this included all corporate communication materials produced on the occasion of the Intech management system by Intech's corporate communication departments. In Chapter 6, this material will be referred to as 'text'. On the other, naturally occurring talk and interviews of two groups of managers directly involved in corporate communication discourse were monitored, namely strategy and communication managers on senior and middle levels[19]. The total stock of text, naturally occurring talk

---

[19] Other organisational groups essentially adopted the role of consumers of the texts produced by the strategy and corporate communication professionals at In-

and interviews, covering both strategy and communication managers, constitute corporate communication discourse at Intech, as used for the purpose of this study.

5.5 Scope and timing

In order to be able to detect emergent patterns (Pettigrew 1992), it is necessary to conduct data collection for an adequately longitudinal time period. This was achieved by extending the observation period over a full business cycle, i.e. from the business conference when the IMS was launched in October 2003 until after the next annual business conference in October 2004.

Table 4 highlights the key discourse segments covered during this observation period in chronological order.

Table 4. Data collection plan / selection of key discourses

Month	Corporate communication discourses covered (selection of key topics)	Intech corporation [IC] / Intech business unit [IBU] levels
October 2003	Intech business conference (IBC speeches)	IC
	Interpretations of business conference (meeting notes)	IBU
November 2003	Publications on IBC	IC
	Interviews with strategy and communication managers	IC / IBU
December 2003	Publications on IBC	IBU
	Intech business unit conference (speeches)	IBU
	Conference on role of communication	IC
January 2004	Interviews with strategy and communication managers	IBU
February 2004	Publications on IBU conference and company programmes	IBU / IC
	Newspaper interviews	IBU
	Interviews with strategy and communication managers	IC

tech, i.e. these groups did not actively participate in the processes forming corporate communication events and materials. Nevertheless, these groups decided on how to treat the information provided, e.g. by developing various modes of turning strategy into action. This aspect is not neglected, but referred to in detail in thematic and discourse analyses throughout this thesis.

Month	Corporate communication discourses covered (selection of key topics)	Intech corporation [IC] / Intech business unit [IBU] levels
March 2004	Meetings on internal communication, branding, messages, customer focus (notes and transcripts)	IBU / IC
April 2004	Conference calls and meetings on internal communication and internet (notes and transcripts)	IBU / IC
	Publications on status of IMS implementation	IC
May 2004	Radio interview / employee event on strategic direction	IBU
		IC
	Interviews with strategy and communication managers	IC
	Conference on role of communication	
June 2004	Publications on IMS	IBU / IC
	Meetings on internal communication	IBU / IC
July 2004	Workshops on role of corporate communication	IBU
	Results of study on media relations (presentation)	
August 2004	Announcements on organisational changes based on IMS	IC
		IBU
	Employee event	
September 2004	Conference on role of communication	IC
	Interviews with communication managers	IC
October 2004	Intech business conference (speeches)	IC
	Intech business unit conference (notes)	IBU
	Publications on IMS	IBU / IC
November 2004	Press conference	IC
	Interviews with strategy and communication managers	IC
		IBU
	Employee event	

An additional criterion was applied in order to gain the 'thick description' (Stake 2003) which is intended as a result of the analysis, and in order to do justice to the complex corporate structure on Intech. It was decided to include both Intech corporation and business unit levels in the observation. House, Rousseau et al. (1995) proposed that a full understanding of organisational processes requires examination of the 'meso' level – the simultaneous study of at least two levels of analysis. This also allowed the study to follow the implementation of the Intech management system down to the level of middle management, including its interrelations with the corporate level, i.e. top management. Intech corporation and business unit levels are highlighted in Table 4.

In concrete terms, the researcher was able to participate in and/or observe all discourse which was created by either Intech corporation's, or Intech business unit's corporate communication departments based on the initiation of the Intech management system during the period of October 2003 to October 2004. All discourse segments during that period were collected and prepared for analysis as explained in Chapter 6.

II Analysis

After having defined the theoretical context and after having defined the case as such, Part II covers the Chapters focusing on the actual analysis of the case study.

To start with, a framework for analysis is developed in Chapter 6. Chapter 7 addresses the specific role of context in this study, resulting in a reviewed definition of context. The core analysis work can be found in Chapters 8 to 11. Each of these Chapters concentrates on analysing one of the four Strands of interrelationships identified in the reference framework (see Figure 4). At the end of each Chapter, findings in reply to the research questions (see Table 3) and with regards to defining aspects of contributions towards an alternative theory of corporate communication are proposed.

Chapter 11 ends with putting forward an adapted framework based on the results of analysing each individual Strand of interrelations.

6 Analysis of case study

In Chapter 3 Intech was selected as a suitable case for studying corporate communication discourse, whereas a more detailed definition of corporate communication discourse followed in Chapter 5.

Chapter 6 deals with the methods to be applied in order to process and analyse the data collected throughout the case study. After presenting theoretical considerations, this will particularly include the actual collection and preparation of data and a detailed account of the dual method to be applied to analyse the data, namely thematic analysis and discourse analysis. In a summarising Section, the overall analytic framework is presented.

6.1 Theoretical considerations

A set of four terms characterises the general approach chosen for analysing the data which had been gathered from the case study: (1) rigorous process, (2) interpretive approach, (3) theory as a 'lens' and (3) hermeneutic understanding.

6.1.1 Rigorous process

According to Brewer (2000), ethnographic data bear certain specifics. For example, they are provided as sections of natural language, they are voluminous in scale, and their scope varies depending on the number of individual cases in which the ethnographer had participated in some way. In consequence, both bulk and complexity characterize ethnographic data (Bryman 2001). This is certainly true for the kind of data which was collected in the course of this research project.

In such high-volume, complex research projects, analysis can be defined as 'the process of bringing order to the data, organizing what is there into patterns, categories and descriptive units, and looking for relationships between them' (Brewer 2000, 105). Of key importance is the need to develop ways of 'systematic social investigation' (May 2002, 5).

What is now seen as a kind of common ground in being systematic and rigorous in ethnographic analysis, was summarised by Miles and Huberman (1994). They defined analysis as three concurrent flows of activity: 'data reduction, data display, and conclusion drawing/verification' (1994, 10). Analysis, in their terms, is seen as a continuous, inductive process – beginning with structuring the data, moving to organizing what is there into patterns, and, finally, looking for relationships between the patterns. This research project embraces all three aspects, as can be seen in Sections 2 to 4 of this Chapter. Section 2 (data preparation) covers aspects of data reduction and display, whereas Sections 3 and 4 (thematic analysis and discourse analysis) covers aspects of defining patterns and analysing their social construction.

6.1.2 Interpretive analysis

Sticking to a rigorous process, however, does not in itself define a complete approach to analysis. Analysis also needs to be consistent with the overall research paradigm chosen for a concrete project – namely the normative, interpretive, critical or dialogic paradigms (Deetz 2001). In other words: 'The point is for the researcher to be clear about what type of questions or claims drives the work at any particular time and how the work addresses the standards and criteria appropriate to it' (Deetz 2001, 18).

The overall research paradigm for this research project had been defined as interpretive in Chapter 3 (methodology). Deetz (2001) proposed that discourse- analytic approaches provide viable tools for gaining the desired interpretive understanding from data like ordinary talk, stories, printed communication materials etc. The later Sections will give further insight into how thematic and discourse analyses were conducted.

6.1.3 Theory as a 'lens'

As has come out of earlier Chapters of this report, both discursive and practice-oriented theories provide useful ways of conceptualising and structuring social processes such as corporate communication. Following Weick's (2003) iterative theorising process, extant management theories following either of these approaches were used throughout the analysis process in order to shed light on the discourse fragments and themes that are going to be analyzed. This plays a role during the identification and clustering of relevant themes (Section 3) as well as particularly in Section 4, when it comes to the discourse analysis. Alvesson and Deetz (2000, 37-

46) recently made a similar point when they argued that theory should be used as a 'lens' through which social processes are observed.

In summary, they suggest three functions of theory in the research and analysis process: (1) 'directing attention' towards details of importance, which can be particularly helpful when it comes to interpreting complex social processes (purely relying on individual perception of the researcher can be rather limiting); (2) 'organizing experience' in order to present the analysis as being part of relevant discourses; and (3) 'enabling useful responses'. The following analysis, for example, suggests alternative responses to orthodox corporate communication theory. To each of the four Strands of interrelations between strategy and communication processes, alternative communication theories are applied in order to provide a communicational reply to extant corporate communication theories which are predominantly adapting a container metaphor of communication.

6.1.4 Hermeneutic understanding

Hermeneutics can be interpreted as an extension of the discursive approach, including reflexivity, into the relationships between researcher, the researched and the reader. In hermeneutics it is assumed that there is not a single way of analysing social processes that is 'absolutely, universally valid or correct' (van Maanen 1988, 35). Again, this is in line with an iterative process of theorising (Weick 2003). In fact, thematic as well discourse analysis bear significant hermeneutic and emergent elements (Gummesson 2000). In the iterative process of moving back and forth, the hermeneutic approach shows a 'notion of openness to the data, the artful development of the interplay between the intuition of the researcher, the data of the subjects of study, the interpretive frameworks that are brought to bear on the analysis of the text and, ultimately, the reader' (McAuley 2004, 201). In other words, it is essential to become thoroughly familiar with the data, and then 'use the data to think with' in order to propose new concepts (Hammersley and Atkinson 1995, 210-211).

6.2 Data preparation

This stage of the analysis process embraces what Miles and Huberman (Miles and Huberman 1994, 10) called 'anticipatory' stages of a research project, namely the processes of data collection and storage.

All data for the Intech case study was collected solely by the researcher between October 2003 and December 2004. As explained earlier in this study, the researcher worked as a corporate communication manager with Intech business unit during that period. This provided him with the opportunity to participate in Intech's corporate communication discourse both on corporation and business unit levels, on an ongoing basis during that period. Data collection involved: naturally occurring talk, text and interviews. All these elements can be interpreted as constitutional to the term of organisational discourse which 'refers to the structured collections of texts embodied in the practices of talking and writing ... that bring organizationally related objects into being as these texts are produced, disseminated and consumed' (Grant, Hardy et al. 2004, 3).

6.2.1 Computer-assisted collection, storage and analysis

Computer-assisted data analysis software (CAQDAS) was used throughout several stages of data analysis and played a particularly important role in preparing data for analysis. The ATLAS.ti software package (version: WIN 5.0) was selected by the researcher, because compared with other packages it appeared particularly flexible with regards to the methodology and analytic framework chosen for this research project[20]. Additionally, ATLAS.ti had been successfully applied for discourse analyses before (Diaz-Bone and Schneider 2003).

All data collected for this research project was assigned to ATLAS.ti between June and December 2004. The overall body of text stored in ATLAS.ti totalled 107 primary documents, which is the equivalent of roughly 180,000 words. All iterative processes of data analysis – namely quoting, coding and memoing – were conducted within the software package, although printed hardcopies supported the processes.

The main benefits experienced by the researcher in the application of CAQDAS correspond with those of other researchers that had used similar packages before (Fielding 2002; Seale 2002; Diaz-Bone and Schneider 2003). First, it encouraged rigour and helped to increase transparency of the analytical process – e.g. by allowing public presentation of the underlying operations. Second, CAQDAS made it possible to retrieve data easily, based on coded segments or applying more complex search tools. This is of particular benefit in the case of large databases such as in the case of this study. Third, using ATLAS.ti provided support for quantification of qualitative data, an advantage which had also been observed by Seale (2002, 660), e.g. by providing counts of code words or words embedded in

---

[20] Other common CAQDAS seemed to be geared more towards grounded theory approaches (Diaz-Bone and Schneider 2003).

text data. This feature proved particularly useful in this study when it came to conducting the thematic analysis (see Chapter 7).

Seale (2002, 662) also pointed out that CAQDAS 'remains relatively underused' for purposes of discourse analysis itself. In addition, during this project, the researcher obviously conducted the interpretive stages in the analysis process personally. CAQDAS supported the retrieval of discourse sections that had been identified and coded as relevant for textual and discourse analysis, but once the discourse fragments had been identified, the analysis was conducted separately by the researcher.

6.2.2 Naturally occurring talk

In line with Silverman (2001), it is argued that taking advantage of naturally occurring data can help to make use of the full potential of qualitative data. Coffey (2002, 313) even went as far as stating that there is 'an increasingly widespread assumption that personal narratives offer uniquely privileged data of the social world'. Naturally occurring talk is defined as talk which exists 'independently of the researcher's intervention' (Silverman 2001, 159).

Given the overall research objective of shedding light on the social world of managing and communicating, and following Oswick, Keenoy et al's (1997, 6) argument that managerial 'doing' above all means 'talking', the researcher put a strong focus on gathering naturally occurring data. With 44 out of 107 documents assigned to the CAQDAS software, a large proportion of the overall data resulted from naturally occurring events. These events ranged from meetings on Intech corporation and business unit levels to interviews with journalists and semi-annual conferences among corporate communication and strategy professionals.

The role taken in the process of gathering naturally occurring talk was one of 'active membership' (Adler and Adler 1994). The researcher had disclosed the research project he was working on and participated in the naturally occurring events in his organisational role as corporate communication manager.

After asking for participants' permission, all naturally occurring talk was recorded on a digital recorder, transcribed on to disc and saved on the researcher's PC as well as on an external backup hard drive.

6.2.3 Text

Text, as defined by Silverman (2001, 119) identifies 'data consisting of words and/or images which have become recorded without intervention of a researcher'. Text, besides naturally occurring talk, constituted the second core of data collected throughout the observation period. While naturally occurring talk allows the detailed analysis of ongoing social processes, it is text which represents the stream of official discourse which occurred throughout the observation period. Text, above all, included outcomes of corporate communication and strategy activities at Intech that were transferred into speech format or published text, for example in the form of articles in management or employee publications, both on corporation and business unit levels at Intech.

The overall body of text encompassed 36 primary documents, of which 16 documents represented public talk and 20 documents published text. Particularly the documents representing public talk were generally very lengthy, because each document contained all public talk which was held at one specific event. For example, all speeches of a whole management conference were compiled into one primary document, allowing analysis by each of the four Strands. These 36 texts represent a complete stocktaking of speeches and articles which became available for employees within Intech corporation and business unit throughout the observation period in the context of the launch of the Intech management system.

Some of these texts were collected by the researcher via searches and regular visits to the relevant sites of the Intech intranet, others were provided by individual managers. In most cases, speeches and articles were available for download in PDF format. The researcher converted these texts into Rich Text Format (rtf) and assigned them to the CAQDAS database. Four texts had resulted from transcripts of speeches held at quarterly employee events at Intech business unit. IBU had itself produced verbatim transcripts of these events. The researcher got access to these transcripts and assigned them also to the CAQDAS database.

6.2.4 Interviews

The researcher had privileged access to capture occurrences of naturally occurring talk und primarily used this kind of data, as had been argued above. Following a positivist strand, interviews might have provided an alternative or even preferred way of capturing data on social practices like those at Intech.

Positivists or functionalists, however, are not normally concerned about the relationship between interviewer and interviewee, whereas interpretivists and constructionists see exactly this interrelationship 'as a topic in its own right' (Silverman 2001, 95). Researchers following an interpretive constructionist approach are interested in the question 'how interview participants actively create meaning', i.e. both interviewer and interviewee are viewed as playing an active role in the interview process, whereas according to positivist research only the researcher takes an active stance in interviews. In consequence, interviews in constructionist terms are processes of co-production and have to be analysed both in terms of 'how' and 'what' questions (Holstein and Gubrium 1995).

Considering the constructionist view which plays an important role in the whole set-up of this research project, interviews were applied selectively, but consciously used as a 'construction site of knowledge' (Kvale 1996, 42). Altogether 16 open interviews with four communication, strategy and human resources managers were conducted – precisely to let these managers construct their views on current social processes related to the four Strands of interrelated strategy and communication processes identified from the reference framework (see Chapter 4). In the course of the 13 months of the observation period each of these managers was interviewed four times. The interviews were conducted in an open mode. The researcher took the overview chart of the reference framework to each of the meetings and asked the interviewees to give their current view of what is going on in the organisation in relation to each of the four Strands.

The researcher recorded the interviews on a digital recorder, transcribed them on to disc and saved the data on the researcher's PC as well as on an external backup hard drive. Again, each of the interviews was assigned to the CAQDAS database.

6.2.5 Issues with data collection

Issues that occurred while data was collected can primarily be summarised as problems of language and transcription.

Language

It can be assumed that language problems regularly occur in international research settings[21]. Only few scholars, however, have picked up language

---

[21] Although the physical research setting in which this case study took place was focused on Germany, the full research process contained several international aspects. One aspect is that due to the international structures of Intech, not all participants were of German nationality, but represented a range of nationalities. Another international aspect is that although the research took place in Germany, this thesis is produced for a university in the United Kingdom. This, for example, had the implication that all data gathered in German needed to be translated into English.

issues in the context of international qualitative research projects (Wright 1996). Language problems in this research project concentrated on issues of translation which came up while collecting naturally occurring talk and, particularly, when conducting the interviews. All interviews were conducted in German and at German locations. In order to avoid the problem that translators might not be familiar with the concepts and language used in the concrete research setting (Wright 1996, 73), the researcher personally translated all interviews into English. He is a native German speaker and had to prove professional English language skills before being admitted to conduct this research project at Salford University. All interviews were translated while transcribing the interview recordings. The same process was applied to the translation of naturally occurring talk, although only a very small proportion of the naturally occurring talk had been recorded in German. Most meetings and events were held in English, although they took place in Germany, mainly due to international participation.

Both German and English are treated as official company languages at Intech. Therefore, an English language version was available from Intech for all texts which were used for this research project.

Transcription

The researcher is aware of the ongoing discussion on transcription quality and that something like the 'right' transcription standard does not exist (Poland 2002). The solution which Poland suggests is to apply a high level of reflexivity with regards to the transcription standards applied in a concrete research setting. Edwards (2003) provides a framework for structuring reflexivity by suggesting a set of format-based and content-based decisions.

The following format-based decisions were taken for this research project: Speaker turns were transcribed in vertical format. This decision was necessary in order to provide the data in a format which is suitable for further processing in the CAQDAS software: coding in ATLAS.ti, for example, required a vertical presentation of data. In order to ensure consistency among all types of data used, namely naturally occurring talk, text and interviews, no symbols were used within transcripts.

Content-based decisions included the following: Standard British English orthography was applied to encoding words. Details of pronunciation, pauses, prosodic features and nonverbal aspects and events were not preserved, because they do not form part of the discourse analysis which is used for this research project (see Section 4)[22]. Relevant features of the context were coded separately at a later stage in the analysis process (see Chapter 7). Decisions on 'unit of analysis' (Edwards 2003, 331) were not necessary as part of the transcription process, because ATLAS.ti allowed flexible coding based on individual definitions of units of analysis. As will also be shown in Chapter 7, individual fragments of discourse were selected as the units of discourse analysis (Boje 2001).

6.3 Thematic analysis

The data which was collected in the course of this research project can be defined as 'antenarrative'. This term was coined by Boje who suggested the use of antenarrative methods to analyse data which is 'too unconstructed and fragmented to be analysed in traditional approaches' (2001, 1). In order to scrutinize data of this kind, there is 'no shortcut way of applying systematised content analysis' (Hardy 2001, 36). Hardy suggests the application of the term 'craft' for this kind of research which had initially been promoted by Daft (1983). It was argued above that crafting an analysis and theorising process in this project followed an iterative route. The first step of this route focused on initial sense-making from the huge amount of antenarrative data that had been collected.

The aim of this step was to identify themes that occurred in corporate communication discourse at Intech according to the alternative view of corporate communication which had been developed earlier on in this study. In Table 3, in which the research questions for this study are presented, this aim is reflected in the column of research questions which was framed as 'Research questions related to stocktaking of themes'.

As part of the analysis process, this stage of analysis is framed under the term 'thematic analysis' which was conducted in order to achieve two aims: First, to reveal a rigorous, i.e. complete, taxonomy of themes (King 2004; McCurdy, Spradley et al. 2005). This was indispensable in order to give the antenarrative data initial structure and to make it possible to link the analysis process to the reference framework which had been developed in Chapter 4. The second aim was to do justice to the antenarrative character of the data which is meant to include 'the excess and in-between of

---

[22] This is not to say that details of pronunciation are generally unimportant. Rather 'what to include and how to do so must be informed by the theoretical stance and empirical focus of the study' (Poland 2002: 637). Conversation analysis, for example, relies on much more detailed transcripts than discourse analysis and, therefore, relies heavily on details of pronunciation.

theme analysis' (Boje 2001, 11) in the process of thematic analysis. Results of this second aim were underpinned with extant theory in order to provide a more robust version of themes which were then entered into discourse analysis. This will be considered in more depth in the next Section.

6.3.1 Approach to thematic analysis

Themes are the 'nucleus' of the social reproduction of communication by paraphrasing what is relevant in social systems and society as a whole (Knoblauch 2001, 216). They define what can become relevant for organisational actors by narrowing down thematic discourses.

As one of the key prerequisites for rigorous thematic analysis, themes need to be classified based on clear criteria. Owen (1984) proposed a discourse approach to thematic analysis by defining a theme as a 'patterned semantic issue of locus of concern' around a specific issue. 'Themes, then, are less a set of cognitive schema than a limited range of interpretations' (1984, 274).

According to Owen, a theme must meet three criteria in order to become relevant and identifiable in discourse: (1) recurrence, (2) repetition, and (3) forcefulness (1984, 275). Recurrence was assumed when 'at least two parts of the report had the same thread of meaning, even though different wording indicated such meaning'. Repetition denoted an extension of recurrence 'in that it is an explicit repeated use of the same wording'.

Both recurrence and repetition analyses were applied throughout this study, although it was not necessary to apply both criteria in all cases in order to identify relevant themes. In fact, in most cases recurrence analysis was sufficient, because most themes were rather constructed in a similar social order (which can be identified in recurrence analysis) than constructed by using a consistent set of wording (which is the focus in repetition analysis).

Recurrence was assumed when more than one discourse fragment (which had previously been assigned to one of the four Strands of interrelations between strategy and communication processes in the CAQDAS database) revealed the same aspect of alternative corporate communication discourse. Criteria to identify the latter were references to the performative capacity of communication. This criterion, as such, may sound rather vague. If applied in the context of one of the four Strands, however, it was sufficient to identify the main sub-themes. The empirical evidence for this will be given in each of the later analysis Chapters.

Repetition analysis was additionally necessary to better understand themes associated with Strand 1, i.e. processes of coordinating the company around dynamic purposes. In that case, only generic themes had been identified which related to this strand of interrelation, but a subset of themes was missing. Repetition analysis, then, revealed a consistency with regards to the wording used, based on which it was possible to define a subset of themes. In all other cases it had not been possible to identify themes which were based on a consistent use of wording. This may have to do with the nature of data used, because, for example, naturally occurring talk of individuals may focus on the same themes, but each individual may well use its own wording to explain the social construction of the theme.

Forcefulness, the third criterion in Owen's framework, applies to the individual form of discourse in the sense of the strength the argument proposed. 'The assumption here was that participants themselves could and did make sense of their relations' (Owen 1984, 276). Particularly different modes of engagement of participants in the research project (Boje, Oswick et al. 2004) form part of such considerations. A monophonic theme, for example, represents a 'single voice' with a high level of coherence (Boje 2001, 129), whereas polyphonic means that the discourse represents 'more than one possible reading' of an event by the participants (Boje, Oswick et al. 2004, 572). Forcefulness, in this research project forms part of discourse analysis which will be dealt with in the following Section of this Chapter.

6.3.2 Process of thematic analysis

Weiss (1994) suggests four steps for thematic analysis of qualitative data: coding, sorting, local integration and inclusive integration. Thematic analysis in this project focused on bringing order into the data, categorizing it and defining core themes that emerged from the discursive data. Therefore, only the coding, sorting and initial local integration steps are treated as part of thematic analysis in this report. Full local integration follows in a detailed discourse analysis (see Section 4), whereas inclusive integration is dealt with in Chapter 12 when all results of both thematic and discourse analysis are related back to the original reference framework.

Coding

The process of coding included several steps and was in itself treated as an iterative activity (Weiss 1994, 154-156). After all primary documents had been assigned to ATLAS.ti software, the researcher revised all data, and – while reading – marked all passages of naturally occurring talk, text and interviews which represented fragments of discourse that appeared as relevant in terms of the reference framework as quotations. 1,227 quotations resulted from this process.

In a consecutive step, six generic codes were created in the CAQDAS software, representing business context and outcomes (see reference framework) as well as the four Strands of interrelations which had been identified in the reference framework: (1) coordinating the company around dynamic purposes, (2) organising by linking decisions and actions, (3) facilitating implementation and processes, and (4) leveraging the competitive position and distinctive competencies. These codes are summarised in Table 5.

Table 5. List of generic codes

Descriptors of elements of reference framework	Generic codes
Business context	C Context
Strand 1: Coordinating the company around dynamic purposes	S1 Coordinating
Strand 2: Organising by linking decisions and actions	S2 Organising
Strand 3: Facilitating implementation and change processes	S3 Facilitating
Strand 4: Leveraging the competitive position and distinctive competencies	S4 Leveraging
Outcomes	O Outcomes

Sorting

The criteria of recurrence, repetition and forcefulness were applied in an additional coding process which concentrated on identifying individual themes within the six categories which had been coded already. Developing taxonomies for themes related to Strands 1 to 4 in the reference framework was the aim of this step. According to Spradley a taxonomy 'shows the relationships among *all* the included terms in a domain... [It] reveals subsets and the way they are related to the whole' (Spradley 1980, 113). Coding the text and then counting frequencies was used as 'a means of identifying key areas for further investigation' (Crabtree and Miller 1992, 95).

An additional taxonomy was elaborated for the Context code which is another key element of the reference framework.

As part of the process, the taxonomy of each theme was depicted in a matrix style as suggested by McCurdy, Spradley et al. (2005). Based on the CAQDAS database, quantitative measures like counts of quotations per code (Seale 2002) were added to each matrix.

Initial local integration

Summarising the 'main line' (Weiss 1994, 158) of each theme formed the core task of the local integration step. Four kinds of 'attribute questions' (McCurdy, Spradley et al. 2005, 63-64) – definition questions, comparison questions, triadic sorting questions and judgment questions – were used as an intellectual structure for these summaries. An analysis of how the individual theme related to orthodox corporate communication theory formed additional levels of analysis for each theme. This step was carried out in January 2005 and served as a preparation for the actual discourse analysis.

6.4 Discourse analysis

In order to provide answers to the research questions proposed in Table 3, it is necessary to drive analysis further than a stocktaking of themes. The third column of this table lists 'research questions related to the construction of themes'. It is suggested that discourse analysis provides a suitable method for analysing this set of research questions.

Discourse cannot only be interpreted as one of the major components of managerial activities (Oswick, Keenoy et al. 1997; Fairclough, Jessop et al. 2004), it also constitutes a core element of qualitative data analysis, particularly in case study and ethnographic designs (Cortazzi 2001). Also in the study, which forms the basis for this study, discourse analysis plays an important role in addition to thematic analysis.

6.4.1 Approach to discourse analysis

There are various approaches to discourse analysis trading under this label. Grant, Keenoy et al. (2001) even made the point that discourse sometimes comes close to standing for everything.

A look at the historic roots can, therefore, be helpful. Knoblauch (2001) traces these roots back to Foucault, who, as a social scientist, developed the basis for a communicational construction of reality and identity. Knoblauch pleaded for revising Foucault's approach, which had concentrated on power relations, and proposed a revised approach focusing on the following set out of Foucault's original elements: the interrelation between knowledge and action, the role of communication in the social construction of reality and the empirical application of discourse analysis. This is also the focus adopted for this study, because contextualisation of corporate communication theory is the approach rather than primarily focusing on power-related issues.

Alvesson and Kärreman (2000) provide additional guidance regarding research on organisations as discursive constructions. They distinguish discourse analysis along two dimensions: (1) as how close 'the connection between discourse and meaning' is assumed, and (2) whether the 'formative range of discourse' (2000, 1129) unfolds rather locally and individually or rather generally in grand discourse.

With regards to the first dimension, social constructionists (Gergen 1994; Gergen 2001) assume a fairly close link between discourse and the construction of the world. This view is also taken for this study and, for example, reflected in the term 'performative capacity' of communication, which plays a major role in the purpose of this study. According to this, discourse is indeed viewed as a 'structuring, constituting force' (Alvesson and Kärreman 2000, 1145).

In terms of the second dimension, a mixed stance was decided on. This dimension describes the focus on detail in local discursive context versus the focus on a rather universal connection of discourse fragments. Although the purpose of the study refers to corporate communication discourse in general, the researcher agrees with authors such as Alvesson and Kärreman (2000) or Antaki, Billig et al. (2003) who had pointed out that a pure focus on 'Grand Discourse' and 'Mega Discourse' needs to be seen as problematic. The argument is that it is necessary to pay considerable attention to detail in order to be able to unleash the performative elements of communication in very concrete ways – in order to be able to move along to broader concepts which appear from the data, possibly backed up by theory. This approach of moving between detail and overall theme has been successfully practiced by Vaara, Kleymann et al. (2004) in their analysis of strategic discourse in the case of airline alliances.

This selective focus on discourse in detail is also the actual reason for pushing the analysis further than the thematic level which could have been reached without discourse analysis, by purely focusing on a thematic level. As the four analysis Chapters will show, the additional analysis of individual discourse fragments makes it possible to reveal in much more depth than thematic analysis would have allowed the mechanisms according to which actors at Intech had constructed their world. This additional step was particularly useful in replying to the 'how' questions which had been raised as part of the set of research questions.

6.4.2 Process of discourse analysis

Fairclough (2003) recently provided a framework for discourse analysis which allows flexible treatment to meet the above demands of being able to move between detail and thematic level. This framework for analysis is based on Fairclough's former and widely applied work (1992; 1997). He suggests twelve elements which should be analysed in a full discourse analysis (2003, 191-194): (1) social events, (2) genre, (3) difference, (4) intertextuality, (5) assumptions, (6) semantic / grammatical relations between sentences and clauses, (7) exchanges, speech functions and grammatical mood, (8) discourses, (9) representation of social events, (10) styles, (11) modality, and (12) evaluation[23].

In previous work, Fairclough (1997) had proposed to distinguish three more generic levels of analysis: textual analysis focusing on individual texts, discursive analysis that concentrates on the characteristics of social discourses, and socio-practical analysis that grounds the discourses in specific contexts.

In the following analysis, focus will be on the discursive level as a starting point – backed up with selectively applied discourse analyses focusing on the textual level, when it was necessary to understand individual constructions in more depth. This decision was made in line with Vaara, Kleymann et al. (2004) who had proposed an ontological stance, which accepts that specific discourses construct social reality, and at the same time happen 'within, around, and because of, pre-existing structures' (2004, 30). In Reed's (1998, 212) words: If such an ontology is accepted, 'then it becomes possible to treat discourses as generative mechanisms or properties possessing certain "performative potentials"'. This view of discourse also allows interpretations beyond the specific language level by accepting discourses as clues to extra-linguistic issues (Alvesson and Kärreman 2000). By taking this stance, it will be possible, for example, to gain insight in strategy and communication practices embedded in constructions of actors, structures and activities (Jarzabkowski 2003).

As had been reported above, in the course of this project 1,227 relevant discourse fragments had been identified during the data collection and

---

[23] It is refrained from a detailed description of each element at this point of the discussion, because most of these concepts have been applied in various constellations in discourse analysis over a long period of time and can be referred back to in standard literature (for this argument see for example Antaki, Billig et al. 2003). Nevertheless, most of the concepts are defined and referred to in Chapters 8 to 11 when it comes to the practical application of discourse analysis in the concrete case.

thematic analysis processes of this project. It is surely in terms of resources and reporting space available not possible to conduct a complete discourse analysis for all 1,227 discourse fragments in this study.

Therefore the themes identified in thematic analysis were, first of all, taken as a starting point and structure for the discourse analysis, i.e. each theme was treated as one 'discourse strand' (Jäger 2001). Second, Jäger's (2001; 2001; 2004) definition of completeness of discourse analysis was used: 'The analysis is complete when it reveals no further contents and formally new findings', based on an analysis of 'what can be said' (Jäger 2001, 51). Eisenhardt had suggested a similar definition for completeness in that she stated that 'theoretical saturation is simply the point at which incremental learning is minimal because the researchers are observing phenomena seen before' (1989, 545)[24]. In practice, this means that for the analysis of each discourse strand, as many discourse fragments were used as were necessary to achieve completeness in Jäger's sense. All discourse fragments that were analysed this way are also displayed in this study.

Another aspect played an important role during the discourse analysis phase. It soon turned out that Fairclough's framework, although very comprehensive, does not reflect different layers or qualities among the elements. Fairclough treats discourse as a vertical process, starting with language-oriented and textual elements, ending with more interpretive features. What turned out during the actual analysis was a rather important horizontal element interlinking each of the four Strands of the reference framework with a web or network of themes.

A similar quality of the intertextuality of themes and discourses had also been observed by Broadfoot, Deetz et al. (2004). This aspect plays an important role in Chapter 12 when it comes to reviewing the original framework and moving on to suggest the core elements of an alternative theory of corporate communication. One consequence is that this theory has to 'deal with several discourses, conversations, texts, etc. which form links in chains of communication situations, in which "the same issue" is recurrently reconstructed, reformulated, and re-contextualized' (Linell 1998, 149).

---

[24] Eisenhardt (1989: 545) applies this definition of completeness to both 'theoretical saturation' and saturation of the iterating process of moving back and forth between data and theory.

6.5 Framework for analysis

In this Section, the results of the above considerations with regards to the analysis of the proposed case study are drawn together in order to summarise a plan for the subsequent Chapters in which the actual analysis is conducted.

The overall structure for what needs to be analysed was set by defining a list of generic codes in Section 6.4. Similar approaches for structuring antenarrative data proved successful in extant research. Beginning with a basic set of codes based on a priori theoretical understanding and then expanding on these while reading the text, for example, has been successfully used by Crabtree and Miller (1992).

In order to test whether this approach generates clear results, an advance analysis of the 1,227 quotations which were considered as relevant (see Subsection 6.3.2) was conducted. Each individual quotation was assigned one or more of the six generic codes. This initial coding process was conducted by the researcher in October and November 2004. The results of this process are listed in Table 6.

Table 6. Distribution of generic codes

Generic codes	No. of quotations
C Context	280
S1 Coordinating	184
S2 Organising	304
S3 Facilitating	189
S4 Leveraging	151
O Outcomes	119
Total	1,227

An interpretation of this distribution of generic codes, considering the expositions with regards to the antenarrative character of the data collected for the Intech case, should not lead to far. It allows to point towards two issues, however: (1) based on the extant data, it was possible to assign a significant number of quotations to each of the generic codes. This means that data actually contained discourse related to each of the codes. (2) Looking at the distribution of the generic codes alone does not allow any conclusions, but it points to the scope of the discourse around Strand 2 which identifies the processes of organising by linking decisions and actions. The number of quotations for this Strand was significantly higher than the number of quotations for all other Strands. This topic will be dealt with in Chapter 9.

Considering this distribution of generic codes, the researcher decided to structure the subsequent Chapters of this study in the order of the generic codes listed in Table 5 (Chapters 7 to 11).

One exception, though, was made with regards to code 'O Outcomes'. Thematic analysis showed that discourse fragments assigned to this code referred to ongoing issues rather than clear outcomes. Due to the antenarrative character of the data underlying this case study, this result did not surprise the researcher. In order to allow more specific conclusions, the discussion of outcomes was conducted in relation to each of the Strands of interrelation between strategy and communication processes (see Sections 5 of Chapter 8 to Chapter 11).

The interplay of data preparation and analysis which had been applied within Chapters 7 to 11 is summarised and visualised in Figure 3.

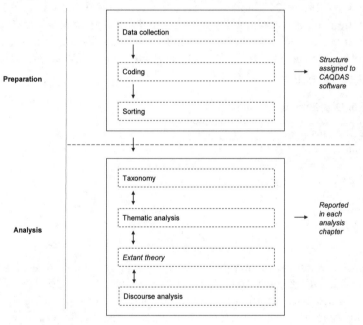

Fig. 3. Framework for analysis

Accordingly, the following analysis Chapters are structured in correspondence with the analysis box in this figure: (1) a taxonomy is developed for each Strand; (2) thematic analysis is conducted for all of the themes which had been identified in the taxonomy; (3), where applicable, it is made use of extant alternative management theories in order to shed light on the mechanisms construction each of the themes. And (4), discourse analysis is conducted for these themes in order to understand the construction of the themes in the concrete Intech case.

A Section with conclusions and theorizing towards an alternative corporate communication theory can be found at the end of each analysis Chapter.

7 Role and analysis of context

Whilst the previous Chapters have focused on providing the theoretical and methodological background, including data collection issues, this Chapter moves to the actual analysis. First, it will deal with context, before each of the four Strands of interrelations between strategy and communication processes are analysed subsequently.

The definition and role of context will also be relevant for all further analyses. By dealing with the general issues of context in this way, repetition of the discussion for each Strand of interrelations can be avoided.

7.1 Definition of context

Chakravarthy, Müller-Stewens et al. (2003), in their original framework for strategy processes, had distinguished between business context (summarising elements of context which are situated outside the company) and organisational context which embraced elements inside the company, like, for example, a management system.

Having approached this study from a social constructionist perspective, context takes on a different quality: management processes are viewed as embedded in and as part of context (Pettigrew 1992). Context and action need to be viewed as inseparable (Pettigrew 1990; Pettigrew, Woodman et al. 2001). It is no longer a set of external or independent elements influencing social processes, but social processes are themselves productive in that they form and construct context. Context forms, and is formed by, the everyday activities of all participants (Allen 2005).

From a communicational perspective, two kinds of information play a continuous role in building context: textual information which is conveyed through language and communication, and contextual information 'that is identified in relation to something else that is the primary focus of our attention' (Schiffrin 1994, 362). Therefore, context cannot be seen as an element in a 'vacuum' and it 'cannot exist unless we are thinking of "something else" (e.g. an image, a smell, a sound, a word, an utterance, a sequence of utterances' (Schiffrin 1994, 362). Context, in this sense, describes the 'environment in which "sayings" or other linguistic produc-

tions) occur' (Schiffrin 1994, 363). It is individual to the situation in which
it occurs and to the person who produces the text.

Schiffrin denoted different aspects of context which are relevant from a
discourse perspective (1994, 365-378): (1) context in terms of knowledge
('what speakers and hearers can be assumed to know'), (2) context as
situation ('both the "here and now" situation and knowledge of "types" of
situations), and (3) context as situation and text (considering 'both situation and text to be context').

The latter view matches Pettigrew's (1990; 1992; 2001) and Allen's
(2005) definitions who defined context from strategy process and general
social constructionist perspectives. This is, therefore, also used as the common denominator for this study.

7.2 Developing a taxonomy

Given the above notion of context as interlinked with concrete strategic action, most of the elements of context were developed inductively from the
quotations which had been coded before, which means that a set of mostly
'emic' terms (Boje 2001)[25] resulted from this process.

It had emerged from the readings of the quotations that five elements of
context were particularly prominent in discourse within Intech at corporate
and business unit levels, at a number of events and over an extended period of time. At the same time, these are the context-related themes which
generated the highest frequencies in terms of quotations: (1) references to
the management system that was implemented during the observation period (30 quotations), (2) roles expected from managers (32), (3) challenges
the participants faced (52), (4) interaction with customers (37) and (5)
other stakeholders (32) which formed part of the context in which strategy
and communication took place at Intech.

Each of these sub-themes was embedded in a wider discourse.

The 'management system' was not only referenced in generic terms, but
also the role of 'formal plans' in the implementation of the management
system was stressed by individual participants (4 quotations). Another discourse emerged around specific corporate 'events' that were held during
the launch phase of the management system (15 quotations), and 'incentives' were emphasized as an important element of the frame when the motivation to implement the management system was discussed (9 quota-

---

[25] The terms 'emic' and 'etic' were proposed by Boje (2001) in order to identify
issues that were derived bottom-up from empirical data (=emic) or top-down from
theory (=etic).

tions). These four themes were clustered under the term 'management framework', denoting the respective generic theme.

Aspects of 'role expectations' were mostly addressed to managers (32 quotations). In discussions between different participants, managers were repeatedly expected to provide clear aims and strategies guiding the way forward. They were also criticized for not communicating enough or in the wrong way. Similarly, discourse around 'challenges' was closely related to the management teams, which had argued that to achieve growth and profitability, at the same time and in a sustainable way, is the key challenge (52 quotations). A limited discourse had emerged around lacking a 'sense of urgency' (4 quotations). These three sub-themes were clustered under the 'managers' umbrella theme.

'Stakeholders' embraced another cluster of context elements in which strategy and communication at Intech were embedded. Stakeholder-related discourse focused around the following stakeholder groups: (1) employees (13 quotations), (2) customers (37 quotations), and (3) 'other stakeholders' like journalists, analysts or non-government organisations (32 quotations).

Further generic context-related themes were 'market factors', which were broken down into the 'business conditions' which focused on changes in the immediate business environment (12 quotations) and 'competitors' themes, covering discussions of competitors' changing strategies (5 quotations).

Throughout the observation period various characteristics of the 'Intech family' were referenced as important elements of the context. One stream was related to the complex corporate 'structures' (18 quotations), based on its global orientation and its overall ambitions. 'History' (5 quotations) – both of the overall corporation and the business unit – formed the second stream of family-related discourse.

Several discourse fragments pointed to 'regulations' (12 quotations) that were perceived as relevant context elements – both as regulations set in place by the company itself and defined by national or international institutions like the Securities and Exchange Commission (SEC) which for example regulates the information of shareholders.

The resulting taxonomy of themes is shown in Table 7.

It is quite remarkable that this taxonomy – created inductively – reveals elements of context going beyond the structural elements which could have been expected from a deductive approach.

Common strategy literature limits context to elements with a structural character like the business environment, organisational structures and the strategic framework of the company (Needle 2004, 3). The above taxonomy, apart from structural elements, also contains actors – e.g. managers and stakeholders – and strategic activities these actors perform – e.g. execution of plans, organisation of events and allocation of incentives. The interplay between context and action already begins to emerge from this taxonomy.

Table 7. Taxonomy for business context

Domain	Generic themes	Sub-themes	Recurrence [No. of quotations]
C Context [7.4]	Management framework [7.3.1]	Management system	30
		Formal plans	4
		Events	15
		Incentives	9
	Managers [7.3.2]	Role expectations	32
		Sense of urgency	4
		Challenges	52
	Stakeholders [7.3.3]	Employees	13
		Customers	37
		Other stakeholders	32
	Market factors [7.3.4]	Business conditions	12
		Competitors	5
	Intech family [7.3.5]	Structures	18
		History	5
	Regulations [7.3.6]		12
Total			280

This confirms Jarzabkowski's (2003) context-sensitive framework for strategic practices. In that study, strategic practices emerged as shared activities between the same three main constituents as found in the taxonomy: actors, collective social structures and the practical activities.

Adjusted to the terminology of the above taxonomy, the three dimensions defining the embeddedness of strategic practices at Intech can be defined as follows: (1) actors: management and stakeholders, (2) collective structures: Intech family, management system, and (3) strategic activity: formal plans, events, incentives, sense of urgency, regulations and challenges. Assuming that 'role expectations' also affected strategic activities this final term is subsumed as part of strategic activity, too.

7.3 Analysis of generic themes

A deeper insight is now given into the generic themes by quoting one discourse fragment per theme. Criteria for selecting the discourse fragment from the pool of fragments coded in the CAQDAS software were: (1) discourse fragment was chosen from a code which was part of the codes compiling the generic theme, and (2) that the quotation illustrates the interplay or embeddedness of action in context.

7.3.1 Management framework

The Intech management system which had been launched in October 2003 was viewed as an important element in which corporate communication discourse was embedded during the observation period, above all by setting the framework within which many management processes happened. Therefore, the Intech management system was referred to in many communication practices applied at both Intech corporation and business unit levels.

As content basis for most of these presentations served the Intech 'corporate story' (Larsen 2000), which was used by the Intech corporate communication department as a generic document for maintaining consistency in storytelling and for storing general information on the company. The Intech management system in that story document was portrayed in the following way:

'After years of individual programs initiated in response to the challenges of globalization, [Intech] will now get a systematic and comprehensive management system that unites all elements under one roof. The company's strategic focal points will continue as before. Reviewing and optimizing the corporate portfolio through acquisitions and divestitures will remain an ongoing task.'
([Intech] story) [53:14][26]

In this discourse fragment, the launch of the Intech management system is portrayed as change in the collective structures which contains transforming and stabilizing elements. Strategic activities like formal planning processes, events and reporting structures or incentives (see sub-themes in taxonomy) are 'united' through the new management system, while the 'strategic focal points' mentioned in the discourse fragment are stabilized.

The management framework as such will be analysed in all four of the following Chapters focusing on the individual Strands of interrelation between strategy and communication. An in-depth analysis of stabilising and transforming action, or 'continuity and change' (Normann 2001) will follow in Chapter 10 as part of the analysis of change processes at Intech.

---

[26] The numbers in brackets represent the identification number of the quotation in the CAQDAS software. Based on this number, the quotation can be traced back in the original ATLAS.ti file.

7.3.2 Managers

Not only top management, but managers in general were frequently quoted as 'key actors' (Jarzabkowski 2003) in many of the practices that were set in place during the observation period. In consequence, extensive discourse had evolved around the role of managers in strategic practices. This discourse focused on themes like creating sufficient sense of urgency in change processes, preparing the company for upcoming challenges, but also specific expectations managers were confronted with during the launch of the Intech management system. Much of that discourse concentrated on the question of how managers can improve the top-down flow of information which had been expected to happen as part of the IMS launch. This discourse took place both on Intech corporation and business unit levels, and was driven by top management, employees and managers themselves.

A senior manager at Intech business unit explained his view in the following way in a discussion with his corporate communication team in May 2004:

'We talk about the fact that many people do not feel well-informed in the collaboration with their immediate boss. But this does not have to do anything with the information itself, it is simply that the manager does not take enough time to inform them about topics or to talk at all with them about topics that go beyond the daily work assignments.'
(Senior manager at Intech business unit) [40:16]

Managers are clearly seen as actors (i.e. elements of context for strategy and communication processes) that need to support communication processes (i.e. action in the sense of strategic activity). In Chapter 9 the ongoing cascade processes will be analysed in detail, and managers play an important role in this.

7.3.3 Stakeholders

The term 'stakeholders' was one of the few terms in the taxonomy which were not developed inductively from the data, but which was deducted from literature. One of the most common definitions of stakeholders was proposed by Freeman (1984, 46): 'A stakeholder in an organization is any group or individual who can affect or is affected by the achievement of the organization's objectives.' This broad definition was also used for defining this generic theme of the taxonomy in order to embrace individual stakeholder groups like employees, customers and other stakeholders such as journalists and analysts.

The most prominent stakeholder-related discourse in terms of number of quotations focused around the strategic role customers should play at Intech corporation and business unit. Much of this discourse was again initiated through the launch of the IMS – more specifically, the 'customer focus' company programme that formed part of the IMS.

The following discourse fragment was taken from the December 2003 issue of Intech business unit's employee magazine. The interviewee, one of the general managers of Intech business unit, had been asked which of the company programmes he viewed as the most important one for his unit:

'Customer focus, quite clearly. This is an area where we still have a lot to learn. Customers must not be a side phenomenon but should have a distinct impact on an organisation like [Intech business unit]. I have the impression that we are too much internally oriented. Customers – both [internal] and external customers – pay our bills and justify our existence.'
(Intech business unit manager) [15:20]

This discourse fragment represented a view which was quite common at Intech business unit during the observation period. Customers are an element of context, e.g. represented in the customer focus company programme, a structure which had been created Intech-wide. Customers are also seen as actors, e.g. by 'paying the bill', and they also enforce communicational processes, e.g. by contributing to the company's identity in terms of justifying its existence.

Exposition: On stakeholder thinking

The orthodox view of stakeholder theory declaring 'that a company should be run for the benefits of all those who may be deemed to have a stake in it' (Argenti 1997, 442) has been criticized heavily. One stream of critiques follows the path that such theory makes it necessary to define ways to value one stakeholder against the other which is seen as impossible, because in the end only shareholder relationships can be valued objectively in terms of return on equity (Argenti 1997). The second stream of critique argues that stakeholder theory in practice is often used as a rhetoric tool to advertise good practice rather than actually acting according to it. 'Stakeholder management damages the interests of those stakeholders whilst giving the impression that they are being attended to' (Thomas 1999, 15).

The focus in this study is going to be another one. The purpose of the research project is to explain how communication and strategy processes interrelate in the sense of strategic practices. Therefore, the role of stakeholders as actors in these practices of social constructions becomes core.

This approach becomes clearer in Näsi's (1995) notion of 'stakeholder thinking':

'By stakeholder thinking we mean a way to see the company and its activities through stakeholder concepts and propositions. The idea then is that "holders" who have "stakes" interact with the firm and thus make its operations possible.' Näsi (1995, 19)

Defined that way, management also needs to be viewed as a specific type of stakeholders – those which have an interpreting function (i.e. to understand the complexities of the stakeholder world and its implications for the company) and a balancing function (i.e. directing the company's actions in a way that the company's and the stakeholders' interests are kept in equilibrium). Kujala (2005, 564), following this approach, proposed the following inventory of stakeholders: customers, employees, owners, competitors, suppliers and dealers, community and government, financiers, and the environment.

Eberhardt (1998), in his 'modified stakeholder approach', puts a strong focus on the interpretive tasks of management. These include the identification of significant stakeholder groups, the detailed identification of the demands of these stakeholders and the development of appropriate responses.

Rather than purely focusing on response, Deetz (1992; 1995; 1997; 2001), from a communicational perspective, has repeatedly made the point that participation should be the solution for the 'balancing' task. This particularly because the relations between company – managed by managers on behalf of the company – and stakeholders are laden by aspects of power, legitimacy and urgency (Pajunen and Näsi 2005).

These aspects will be dealt with in more detail in the analysis of the four Strands of interrelations between strategy and communication processes at Intech in the following Chapters.

7.3.4 Market factors

Market factors can be viewed as among the more common facets of context for communicational and strategic activity (Needle 2004). Intech business unit's CEO explained the changing market environment in an interview with a business journalist in February 2004 the following way:

'I mean, on the financial market, all of us are driven by what happened during the last three years. And here we have to recognize that today things are improving, also in Germany. Banks in Germany left their low behind, and we have learnt a lot during the last three years with regards to efficiency and focusing – resulting

in organisational consequences which to a large part have been taken already… This is the environment, which means that competitors on the side of the banking industry are getting a foothold again. They are in future dealing with less internals, and, instead, are going to pay more attention to their profitability again… This I am only saying, because, as a result, the environment for [Intech business unit] will be more oriented to competitors than it was the case during the last two to three years.'
(Intech business unit CEO) [20:2]

The CEO refers to changes in the market environment which had taken place over several years. A difficult economic environment had marked not only banks, but business as such. Two aspects of the discourse fragment should be emphasized again with regards to the embeddedness of strategic practices: (1) context as such is not seen as static, but as evolving over time (e.g. from highly volatile to more stable), (2) as market factors are changing, they also continuously shift the focus of attention within Intech business unit, i.e. from dealing with internal processes to observing what competitors do. Again, a conclusion can be drawn that the environment influences the way strategic practices are handled in the company.

7.3.5 Intech family

Finally, also the Intech family continuously played a role when managers were making sense of their world. Particularly at Intech business unit, whose divisions relied to a significant degree on doing business with other Intech units, activities were continuously monitored in light of the 'family'. The following discourse fragment covers a short section of a radio interview one of Intech business unit's senior managers gave in May 2004:

[Journalist]: Your clients – are they primarily [Intech] clients or do you go beyond the [Intech] family when trying to line up business?
[Manager]: For the time being, probably 70% are [Intech] clients and as a captive finance company, we would like to have at least 50% of our client base coming from [Intech].
(Radio interview) [35:2]

This fragment shows that being part of the Intech family serves as a defining element in the purpose of Intech business unit. Purpose at the same time is, however, to extend external business as far as possible. Context, in this case, then, is also a limiting factor, because it does not allow the CEO to grow external business above 50%. Again, context interferes with ongoing practices.

7.3.6 Regulations

Regulations that were mentioned as elements of context comprised external regulations, e.g. legal or governance-related issues, as well as regulations the company decided to implement as part of its business processes, mainly covering compliance issues and regulations of business processes. The following example was taken from an internal circular at Intech in which new communication guidelines were communicated – necessary due to respective stock exchange regulations:

> As you are aware, [Intech] became subject to oversight by U.S. regulatory authorities following its public listing on the New York Stock Exchange…. We have adapted our worldwide communication practices accordingly and established principles governing communication on business matters (the "Principles of Communication"). These Principles have now been updated to reflect new legal requirements particularly in the U.S. and Germany.
> (Intech communication guidelines) [68:1]

Again, as with previous examples, changes in context lead to adaptations of ongoing strategic and communicational practices.

7.4 Context reviewed

Figure 4 highlights the role context played in the revised framework for analysing interrelated strategy and communication processes. It represents an adapted version of Figure 1 in Chapter 4.

Having gone through the analysis of context-related discourse, a someway different picture of context emerges. As the examples used in thematic analysis have shown, elements of context were generally referred to as part of a concrete business process or strategic practice. It is hardly possible to view either elements of context or strategic practices alone.

Instead, strategic practices always take place in a specific context (Needle 2004). In other words, context is treated as a 'frame … that surrounds the event being examined and provides resources for its appropriate interpretation' (Fitch 1998, 94).

Given this perspective on context, the original distinction between business and organisational contexts as separate elements of the reference framework is no longer maintained. As first amendments of Chakravarthy, Müller-Stewens et al.'s (2003) original framework, context is removed from the process itself and literally drawn as an actual frame within which all strategy and communication processes are taking place.

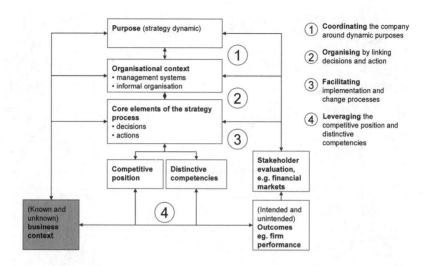

Fig. 4. Referring back to context in the reference framework

Additionally, relations with stakeholders need to be added as part of management processes (Müller-Stewens, Lechner et al. 2001). Based on the assumptions made in the exposition on stakeholder thinking, stakeholders are explicitly included in the framework. The dotted line around their box was chosen as a reminder that they need to be seen as both part of context and as actors framing concrete communication and strategy processes.

These amendments are illustrated in Figure 5.

This alternative view of context, however, also has implications for the way in which the subsequent analysis needs to be conducted. Pettigrew, recently in an interview stated that strategy processes should be analysed 'through the double lens of outer and inner context of the firm' (Starkey 2002, 21), i.e. management research should 'involve the simultaneous analysis of the contexts, contents and the process of change'. Context, therefore, needs to play an ongoing role in the analysis of all four Strands of interrelationships between strategy and communication which had been identified in the framework.

This aspect was implicitly covered when the analysis methods were chosen. The thematic analysis in this Chapter allowed a stocktaking of relevant elements of context, and it also provided ample indications and arguments that context and activity are related in an ongoing exchange.

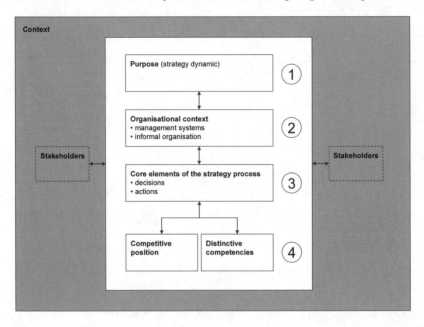

Fig. 5. Context as a frame for strategy and communication processes

Still missing is an explanation of how context, in a very concrete way, influenced strategic and communicational practices at Intech. Discourse analysis, based on Fairclough's (1992; 1997; 2003) framework, will allow this to be achieved. Mumby and Clair (1997, 181) put it the following way: 'Discourse is the principal means by which organization members create a coherent social reality that frames their sense of who they are', i.e. a reality which is framed by context. The 'discourse analysis' Sections of the next four Chapters will each give appropriate accounts of the interrelations between context and action.

8 Coordinating the company around dynamic purposes

Table 8 highlights the generic code which was assigned to all discourse fragments that cover aspects of the descriptor for Strand 1 – Coordinating the company around dynamic purposes. In addition, the specific research questions for the analysis of Strand 1 are listed. These research questions were adopted from Table 3 in Chapter 4. In order to allow easy orientation throughout the remaining part of this study, a similar table is also inserted in the introduction of Chapters 9 to 11.

Table 8. Focal points for analysis of Strand 1 – Coordinating the company around dynamic purposes

Generic codes	Descriptors for Strands of interrelation between strategy and communication processes
S1 Coordinating	Coordinating the company around dynamic purposes
S2 Organising	Organising by linking decisions and actions
S3 Facilitating	Facilitating implementation and change processes
S4 Leveraging	Leveraging the competitive position and distinctive competencies
Research question related to stocktaking of themes [Thematic analysis]	
Which purpose-related themes did corporate communication discourse cover?	
Research question related to construction of themes [Discourse analysis]	
How did the performative capacity of corporate communication emerge with regards to coordinating the company around dynamic purposes?	

Having in Chapter 7 given an overview of the role context played at Intech, this Chapter is the first of four Chapters covering a full cycle of interpretations as defined in the framework for analysis.

Although talking about a company's purpose appears a rather straightforward exercise, the collection of related discourse fragments that had appeared after the coding process at first sight looked fairly incoherent. In order to make initial sense of the data, therefore, an 'etic' approach (Boje 2001) – based on a theoretical pre-structuring – was chosen to develop a taxonomy.

8.1 Developing a taxonomy

The objective of this section is to give an initial overview of the themes that emerged as part of the overall discourse on 'coordinating the company around dynamic purposes' and to summarise the themes in a taxonomy.

A literature search showed that certain key concepts recur continuously when analysing data related to the purpose of a company from a discourse viewpoint.

One set of concepts is generally related to the process of managing the 'totality' of a company, i.e. its 'core idea' or 'basic nature', which in the course of this study will be referred to as the 'business concept' (Alvesson 2002, 71-76). Other writers have also used the general term strategy to refer to the business concepts and the activities intended to achieve it (Ashforth and Mael 1996, 19). Strategy as applied in this study, however, refers primarily to strategic practices as defined above. Therefore, the term 'business concept' was retained to identify the generic theme.

The other set of concepts emerges around the notion of identity which was traditionally defined as the 'central, distinct and enduring' dimensions of a company (Albert and Whetten 1985). The orthodox concept of corporate identity typically refers to something that sets an organisation apart from its surroundings (van Riel 1992). Viewed from a communicational perspective, however, 'identity is closely related to the ways living systems make sense of themselves and their environments' (Cheney, Christensen et al. 2004, 107). Identity, then, becomes more fluid and is closely related to what companies say and do and how its members and stakeholders construct their identity. This kind of identity is also embedded in the company culture and its underlying values (Albert 1998; Hatch and Schultz 2002)[27].

The development of a taxonomy based on these two generic themes – 'business concept' and 'identity' facilitated the initial structuring and analysis of themes – and still allowed, as the taxonomy shows, to reach the status of completeness with regards to the stocktaking of themes. It was possible to cluster all discourse fragments related to Strand 1 under subthemes of either business concept or identity.

Themes that, based on recurrence analysis, emerged within the business concept discourse were: discourse covering strategic practices, again in-

---

[27] In the course of this study, culture is not treated as a concept separate from identity. Instead, the Hatch and Schultz (2002) model of culture is assumed which suggests that a company's culture is always part of the company's identity. According to this model, company members and other stakeholders always implicate their company's culture in their identity dynamics.

cluding actors, structures and activities, termed as the 'strategy' sub-theme (78 quotations). A second sub-theme had emerged around 'dualities' (40 quotations) inherent in Intech's business concept. Sánchez-Runde and Pettigrew (2003, 245) pointed out that dualities are 'opposing forces that need to be balanced because … in fact they are complementary'. Dualities, then, are not insoluble like paradoxes, but rather need to be viewed as two sides of the same coin. The third sub-theme was termed 'heterogeneity' (6 quotations) – an expression which had emerged in an emic way from data analysis and was quoted by several managers as a factor influencing the business concepts.

Table 9. Taxonomy for Strand 1 – Coordinating the company around dynamic purposes

Domain [Section]	Generic themes [Section]	Sub-themes [no. of quotations]	Repeated terms [no. of word counts]
S1 Coordinating [8.2]	Business concept [8.2.1]	Strategy Intech corporation [78]	Strategy [99], vision [15], customers [79], employees [68], success [33], portfolio [34], focus [40], innovation [13], global [12], growth [53], profitability [46], economic value-added (EVA) [21], responsibility [15]
		Dualities [40]	Positioning [50], captive/internal business [85], external business [52], growth [53], profitability [46], continuity [9], change [29]
		Heterogeneity [6]	Market [39], challenges [29], family [24], business environment [14]
	Identity [8.2.2]	Culture [37]	Culture [105], change [65], organisation [49] Employees [142], customers [88], managers [75][28]
		Values [23]	Values [117]
Total			184

'Identity' discourse remained somehow more unstructured or 'multifaceted' (Soenen and Moingeon 2002), and at the same time reflected the

---

[28] The terms 'employees', 'customers' and 'managers' were used in the context of the whole identity theme, i.e. it referred to culture as well as to values.

struggles inherent in ongoing identity processes – often based on 'information equivocality' (Kreps 1990, 103).

Aspects of company culture formed an important part of identity discourse (coded as 'culture' – 37 quotations). Another theme which had emerged continuously as part of the identity processes at Intech were the company values and principles which had been communicated as part of the launch of the Intech management system ('values' – 23 quotations).

Table 9 shows the taxonomy for the themes which were identified in a structured format.

8.2 Thematic analysis

The aim of this step in the analysis process is to deepen the stocktaking of themes by giving insight into concrete examples of fragments that constituted the discourse.

As mentioned in Chapter 6, which covered the general analysis methods, repetition analysis was used in addition to recurrence analysis which had been conducted for developing the taxonomy. This step was necessary in order to reach full understanding of the themes, which, purely based on the coding process, had not yet revealed a sufficient level of coherence.

The criterion of repetition was analysed via the ATLAS.ti word crunching facilities (results see in Table 8 and, in more detail in Table 17 in the Appendix). A word count was run over all quotations that had been coded as part of the business concept and identity themes[29]. Afterwards, the words were sorted according to the number of word counts in order to distil significant word clusters. This method produced several word clusters for the business concept theme, whereas the identity theme remained more unstructured. Results of this thematic analysis are explained in the following Subsections.

---

[29] It might be criticized that such an approach implicates an artificial quantification in an actually qualitative analysis. Word crunching, however, was not conducted in order to generalize from its results, but to use results as an entry point into deeper analysis. The aim is to get a better overview of the themes a very heterogeneous stream of discourse actually focused on. Word counts have been applied as a legitimate approach to that problem in various traditions of discourse analysis. According to Fairclough (2003, 129), for example, vocabulary is likely to be among the most distinguishing features of discourse. Also Jäger (2001, 2004) pointed to the importance of repetitions in wording as a criterion for defining significance of a discourse.

8.2.1 Business concept

The three generic themes which had been identified as part of the taxonomy were also confirmed in repetition analysis: (1) strategy, (2) dualities, and (3) heterogeneity. These three themes are going to be analysed in more depth now.

Strategy

'Strategy' as a term produced 99 counts and, therefore, was the most frequently counted word within the business concept theme. Discourse happened mostly in what was termed as 'text', which means published sources of information like company publications, public speeches etc.

Strategy, in the Intech case, was communicated less by an overall 'vision' (15 counts) than through a focus on individual stakeholder groups, on a specific business portfolio and on general business objectives.

Discourse around 'customers' (79 counts) and 'employees' (68 counts) as target groups even dominated other strategy elements in terms of repetition.

Particularly the company media stressed the importance of these target groups for overall 'success' (33 counts). The quarterly management publication, on the occasion of the launch event for the Intech management system in October 2003, pulled the attention towards customers: 'A systematic sales approach, the winning of new customers and the exploitation of synergy benefits through cross-selling are all short-term focal issues that require immediate action' [55:6]. At the same event, need for a more conscious attention to managers and employees as well as their education was expressed by one of the general managers: 'Finally, there is also considerable potential for improvement in management training and in the vocational training and continuing education of our employees. We spend a lot of money here, but we don't get the returns that we should' [54:25]. These are just two short fragments underlining the focus on these two stakeholder groups. Focus on stakeholders will play an ongoing role throughout the analysis.

Apart from the target groups, strategy discourse concentrated on the actual 'portfolio' and business activities (34 counts). Particularly often the specific 'focus' of activities was mentioned (40 counts). Continuity in terms of the business portfolio, in conjunction with the expertise developed in specific market segments remained part of the strategy and was also stressed by the general manager in his speech one year after the above event in October 2004: 'We have continued to develop these businesses over decades and generations. And even in difficult times, we haven't been deterred from pursuing a broad portfolio of activities within this enormous business field' [97:8].

'Innovation' (13 counts) and 'global' presence (12 counts) became visible as two further elements of the strategy discourse. An example for innovation discourse: 'Commercially successful innovation..., this is setting the pace in an industry. That's what we want, and that's the best for our customers also', Intech's CEO said in a company TV interview in November 2004 [108:7]. This statement is an example for official strategy discourse, which was published and broadcasted in the company media, aiming for communicating a coherent picture of strategy discourse.

Discourse on the generic business concept theme also contained some of the ends to which strategy is done at Intech. Again, repetition analysis delivers some key terms. 'Growth' (53 counts), 'profitability' (46 counts) and 'economic value-added' (21 counts) – basically representing shareholder value – defined measures of financial and market success as the overall rationale of the company. This came across rather consistently in the official communication both on corporation and business unit levels. A general manager of Intech business unit summarised at an employee event in November 2004: 'Our motto has not changed: Go for profit and growth remains the Charter of [Intech][30] and thus for [Intech business unit]' [103:10].

The ends of the company are not purely defined in financial terms. Also 'responsibility' (15 counts) was an issue – as part of the strategy discourse in a rather weak form, however – in a second order after having paid attention to the main stakeholders, i.e. customers, employees and shareholders. Again an example from one of the speeches at the October 2004 conference, where one of the general managers said: 'Our main responsibilities are to our customers, our employees and our owners, the shareholders. We also have a broader responsibility to society' [97:7].

Dualities

Strategy, so far, has appeared as a fairly consistent and straightforward discourse. In repetition analysis, however, additional pairs of terms became apparent which did not represent homogeneity, but pointed towards several contradictions or at least competing goals inherent in the strategy discourse. In a very concrete way, these dualities were represented in pairs of opposing terms: the 'positioning' (50 counts) of Intech business unit

---

[30] In this study the original company name was replaced by the Intech pseudonym. In all cases in which the original company name occurred in quotations of the empirical data, the term 'Intech' was put in brackets.

was identified as rooted in a contrast of 'captive/internal' business (85 counts) and 'external' business (52 counts). The challenges Intech corporation and business unit faced were felt as a tension between 'growth' (53 counts) and 'profitability' (46 counts). 'Continuity' (9 counts) and 'change' (29 counts) were used to describe the situation Intech corporation and business unit are in.

In an interview with a journalist in February 2004, the CEO of Intech business unit made an explicit statement about this kind of opposing forces: 'This is what the strategy of a captive financial services provider needs to manage: to exist in a field of tension. This is the framework for its strategy' [20:39]. Jackson (1999) as well as Sánchez-Runde and Pettigrew (2003) suggested the use of the term 'dualities' in order to stress the 'opposing yet complementary nature of these elements' (Achtenhagen and Melin 2003, 306). This term was adopted for labelling this theme throughout this study. As Intech's CEO put it: 'These things, so to speak, need to weigh up carefully, and find a balance', he said in the same interview which has been quoted above [20:9]. Sánchez-Runde and Pettigrew (2003, 245) made the same point when they said that even if dual forces are seen 'as paradoxical or contradictory, in fact they are complementary'.

Discourse around the duality of Intech business unit's positioning as a captive provider – doing business with and for its parent company Intech – as well as an external provider – offering services in its own right to customers outside of Intech – showed, however, that this duality of the business concept in practice caused struggles.

The two positions were the following. Top management tended to stress the captive positioning. One more example can be highlighted from the CEO who said in a radio interview: '[Intech business unit] is a captive finance company. At the same time, we are one of the 14 business units of the [Intech corporation]; therefore, we are responsible for providing earnings to [Intech] and we have our own balance sheet' [35:1]. Operational managers, however, frequently did not understand this unilateral positioning in internal business. A sales manager whose job was to acquire customers outside of Intech said: 'If we build up the muscle to be a captive provider, there will be a negative impact on the positioning as a financial services provider in its own right, credible, and generally in a B2B sector' [21:8].

Apart from the fact that dualities and tensions with regards to the business concept existed in the minds of participants, repetition analysis revealed another tendency: most discourse fragments which were located in text, i.e. official company publications and public speech, represented a monophonic discourse. Naturally occurring talk, instead, represented a much more polyphonic spectrum of interpretations, stressing tensions and struggle with individual aspects of the business concept.

Heterogeneity

Several elements of context which were identified in Chapter 7 re-appeared in repetition analysis and were referenced as part of the overall heterogeneous picture that had been gained from Intech. Examples for factors contributing to a heterogeneous picture of Intech are various 'market' factors (39 counts), 'challenges' demanding various reaction (29 counts), and the complex structures of Intech 'family' (24 counts). This supports a theory which had been proposed by Janssens and Steyaert (1999, 131): that balancing of dualities is addressed in dynamic and spatial terms, e.g. within the specific social context in which they are embedded. This process is inherent in the examples mentioned above. The CEO clearly referred to the expectations of the Intech family when he argued for the captive business concept – at the same time, the sales manager was concerned about market factors like customers and competitors when he argued that in this environment an external positioning is necessary. In that sense, referring to social context is used as one way of 'bridging over' (Alvesson 2002, 74) contradictions between ideals and perceived reality in this case.

A more detailed analysis of the relations between strategy, duality and context themes will follow below, because in order to obtain the full picture, issues related to the business concept need to be seen in their relationship with identity issues.

8.2.2 Identity

Whereas repetition analysis immediately revealed specific topics related to the business concept, this was not immediately the case for identity-related discourse (see Table 18 in the Appendix).

Further insight into identity discourse gained from word crunching seemed limited. Above all, the interrelated set of themes that was presented in the taxonomy, was confirmed. The two sub-themes of 'values' (117 counts) and 'culture' (105 counts) achieved significant evidence.

With the heterogeneity of discourse pointing to various aspects of identity interrelating in the company practice at Intech, the approach was chosen to better understand and define the various dimensions of identity that appeared from the data. Researchers like Humphreys and Brown (2002) had suggested the use of existing theoretical frameworks for making sense of identity processes.

Soenen and Moingeon (2002) proposed a suitable framework for structuring the identity theme, explicitly drawing on a multidisciplinary background in which strategy and communication literature on identity were integrated. Their framework suggests 'five facets of collective identities' (2002, 17-21): (1) 'professed identity' – statements of participants to identify their identity, (2) 'projected identity' – identity communicated by the company, (3) 'experienced identity' – utterances of what participants feel and experience about their company, (4) 'manifested identity' – long-terms characteristics of a company, and (5) 'attributed identity' – how different stakeholders see the company. These five facets alone give evidence of a high degree of complexity associated with identity issues.

Albert (1998) proposed an additional dimension: 'The question of identity is at the heart of the idea of level' (Albert 1998, 10), meaning that identity can be posed at any level of analysis – individual, group, organisation or industry – and that each of these levels are interrelated. This part of the thematic analysis will focus on the organisational level because this generally is the level corporate communication discourse concentrates on. This is not to disguise the fact that this discourse also influences other levels of identity, and vice versa. Intertextualities of that kind, however, will be covered in later stages of the analysis.

In this thematic analysis, the focus is on shedding light on whether and how the five facets of identity emerged in Intech's corporate communication discourse.

Professed identity

Professed identity at Intech corporation and business unit did not appear as a homogeneous stream of statements. One of the managers at Intech business unit explained it this way in a meeting with members of the corporate communication team: 'I do not have an answer now to what our identity is. [Intech] overall has this problem. What is [Intech]? You will get different answers when asking different people.' [17:5] Soenen and Moingeon as well had detected inconsistencies in many organisations when they summarised 'the extent to which professed identity is actually communicated to others ... varies positively with the group's legitimacy, status, and power within the organization' (2002, 18). This was clearly the case at Intech – to the extent that professed identity, depending on who commented on it, basically demonstrated all fragments of content which had already been revealed in the business concept analysis.

Projected identity

This facet essentially includes aspects of identity which are communicated through 'products' of corporate communication departments – image brochures, advertisements, internet presences, etc. That kind of material was produced with a high level of consistency both on corporation and business unit levels, tailored to individual target groups. One of the most stringent examples is probably the communication of the company values (named 'principles' in Intech's own terminology). Throughout Intech, in most internal and external media the same wording was used consistently:

Our Principles
- We strengthen our customers to keep them competitive
- We push innovation to shape the future
- We enhance company value to open up new opportunities
- We empower our people to achieve world-class performance
- We embrace corporate responsibility to advance society
(Intech's company principles) [69:8]

Such statements sound rather straightforward, but – as discourse analysis will show – can cause emotional reactions, for example, if the projected identity differs from experienced identity.

Experienced identity

Viewed from a constructionist and communicational viewpoint, experienced identity is the facet of utmost importance, or even the core of identity. Christensen and Askegaard reviewed the concept of identity from this perspective and concluded that 'an organisation's identity is what becomes commonly understood to represent it, regardless of how intangible, incoherent, fragmented, or even self-contradictory that set of signs sometimes is' (2001, 304). Experienced identity is a central concern for company members, which can also cause a lot of emotion (Knights and Morgan 1991). Therefore, it can also be seen as the facet which bears the ability to give vent to disruptive elements (Humphreys and Brown 2002).

Another important aspect is that culture and values themes are linked into this facet – both stabilizing experienced identity and making it more volatile. Hatch and Schultz pointed out that culture includes 'the tacit organizational understandings (e.g. assumptions, beliefs and values) that contextualize efforts to make meaning, including internal self-definition' (2002, 996). Linstead went even further and defined culture as 'a complex phenomenon, usually related to shared values and shared meanings in an organization, but also related to common ways of dealing with, or ignoring, commonly experienced problems' (2004, 118). In this sense, culture and values contribute to the experienced identity of a company and its members, but, to a certain extent, also inform action based on this identity – both in intended and unintended ways.

Also at Intech corporation and Intech business unit identity and identification were experienced which caused emotional reactions and processes of sense-making, including links to cultural elements and company values. Here is an example of how a manager at Intech experienced the launch of the company values which had been quoted above. This account was given in an open-ended interview, reflecting on the Intech management system:

'Today, the big problem we have is in the commitment part of the [IMS]. ... I think the whole values story within [Intech] has to be somehow re-engineered. Otherwise we keep falling back to the default thing. Now, after the big change is over, you then go back to base camp again. And then there is something else coming up again. It's a shame.'
(Human resources manager) [82:3]

In this case, values were perceived as inherent in experienced identity – without actively reinforcing identity. Further examples of this part of discourse will be dealt with in the discourse analysis below. Particularly underlying aspects of culture and values will be treated there.

Manifested identity

With its long history, Intech developed a regular discourse around manifested identity. For example, managers frequently referred to the company's historical manifestations when talking about Intech. This reached back to the company founder who was regularly quoted in company publications. In Intech's corporate responsibility report the constants of Intech's identity were explained the following way:

First, we remain true to our principle of not choosing short-term courses of action that could cost us our future. ... Second, future-focused action calls for continuous investment in research and development, in new products and solutions, and in improved processes – one issue that we address in detail in this report. ... Third, crucial to our perception of ourselves as a company is our ability to balance business success and benefits for society...
(Corporate Responsibility Report 2003) [69:1]

Aspects of manifested identity particularly recurred in strategy and communication practices. The first of the principles mentioned in the report, the long-term approach to business, for example, was an issue in strategic planning processes as well as in communicating with stakeholders.

Attributed identity

This facet, in orthodox corporate communication theory is also frequently referred to as 'image', 'brand' or 'reputation' (Balmer and Greyser 2003). Attributed identity is generally created in the exchange processes between a company or its members and its stakeholders. The company needs to bring its 'competitive position' and 'distinctive competencies' (Chakravarthy, Müller-Stewens et al. 2003) into a negotiative process with customers, employees, shareholders, and other stakeholders (Deetz 2001). In the reference framework of this study, this aspect of identity formation is dealt with in Chapter 11 when it comes to analysing processes of 'Leveraging the competitive position and distinctive competencies'.

Applying Soenen and Moingeon's framework helped to shed light on the various aspects of identity and it also confirmed the relevance of underlying aspects of culture and values.

Repetition analysis also supported the identification of two new word clusters that had not become obvious from the taxonomy itself. The first new term, 'change', produced 65 counts. This needs to be seen as an indication that culture and identity were not discussed as static, but as 'fluid' concepts with both a 'stable and unstable' character (Gioia 1998, 22). Gioia, again, sees changes in context as major drivers for changes in organisational identity. This rationale was also presented by one of the general managers at the business conference in October 2003, when he said: '[Intech] will continue to change in the coming years through acquisitions, divestments, joint ventures and other forms of co-operations. And our global presence also plays a role here.' [54:29]

The second new term was 'organisation' which created 49 counts and was primarily embedded in discussions around organisational structure. Barney and Stewart (2000) made the point that the appearance of identity is often heavily related to organisational structures and that highly diversified companies – like Intech corporation – often bear fragmented organisational identities throughout the company. Moral values can function as a common denominator in that situation. The same manager at the business conference had continued: 'That, ladies and gentlemen, is the great advantage I personally see in our Corporate Principles. Because our company is highly complex ... It is clear that this degree of complexity cannot be organized down to the tiniest details from one central location.' [54:29] Moral values form a kind of glue function in this case.

Three further sets of significant repetitions identified the key participants in identity processes: 'employees' (142 counts), 'customers' (88 participants) and 'managers' (75 counts). This fairly precisely matches the target groups which had become apparent in the analysis of the business concept discourse and indicates that both identity and business concept involved similar sets of stakeholders.

8.3 Communicational review of business concept and identity

Thematic analysis so far has revealed a set of discourses which are active in processes of coordinating the organisation around dynamic purposes. These can be summarised as strategy discourse which focuses around the business concept and a second discourse, rather communication-oriented, which focuses around different identities, their interrelationships and embeddedness in culture and values. The aim of this section now is to explain in some more depth the possible relations between these discourses.

8.3.1 Discursive character of business concept and identity

The clean and structured taxonomy of terms shown above somehow obscures the fact that in reality each discourse influenced each other and that instruments of corporate communication played an active role in this. When, for example, the management publication reported about a 'systematic sales approach' and 'winning new customers' as important steps to make the company more successful, this statement was then read by managers through the lens of their individual identity. If their experienced identity was, as the example of the human resources manager showed, that initiatives like the one communicated in the management magazine come up all the time, then falling back to 'the default thing' might be the result.

This example shows that there is an interrelation between business concept and identity. However, not only mass-communicated symbols, but all participants are active in identity creation. 'Every individual embodies a unique combination of personal, cultural and social experiences' (Soderberg and Björkman 2003). Therefore, both business concept and identity discourses influence each other continuously so that identity is not 'something an organisation has, but something that emerges in enactment and social interaction' (Cornelissen and Harris 2001, 61). In consequence, both business concept (Alvesson 2002) and identity (Hatch and Schultz 1997) as symbols can have quite varied meanings across the company.

From a communicational perspective, it is also important to recognize that there are varieties of identities carried into or developed in the workplace (Ackroyd and Thompson 1999). These processes are accompanied by the emergence of 'enclaves' based on different values than those officially espoused and sanctioned. Therefore, interests and identities are not opposites. They reciprocally and discursively form each with another. 'Self-organization and the impulse towards autonomy are present in all work situations, varying only in terms of the extent to which they are overt or latent' (Ackroyd and Thompson 1999, 55). In other words, identities and cultures are unique, yet at the same time they share similar features. Organisations are collective but also divided – but neither one or the other exclusively (Parker 2000, 223).

Nevertheless, business concept and identity remain powerful constructs. Every company unit or individual needs 'at least a preliminary answer to the question "Who are we?" or "Who am I?" in order to interact effectively with other entities of the long run' (Albert, Ashforth et al. 2000, 13). Also, it is the integrative power of both business concept and identity which many companies use to define their management challenge 'to make sure that organizational members identify with the organization' (Cheney, Christensen et al. 2004, 128). This is in fact also a goal in the Intech case. Intech's CEO made that quite clear when he used the metaphor of an onion when he was asked what his main priority for the company is:

> For me, I have always that picture of an onion. I don't know whether that comes across. An onion you have to build from the inside out, you know, otherwise it is foul. Therefore, you need to have a strong core, and then from the core build the other rings.
> (Intech CEO) [23:25]

As was argued above, the core of that onion, namely the company's business concept and identity, is continuously reinvented in ongoing articulations and negotiations in which corporate communication participates and interferes.

8.3.2 Relations between business concept and identity

Before moving on to discourse analysis, this subsection sheds some light on the interplay between business concept, identity and practices or actions in the company.

Following Alvesson (1994) three different types of relations between business concept and identity are possible: either identity reflects business concept, or the business concept produces identity, or identity forms a source for business concept.

In each of these cases, business concept and identity are in a reciprocal relationship and influence each other (Ashforth and Mael 1996). Most research on identity, as has also been argued above, indicates the importance of coherence between both concepts (Dutton and Dukerich 1991). A strong identity can guide companies in their strategy and be a source for difference. On the other hand, strategy can inform identity by giving guidance with regards to who the company wants to be.

Therefore, it is important that members of a company share at least some common ground on what the company represents (Ashforth and Mael 1996). As the discussion on dualities has shown, this cannot not always be completely the case, but the task for top management still is to maintain an equilibrium of more or less shared meanings (Smircich and Stubbart 1985).

This equilibrium, from a management viewpoint, can be enacted through substantive and symbolic management (Ashforth and Mael 1996, 35-38). While substantive management includes concrete decisions like organisational changes, symbolic management 'refers to the ways in which management *portrays* the organization.' This clearly is a strong link to common-sense corporate communication products and activities, like corporate identity brochures, mission statements, employee events, branding activities, corporate design, etc. The whole corporate communication programme for implementing the Intech management system could be subsumed under this claim. Examples will follow in discourse analysis below.

According to Ashforth and Mael (1996, 38), peers play a major role in the negotiating process of identity and business concept. This point was also made by Deetz, Tracy et al. (2000). Leaders can have important effects on the interpretive frames of employees. People respond to the meanings they have for words and events rather than to the words and events themselves (Deetz, Tracy et al. 2000, 67). Ashforth and Mael (1996, 40-41) add another dimension to this when they make the point that, 'if identity constitutes the soul of a company, then employees regard themselves as the 'rightful custodian', whereas they may view strategic decision-making a legitimate domain of management'. In other words, even if business concept and identity are communicated clearly, it is not necessarily the case that people respond to it in the intended way or that business concept and identity even re-enforce each other – which is the outcome most desired by management and which, at the same time, would mean that corporate communication would utilize the optimum performative capacity for the company.

A participatory approach to communication can be a solution to facilitate this process (Deetz, Tracy et al. 2000, 108), although employees may only be willing to negotiate identity in the cases of ambiguity, change or contradicting identities (Ashforth and Mael 1996, 41), because otherwise identity might be perceived as too natural to question.

8.4 Discourse analysis

Preceding thematic analysis showed that corporate communication discourse covers a wide range of topics associated with the process of coordinating the company around dynamic purposes. In addition, the research by Ashforth and Mael indicates that corporate communication – interpreted as a process of symbolic management – can play a crucial role in facilitating the continuous interplay between business concept and identity discourses in an organisation. Discourse analysis now continues to shed further light on how corporate communication discourse emerged in conjunction with strategic processes at Intech. The aim is to identify and explain the performative capacity of critical interfaces between communication practices and the other elements in Ashforth and Mael's model which are then integrated in the alternative theory of corporate communication.

Criteria to select suitable fragments of discourse were whether the fragments are able to thematically cover dimensions of Ashforth and Mael's framework, and whether they illustrate communicational rather than functional forces of corporate communication discourse.

8.4.1 Interplay between business concept and identity

Both of the following fragments of discourse illustrate how corporate communication discourse linked into the interplay between business concept and identity. This discourse happened predominantly at Intech business unit level in daily conversations around the purpose of the company so that both examples were taken from Intech business unit.

As thematic analysis has shown, positioning Intech business unit as a captive company was a particular concern of top management. This view is represented in the first discourse fragment. The second fragment represents the view of middle managers which had advocated a stronger focus on the positioning of Intech business unit in external markets. The third fragment contains discourse on the 'balancing' act between captive and external positioning.

The following text was taken from a presentation held at an event with Intech business unit employees in May 2004. The event was part of a series of quarterly employee presentations and discussions at different locations. The sessions had the aim of communicating and discussing business performance in a timely manner after having informed Intech corporation's top management on financials. Intech business unit's corporate communication department prepared and organized these events, including presentations. The presentations were filmed, edited in a news report format and broadcasted to all Intech business unit employees via Intranet. On that occasion a member of Intech business unit's management board said, based on a presentation chart showing the organisational structure of Intech business unit:

'Given this fairly heterogeneous picture, in terms of products, in terms of regions, you might find it hard to give an answer on what is our market positioning. How can we bring clarity to who we are? No doubt, there is financial expertise, and there is industrial know-how. So, our market position is just in-between. In the market for financial products, we are a company which drives financial expertise and industrial competence at the same time. That's where we position ourselves. And at the same time, we are in another very important niche. We are a captive company. We survive as a captive company, and within the captive market segment, we are one of the large players. We are fairly large compared to other captive companies who would focus their efforts on the same kind of things we are in. … And that reflects being part of [Intech], which in itself is a fairly unique company. That gives us a special niche, a specialized product range, specialized services. We are solution-oriented because that's what we are grown up with, and clearly we will maintain activities close to [Intech] needs.'
(General manager, Intech business unit) [36:4]

This discourse fragment follows the strategic purpose to explain and clarify the positioning of Intech business unit. The presentation was held in a one-way non-mediated way and can be seen as an attempt to overcome the struggle with Intech's business concept which had been a point of discussion above.

The overall mood of the discourse can best be described as declarative. It remains on a fairly abstract level: examples are missing, and ongoing struggles like the ones with dualities which had been identified in thematic analysis are avoided.

Both themes – business concept and identity – are addressed. The argument begins with a statement regarding the 'heterogeneous picture', which is described by several elements of the business concept, like products and regions. Heterogeneity is assumed here rather than illustrated by examples. Following the logic of problem and solution, the manager then switches to identity discourse to show a solution for the heterogeneity issue and 'to bring clarity to who we are'. Assuming that financial expertise and industrial knowledge are key elements of the company's identity, a position 'in-between' is sought. In terms of modality, a high level of commitment can be assigned to these statements, repeating and asserting that this is indeed the identity of the company. This statement can also be seen as a typical example for the professed identity of Intech business unit. Alvesson (1994, 389) identified a similar approach by top management to interpreting a company by combinations of characterizations, concluding that identity in his case was rather 'loosely connected to what people are really doing in the company'. This observation also holds for Intech business unit, where defining the identity of the company through combining financial expertise and industrial knowledge was fairly accepted, but not deeply reflected in actual business practice.

Discourse in the above fragment, however, does not end here. The manager returns to elements of the business concept in a paratactic grammatical relation – by stating that 'at the same time' the company is a captive company. By now, business concept and identity have been used 'reciprocally' (Ashforth and Mael 1996, 33), referring back and forth. This argument is of additive character, stressing the role and the benefits of the captive definition several times – namely the resulting size for Intech business unit, presence in special niches and a range of activities which is close to the needs of Intech corporation. Not discussed are disadvantages of being a captive provider. Also possible ambiguities between market and captive positioning (see thematic analysis) are not a subject of discussion.

A similar interplay of argument between business concept and identity-related characteristics happens in the second section of text which was taken from a discussion which happened between members of the corporate communication team and a marketing manager following up on the above presentation. This fragment of discourse represents naturally occurring talk about the interplay of identity and business concept. The manager said:

'[Intech business unit] cannot escape this role as a captive financing provider. But we have to think what the long-term drivers are. It can be an approach that we combine telephones to power plants with financial services, so that not all the time people think about [our major competitor]. That's the challenge for us, and we have to think about growth that will come from the operating companies, no doubt. We could do a lot more. ... But putting that at one time, where do we want to be? We don't want to be seen as purely a captive financing provider. We want to be seen as a financing provider which has a captive portfolio and which has an external portfolio.'
(Intech business unit manager) [21:5]

To start with, the manager implicitly refers back to the ongoing discourse around the captive and external positioning of Intech business unit. He extends his argument from a view on the business concept, making the statement that Intech business unit 'cannot escape this role as a captive financing provider'. Level of commitment towards the business concept, here, is much lower than with the general manager's statement which had been analyzed previously. The manager sees the captive role rather as a necessity than a huge benefit. He continues by illustrating the combination of financial expertise and industrial know-how with a concrete example –

and, by doing this, moves on to identity discourse. His suggestion is to use the combination of product and financial services as an element of projected identity in order to differentiate Intech business unit from its competitors. In the next sentence, however, it is referred back to business concept, making the rhetorical link that enforcing captive business would also help to achieve the business goal of growth. This way, the manager links elements of business concept with 'substantive' management – involving 'real, material change in organizational practices' (Ashforth and Mael 1996, 35). Similarly, parallels between symbolic management and managing identity can be drawn (Alvesson 1990). However, ultimately the network of relations between business concept and identity culminates in 'continual, reciprocal interactions' (Ashforth and Mael 1996, 35).

As another indicator for a low level of commitment, the manager questions this statement afterwards by asking 'where do we want to be?' This leads back to identity discourse, focusing on the aspect of professed identity. The manager's commitment now increases by asserting that 'we want to be seen' in a specific way. In talking about identity that way, often self-fulfilling consequences are expected, but not necessarily fulfilled (Alvesson 1994).

A resolution to the duality of captive versus external portfolio is sought by putting both captive 'and' external portfolio on the same level. This can be interpreted as another one of the 'balancing acts' which are necessary to resolve dualities in business concept discourse.

The analysis of the two examples of discourse confirmed Ashforth and Mael's (1996) thesis that there is a reciprocal relation between business concept and identity discourse. As the general manager's as well as the marketing manager's discourse showed, this relationship is mutually reinforcing, i.e. business concept does not determine identity, nor does identity determine business concept and strategy. Instead, the arguments show that there is a continuous switch between identity and business concept discourse, with each used to argue in favor or against the other in a rhetorical game. This points towards a 'loosely coupled' relation between identity and business concept (Ashforth and Mael 1996, 33). Identity and business concept do not necessarily reinforce each other, instead, they can even be played off against each other at different levels of discourse.

These findings illustrate that the orthodox definition of corporate identity does not reveal the full picture. Orthodox theory 'suggests that by strengthening the organization's identity – its experienced distinctiveness, consistency and stability – it can be assumed that individuals' identities and identifications will be strengthened with what they are supposed to be doing at their workplace' (Alvesson 1990, 374). This re-enforcing relation between identity and business concept is according to the above statements not necessarily given.

Both fragments of discourse also highlighted the concept of dualities which were introduced earlier on. Normann (2001) proposed that dualities in identity and business concept discourse are a common phenomenon in all companies. On the one hand, companies try to manifest an identity and a strategy. On the other, they are changing permanently, driven by forces from business context, from their own actions and the discourses which they frame. Moved by this dynamism, every company has to find as its identity 'some kind of harmony, fit, consonance' (Normann 2001, 146) – or the 'balance', as Intech business unit's general manager framed it. This balance, however, is never fixed or static. With continuous changes in context and with continuous change enforced by the company's own actions, change becomes continuity (Normann 2001, 151).

Ashforth and Mael (1996) as well as Normann (2001) assign corporate communication an important role in managing this balance between identity and business concept in a highly context-sensitive environment. The aim, however, should not be to impose a certain corporate identity, as orthodox corporate communication theory suggests, but to share different views 'which can be achieved in an open-ended process in which all participants discover and see things that they did not know before, or that even did not exist before' (Normann 2001, 287). In fulfilling this task, substantive management – at Intech, for example advanced by members of the strategy department – and symbolic management – often enforced by members of corporate communication departments – need to collaborate with operational managers in order to design and participate in a discourse which strengthens identity and complementary strategies and business concepts. This resembles a process of bringing together communication 'in seemingly disparate areas' which are not to be made identical but whose 'common features can be productively examined from the perspectives of communication' (Cheney and Christensen 2001, 233).

8.4.2 Negotiating identity

Having made the point that identity and business concept are constantly being produced, reproduced and altered in the ongoing discourse, the focus of this subsection is now to give some insight into how corporate communication might interfere in processes of identification – defined as 'the process of emerging identity' (Scott, Corman et al. 1998, 304), indicating 'the degree to which a member defines himself or herself by the same attributes that he or she believes defines the organization' (Morgan, Reynolds et al. 2004, 365).

As Scott, Corman et al. (1998, 305) have pointed out, communication in the form of 'actual, hypothesized, or even retrospectively examined interaction' is viewed as essential to the development of identification. The background for that is that it is mostly through communication that we express our belongingness to companies and that we assess identity (Dutton and Dukerich 1991). Some authors go even further and state that there is a regular shift from substantive ways of constructing identity to increasingly occurring in the imaginary realm (Kärreman and Alvesson 2004). This shift is facilitated, as was argued above in the literature review, by orthodox corporate communication which – according to all five theories that were reviewed – emphasize symbolic over substantive forms of communication.

The second aspect which Scott, Corman et al. (1998, 324) raised with regards to negotiating identity is that they advocated local analysis of identification processes. The reason for that is that multiple identities (e.g. organisation, work-team and personal identities) frame every situation. Given these multiple identities, conflict between groups and identities 'is both common and integral to the construction of a collective identity' (Kuhn and Nelson 2002, 11). However, conflict and negotiation can facilitate and strengthen the identification process. In other words: 'As employees discuss their identities, they become their identities. In turn, as employees assess the identification process, they will reveal in their narratives the sources of inspiration for those identities' (Morgan, Reynolds et al. 2004, 362).

The aim of this subsection is to shed light on the question of which elements and processes of managed communication shaped the identification of members of Intech and how identity was negotiated in this concrete case.

The examples for this analysis are taken from corporate communication discourse happening at Intech corporation. The following discourse fragment was taken from a moderated discussion round between the general manager of Intech and corporate communication professionals from Intech's different regions and business units in November 2004. The discussion formed part of the semi-annual internal corporate communication conference at Intech. It was embedded in a series of events which were held in a two-way mediated mode.

[Moderator]: 'Can you give us your view of the customer perspective, how should they think about [Intech]?
[Manager]: Yes, that's not actually difficult at all. We just have to look at our roots and fix that. If you have a company that is over 150 years old, you can be

pretty sure that there is something really good in the roots. ... I think the gene code that we have is a very good one. It has always been around. We want to set the pace in certain industries. We want also to be commercially successful. Commercially successful innovation, this is setting the pace in an industry. That's what we want, and that's the best for our customers also. The customer is literally out for a few things: bring the performance up, bring the costs down. We have seen that in the logic of many. In the past that has been a conflicting thing, but we know, to many examples in our company, that it's not conflicting, actually a very good mechanism to do two things at the same time. I think that's something. The other thing, now, really from the first days on, is: we are an international company. I'm sure you have experience with this in here. How much fun is this? I mean over lunch, over a short break, you talk to a colleague and realize how different the perspective of that individual is. And this perspective you would otherwise only have gathered not as credible as from somebody who is living in that environment. I think that is the strength that we have.'
(Intech general manager) [108:7]

To start with, the moderator asks the CEO about the attributed identity he expects to be perceived by customers. In his answer, he replies immediately by quoting and interpreting manifested identity. Manifested identity, in this case is used in order to underpin the assumption that the existing 'gene code' is 'good'. This step in the discourse can also be interpreted as a 'depersonalization' of identity (Ashforth and Mael 1996, 43), a categorization which is generally seen as a sign for a strong identity and identification with the company. This, taken one step further, can even lead to 'depersonalized trust' (1996, 44), meaning trust which is based on a common social identity which 'does not require prior interaction with every individual'. Reference to such a level of trust has occasionally been used by Intech business unit in their marketing activities towards Intech employees, where the trust associated with Intech as such was used to associate financial services in marketing communication materials.

At the same time, however, by referring back to the historical dimension of the gene code, negotiation of identity is avoided, particularly when considering the audience which – as communicators – are not simply passive receivers of corporate efforts to shape their identification but are active participants in constructing their identities (Scott 1997). Instead, the general manager uses an external logic – a company which is 150 years old must have a good gene code – in Cheney and Frenette's terms serving as a kind of 'overarching or superordinate value premises to which subordinate or subsidiary values ... are connected or contributory' (1993, 55).

Larson and Pepper (2003) in their attempt to categorize strategies and tactics for managing the ongoing identity contest in companies detected similar practices in their case. Related to the strategy to use external logic, they conclude: 'These rhetorical justifications are important in the management of identifications because they allow people to rationalize their identity choices as normal and natural' (2003, 544).

Intech's general manager, in the above discourse fragment continues on this strategy of external logic by quoting customer needs in the form of the assumption that 'the customer is literally out for a few things'. He uses additive and elaborative semantic relations to make his point clear, and repeatedly relates to the 'logic of many' or 'to many examples'. According to Larson and Pepper's categorization such as this corresponds to the tactic of 'implied support' which is 'usually played out in subtle ways as individuals indirectly mentioned that others held similar beliefs' (2003, 548). Referencing 'the logic of many' is used to underpin the conclusion that bringing performance up and costs down at the same time is not a conflicting thing. This is also an example that elements of the business concept discourse are used, as well as elements of identity discourse, to argue in processes of identification. Both business concept and identity need to be considered when arranging the process of negotiating identity.

The general manager repeats his strategies of forming identity with regards to the second element of the 'gene code' which is covered in the above statement: that Intech is an international company. He makes the point that Intech has been an international company since its foundation and uses a tactic of 'direct support' (Larson and Pepper 2003, 548) – 'I am sure you have an experience with this here' – by directly involving the company members which were present at the event itself.

Another conspicuous characteristic of the statement is the high level of commitment the manager demonstrates in terms of Fairclough's (2003) framework for discourse analysis. The overall style of discourse is very assertive, and can also be interpreted as an attempt to enact identity. This was explained by Ashforth and Mael (1996, 45) in that 'the more a member identifies with the organization, … the more he or she will think, act, and feel in ways consistent with that identity and strategy'. He uses identity as a 'lens' to separate good from bad, to judge importance, and therefore, also enters the moral arena of discourse.

This is the point where critical communication scholars make the point that negotiating identity needs to happen in a collaborative way. In these theories, a collaborative approach to negotiating is less a moral choice than a necessity, because people create meanings around words in a continuous process and respond to these meanings rather than to the events happening in reality (Deetz, Tracy et al. 2000). The statement made, therefore, is rarely the statement received, unless the meaning of words is created in a collaborative rather than an adversarial way (Gray 1991).

The next discourse fragment provides an example of how a corporate communication tool influenced the process of negotiating identity from the viewpoint of one manager and how that manager experienced participation during that process. The discourse fragment was taken from a story the manager told the researcher about an event which had been held at one of Intech's German locations to introduce the new Intech management system. The conversation took place in an informal atmosphere following a workshop among corporate communicators in July 2004 in the manager's office. In this face-to-face situation, the manager was very emotional about the communication tools which had been put in place by the corporate communication department, particular an online discussion forum which was set up on the Intech corporation intranet:

'There used to be a forum which was established before this event. There was the discussion forum. Hopefully it has gone. … If you set up a forum, what's the idea behind it? There are two options. One, you say we set up a forum and let it run. See if people put in comments. But even if you do that, you should at least keep an eye on it. Two, and my idea behind it: if you set up a forum and somebody puts in a critical question, can they expect an answer from the people who set up this forum? It's a question that we don't understand what this has to do with our day-to-day business. Can you expect somebody else in the forum to answer that or is there an obligation of the people who are so clever to set up this forum to also provide an answer. No. So many questions in there, and no answer.'
(Intech manager) [83:19]

The manager, in this fragment, reports on how he experienced participation in the Intranet forum. By applying a number of contrasting semantic relations, he first of all accuses the corporate communication department for not taking care of content in that forum, and for not facilitating the question and answer process which is necessary to make participation in this forum a two-way process. Frustration and cynicism are his reactions to the fact that many employees want to participate in the process of identity-building: employees ask questions, but do not receive replies to their questions.

This example illustrates both opportunities and threats associated with corporate communication activities intended to contribute to identity negotiation. On the one hand, it demonstrates in practice that 'communication functions as an intervening variable in participation outcomes' (Seibold and Shea 2001, 685) and can make an immediate difference (Scott, Connaughton et al. 1999). On the other, it also shows that if corporate communication activities are carried out in the form of 'pseudo-actions' (Alvesson 1990, 387) – 'only for the sake of affecting perceptions of an audience, without being recognized as having that intention' – they can easily become counter-productive in the minds of the recipients.

This point has been further analysed in Kuhn and Nelson's work (2002) who draw attention to the perceived position of members in a communication network which also plays a crucial role in negotiating identity. The more intensively members participated in activities relevant in the identification process, the more consistent their identification was afterwards. It becomes an important aspect that 'substantive' communication activities, then, not only need to be substantive in terms of content, but also in terms of participation. Collaboration requires a 'different attitude' towards communication (Deetz, Tracy et al. 2000, 113) – one that takes dialogue seriously. In Czarniawska's words, identity may be conceptualized as a 'continuous process of narration where both the narrator and the audience are involved in formulating, editing, applauding, and refusing various elements of the ever-produced narrative' (1997, 49).

It was argued, above, that this ongoing process of identity negotiation involves multiple identity discourses. Touraine (1995) suggested the metaphor of contest in which dominant repertoires or discourses are continually reconstructed in interaction. Several authors (e.g. Humphreys and Brown 2002; Kreiner and Ashforth 2004) have contributed to a differentiated picture of the ways members of a company acquire identities. It is argued that, in summary, there are four possible kinds of relationship between individual and company identities as an outcome of identity negotiation: identification, disidentification, ambivalent identification and neutral identification. Only the first of these four possible outcomes is the intended outcome which is referred to in orthodox corporate communication theory.

Given the complexity of identity negotiation, particularly in large companies like Intech, it is likely that all four dimensions of identification exist throughout the company. The following example surfaces evidence for neutral identification which can be explained as a 'self-perception of impartiality with respect to an organization's identity' (Humphreys and Brown 2002, 425). It represents a section from the quarterly management magazine which was distributed as a printed version after the business conference in October 2003 to all managers at Intech worldwide. Therefore, as an example of the one-way mediated domain of corporate communication, it also highlights some of the specific problems that arise if company media report on identity issues. The fragment features the head of one company program which is part of the Intech management system:

'I think the most important task facing us at the moment is to convince the business units that the proposed approach is the right way to produce faster, more efficient results that meet market demands. With management on our side, we can instil a corporate culture in line with our approach to innovation. This will mean overcoming the "not-invented-here" mentality and thinking beyond the narrow confines of our own functions. Greater innovation also goes hand-in-hand with a greater degree of risk, and this is a fact of life that we need to recognize and accept. That's why we need managers and employees who know how to operate un-

der such conditions, and this is also why innovation is ultimately very much about the people charged with putting it into practice.'
(Management Edition No. 1) [55:19]

As a printed fragment of discourse, this text does not represent a section of immediate negotiation. Instead, according to Schmidt (2004), it needs to be interpreted as an information offering which then produces meaning in the minds of the people who read the text. Interpreted this way, it can be viewed as an invitation of the corporate communication department made to all employees – rather than a process of transporting information from sender to recipient, which was the proposition in the container model of communication.

Not being able to completely enforce the intended meaning or cognitive operation, points towards the first problem with this text: i.e. that one-way mediated forms are not always suitable means of transporting information. In order to not remain a pure intention, but have a chance of achieving the intended result, the offered information needs to conform with 'common-sense knowledge' of the recipients, Schmidt (2004) argues. The clue to this is that communication is only constituted if the recipient replies in a second offering which proves that the recipient understands the intention. Then, communication becomes a reflexive process with feedback as an indicator of success (Schmidt 2004, 52).

The provider's intention in this case is clear: To make the point that the 'not-invented-here' mentality – i.e. assumed neutral identification – needs to be overcome. The argumentation follows the general rhetoric of assumption, goal and solution. The assumption is that the 'not-invented-here' mentality exists. For the manager, this is part of common-sense knowledge in the company. The goal is to instil a company culture which is in line with his approach to innovation: a changed company culture, based on managers' support, acceptance of higher levels of risk and operational knowledge of how to conduct business under these circumstances.

Both the managers making such statements and corporate communication departments publishing these kind of messages have to be aware that any statement about the core of the company is essentially one – but not the only possible claim (Albert and Whetten 1985). In viewing companies as narrative constructions, the notion of a contest in which dominant repertoires or discourses are continually reconstructed in interaction can be advanced (Touraine 1995). As managers draw on such propositional narratives, they take an active stance in identity formation processes and make their currency in terms of being 'used' to visibly transport the discourse. Acceptance of such statements, however, finally underlies a successful passing of the identity contest (Ashforth and Mael 1996, 31).

In order to enforce identification, management tends to combine such statements with regulating mechanisms rather than installing negotiation processes. Such mechanisms are not only enforced, but in many cases also expected by employees, for example as a sign of the seriousness of an identity change (Alvesson 1994). Incentives, in the case of the Intech management system are one of the regulating mechanisms (see Chapter 7).

The next example illustrates how such an identity contest emerged in a concrete case. The discourse section is taken from a conversation with another manager, who observed a project of re-constructing the entrance area at Intech's head offices and interpreted the meaning from his individual viewpoint. The fragment is part of naturally occurring talk, recorded in June 2004 in the course of an open-ended interview:

'Do you remember the big construction site at [Intech head offices]? I will tell you the story. They were building a whole summer and winter there. So we asked: what are they doing? It must be something amazing with all this noise. We were going on for two years with this noise. We all had the impression there must be coming something fantastic. And I said: do you know what we get? Stairs! We get stairs? And Louis XIV could have walked up there. In the year 2002 we end up with what? Stairs? We were expecting a fitness centre, a restaurant, something that says the 21st century has arrived. What do we get? Stairs from medieval France. And you start: what does this tell us? What the hell are we trying to communicate? What the hell is this organisation about? People on massive stairs. You could have built an escalator and the space underneath, you could have had a fitness centre for 500 people, you could have done something innovative, you could have had a café, Starbucks come in and do something, whatever, right? Now we have got stairs. And what is on the stairs? Nothing.'
(Intech manager) [82:16]

The main theme covered is the symbolic meaning of building a new staircase at the company's head offices. The statement reveals the high level of emotion this project has created for the manager and the high level of personal struggle associated with related processes of identity negotiation. The fragment shows that 'discourses, roles and narratives are all involved – they fuel and constrain identity work' (Sveningsson and Alvesson 2003).

First of all, the manager perceived the construction work in the entrance of the building as a literal offering for cognitive information production in the sense described by Schmidt (2004). He also gave evidence for the intertextuality of this kind of discourse: he did not only think on his own what these construction activities mean, but he started conversations about this issue with his colleagues. In the course of these conversations, expectations started to rise, culminating in the idea that 'something fantastic' must be coming. Disappointment and cynicism was the reaction when the manager and his colleagues found out that a staircase was going to be the result – which was obviously something which had not been in line with their common sense. The symbol of 'Louis XIV' – a concrete persona – was quoted, and a process of discussing "what does this tell us?" was put into operation. The managers had started to negotiate identity. They used the offering to do so, but they did not reply to the provider of the offering. Instead, they concluded for themselves that the company is about 'people on massive stairs'.

This example for illustrating the process of negotiating identity pulls attention to a conclusion Alvesson (2002) had drawn with regards to cultural processes in general: negotiation of identity often takes place unconsciously in everyday interactions. In other words, organisations exist in a 'pattern of ongoing action-interaction' (Smircich and Stubbart 1985, 727). And, as Cheney, Christensen et al. have recently concluded: 'Identity management is carried out not only by managers with communication responsibilities but also by rank-and-file members who identify with the organization' (Cheney, Christensen et al. 2004, 126).

An alternative corporate communication theory and practice, therefore, needs to recognize that corporate communication activities provide the offering to start communication, but it is often beyond its control which processes of sense-making happen at the local level. This has to do with the practice that many corporate communication activities happen as mediated processes.

Rather than thinking about culture and identity in sweeping statements like the good overall organisational identity, Alvesson, therefore, calls for 'local adaptation and case-by-case evaluation' (2002, 173).

8.5 Theorising

In Section 5 of Chapters 8 to 11 – i.e. the Chapters focusing on the analysis of the four Strands of interrelations between strategy and communication processes – the findings of the preceding analyses are drawn together. Additionally, contributions to an alternative theory of corporate communication are summarized. Each of these Sections is ordered in the same sequence, finally resulting in a new integrated framework for alternative corporate communication which is derived in Chapter 12.

The theorising process can be depicted in three steps: First, it is referred back to the respective Strand as illustrated in the reference framework. Based on the amendments which were proposed in the review of context (see Section 7.4), an adaptation of Figure 5 is used for reference. Figure 6 illustrates this step of referring back to the reference framework in the case of Strand 1. Second, based on the results of the preceding analyses, an additional Figure is proposed for each Strand – summarising and illustrating answers to the research questions which were proposed above for each Strand (see Table 3). This Figure can be interpreted as a way of 'zooming' graphically into the reference framework. Figure 7, for example, shows the core themes identified as part of Strand 1 and suggests a solution of how the interrelations between strategy and communication processes are constructed from a communicational perspective. These figures provide key summaries of the aspects relevant for an alternative corporate communication theory. In the third step, the in-depth illustration of each Strand is reintegrated into the reference framework. This way, the reference framework is adapted gradually throughout Chapters 8 to 11.

In the following paragraphs, this three-step process is carried out for Strand 1. First, in Figure 6 it is referred back to Strand 1 as it was used in the reference framework above.

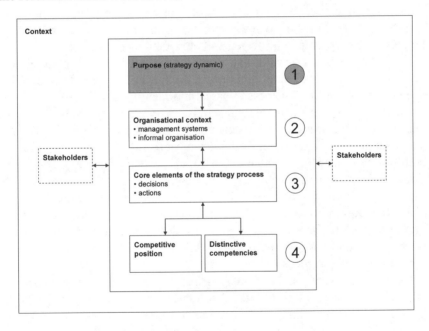

Fig. 6. Referring back to Strand 1 in the reference framework

In the original framework (see Figure 4) the Descriptor of Strand 1 – i.e. 'Coordinating the company around dynamic purposes' – remained a fairly abstract concept.

Concrete research questions were framed in order to guide the analysis in terms of the overall purpose of the study (see Table 8). Thus, thematic analysis focused on the research question of which purpose-related themes corporate communication did cover, whereas discourse analysis focused on the question of how the performative capacity of corporate communication emerged with regards to coordinating the company around dynamic purposes.

Drawing on the findings of thematic and discourse analysis leads to a revised and richer picture of the interrelations between communication and strategy processes related to Strand 1.

First of all, thematic analysis helped to refine the term 'purpose' which had identified Strand 1 in the original framework. It became clear that the purpose of Intech is less a consistent term than a rather complex web of themes around two core discourses, namely 'business concept' and 'identity'. Business concept contained themes like strategy (on several organisational levels) and dualities which appeared as inherent in Intech's corporate communication discourse. Identity discourse revealed interplays between various types of identities which coexisted at Intech – professed, projected, experienced, manifested and attributed identities.

Discourse analysis, in addition, provided insight into how communication can help to 'coordinate' a company around its purpose. To start with, insight was given that business concept and identity discourses are related to each other. It revealed that substantive as well as symbolic forms of management are necessary to balance both sides of the purpose medal, and that a singular focus on either of them can cause significant ambiguities for both business concept and identity. Also, embedded in ongoing communication processes of the company, business concept and identity need to pass a contest among members of the company – only then, they can become the powerful tools they are intended to be by many companies. Therefore, in the sense of this Strand's definition, coordination of the company around its dynamic purposes needs to include the serious execution of negotiation processes.

Cheney and Christensen (2001) suggest one more extension of the original view of identity as related primarily to internal communication. They make the point that, when moving from the 'container' metaphor of communication towards a discursive model, '"internal" and "external" communication no longer constitute separate fields in practice (2001, 232).

Figure 7 summarises the results of the analyses of Strand 1. At the same time, this Figure completes the second step of the three-step process leading to an adapted version of the reference framework.

The research questions for analysing Strand 1 had referred (1) to identifying the purpose-related themes covered by corporate communication discourse and (2) to explaining how the performative capacity of corporate communication discourse emerged with regards to coordinating the company around dynamic purposes (see Table 8). Figure 7 provides answers to these questions by (1) showing the themes of strategy and dualities as part of the business concept discourse, as well as showing the themes of professed, projected, experienced, manifested and attributed identities as part of identity discourse. The performative capacity of corporate communication discourse, (2) emerges in processes of negotiation, substantive management and symbolic management. This is also illustrated in Figure 8.

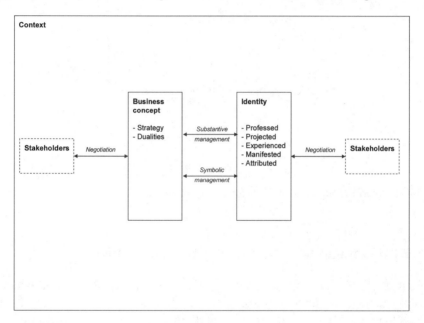

Fig. 7. Review of Strand 1 – Coordinating the organisation around dynamic purposes

In order to complete step 3 in the process of adapting the reference framework towards an alternative theory of corporate communication, a revised version of Strand 1 is implemented in Figure 8.

Based on the analyses so far, the following contributions to an alternative corporate communications theory can be concluded.

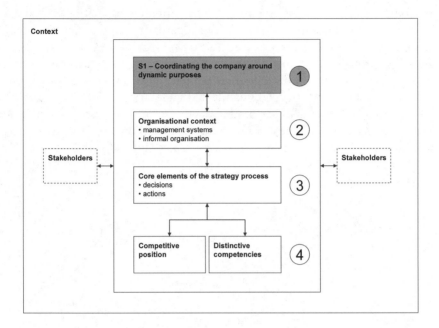

Fig. 8. Adapting Strand 1 in the reference framework

8.5.1 Understanding the complexity of the field

First of all, the analysis has shown that processes related to business concept and identity cannot be explained and managed by a model of communication which purely consists of source, message and receiver. As the examples above have shown, corporate communication participates in and
influences many processes of identification, and not all consequences of
identity-related communication are foreseeable. Therefore, in line with
Cheney and Christensen, it needs to be realized in alternative corporate
communication theory 'that communication is not an unproblematic solution to crises or queries over identity' (2001, 243). Instead, in many cases
communication is part of the identity problem.

Another important point in this overall frame is that communication
processes related to business concept and identity are not all in the hands
of corporate communication departments. All members of a company and
external stakeholders participate actively in creating identities. Not only
are there multiple identities competing among each other, there are also
various levels of identity influencing each other in a rather uncontrollable

way. As has been shown above, many of the mainstream corporate communication activities, particularly those contributing to mediated container forms of communication, like newsletters, brochures and image campaigns, rather work as communication offerings than as actively 'managed' forms of communication. In the complex web of themes and interplays between business concept and identity – i.e. substantive and symbolic forms of management – it remains at least questionable to what extent the intended outcomes of the providers of communication instruments can be reached – or at least tracked.

Christensen and Cheney go even further and argue that, particularly regarding the recent euphoria for identity, companies should 'reconsider radically the role that their formal communication campaigns play in the market of symbols and messages of today' (2000, 246). In the quest for distinctiveness and visibility as well as accreditation and legitimacy, it can be concluded that many companies run the risk of communicating messages that are more relevant to the sender than to the receiver. Cheney and Christensen call this phenomenon 'auto-communication – that is, communication through which organizations establish and affirm their own self-images or their own cultures' (2000, 252). As the above analysis suggests, auto-communication cannot only become a waste of resources, the quest for more and more communication also bears the risk that this kind of communication induces unintended outcomes.

This does not interfere with the findings of former research that a strong identity is crucial for companies (Ashforth and Mael 1996; Albert, Ashforth et al. 2000) and that companies are important points of identification for employees and many other stakeholders (Christensen and Cheney 2000). The point is rather to be aware of the complex processes associated with negotiating business concept and identity, as well as the interplay between these.

There are two sets of thoughts associated to this which have not yet gained much attention in orthodox corporate communication theory. These are summarised in the following paragraphs.

8.5.2 Plea for more 'substance' in corporate communication

Alvesson has, from a general management viewpoint, for quite a while made the point that companies have developed from substance to symbols (Alvesson 1990; Alvesson 2002). He sees this as a consequence of cultural changes and the associated complexity of society, the expansion of the service sector and a resulting increased interest in images, as well as an expanded role of mass media – which has finally resulted in an increase of 'pseudo-events'. A pseudo-event, in Alvesson's terms, 'is a happening which is not spontaneous, but has been planned for the immediate purpose of being reported or reproduced' (Alvesson 1990, 383). These kinds of events are purely created for publicity reasons. Corporate communication is one of the management processes which, until today, is most influenced by symbolic management ideas (Alvesson and Berg 1992).

In the course of these influences, the main purpose of orthodox corporate communication has become to influence the reputation of the company held by a given audience (Argenti 2003). Symbolic communication has evolved as a comparably straightforward tool to manage communication – straightforward compared with the complexity of processes it initiates according to alternative theories. A lot of effort is put into these tasks, and a large proportion of the communication industry today focuses on these aspects. Yet, it is precisely the primarily symbolic approach to identity and communication that becomes more and more criticized by many stakeholder groups (Ind 2003) and can even be seen as counter-productive in 'a cluttered communication environment, saturated with symbols asserting distinctness and identity' (Christensen and Askegaard 2001, 297).

As the analysis has shown, in real business life symbolic and substantive management always go hand in hand. Managers and other members of the company continuously moved back and forth between elements of business concept and identity when talking and arguing about the company's purpose. In all discourse fragments which were analyzed, substantive elements were part of the game.

Already Alvesson (2002, 146), however, had stated that 'the significance of such 'substantive' activities as productive work, the structuring of tasks, the formalization of procedures, the technical and bureaucratic control of work, cost management and the reproduction of power relationships is often neglected'. The results of this study so far confirm this view and lead to the conclusion that identity work cannot be done without substantive underpinning work. Business concept and identity are two sides of the same coin, as are strategy and communication work.

The analysis has also shown that due to its complexity, discourse around the purpose of a company only becomes meaningful in a concrete business context. This suggests that purpose-related corporate communication should also start to move away from generalizing image and corporate identity work and find ways to embody itself in business-related processes with all stakeholders. This is the level where coherence can also be achieved when communication is viewed from a discourse perspective: a strong identity can be achieved when local talk becomes coherent and captures the 'imagination and appeal of what people see as important, meaningful and relevant' (Alvesson 2002, 174). For corporate communication, this probably means moving away from the easy job of managing communication and diving much deeper into specific business and work processes, trying to elaborate on ways of creating an ongoing presence there.

8.5.3 Taking identity negotiation seriously

In addition to the increasing importance of substantive communication, a need to provide suitable means for negotiating business concept and identity for corporate communication can be concluded from the discourse analysis displayed above. This increasing need is partly based on the emotional involvement of employees and other stakeholders with identity issues. For example, Cheney, Christensen, et al. come to the conclusion that 'identification presupposes participatory involvement' (Cheney, Christensen et al. 2004, 129). Other recent studies have shown that the aspect of negotiating identity becomes particularly relevant in companies with multiple identities (Larson and Pepper 2003). Intech surely is an example of that: identities compete at several levels, e.g. corporation with business unit levels, but also organisational with professional levels, e.g. business unit identity with identity as IT, finance, HR, etc. professional.

Additional difficulties of actually managing communication by focusing on business concept and identity arise from the fact that many orthodox corporate communication products which are intended to enforce identity, actually need to be understood as offerings to communicate rather than 'containers' shipping identity to the recipients. Mantovani and Spagnolli concluded that 'semiotic mediation emerges … as the basic function of artifacts and increasingly informs their previously basic function of "producing" things' (2000, 224). Viewing corporate communication products like newsletters, internet pages, brochures, advertisements, etc. as artifacts in Mantovani and Spagnolli's sense, they become part of the identity negotiating process – for example as part of the context for negotiations. This leaves communication products open to multiple interpretations. Communication managers need to be aware of this. Smircich and Stubbart had exactly this point in mind when they several years ago stated: 'But, in strategic management, multiple interpretations often are viewed as communication problems to be overcome by more information, rather than as a natural state of affairs' (1985, 731). The alternative corporate communication perspective moves away from this interpretation and suggests that negotiation, even if conducted in a diverse manner, is necessary and healthy.

Careful attention, therefore, also needs to be given to the negotiation process itself. Deetz (1997) argues that reacting to symptoms, e.g. by understanding negotiation as the mere expression of interests, is not enough, i.e. 'to say' is not the same as 'having decided together', and 'having a meeting is not itself a democratic act' (1997, 135). Instead, supporting Deetz' argument, the task for corporate communication needs to be to contribute to mutually satisfying decisions supporting the purpose of the company. Corporate communication processes need to be transformed with a focus on participation in, rather than control of, identity and business concept. Meaning of identity needs to be created in negotiation taking the "other" serious. Members of the company need to be understood as both processor and expresser at the same time. In this context, images and symbols still play a central role in the creation of identities – but it is no longer the images' and symbols' consumption which counts. Instead, their ability to link people with likeminded individuals becomes of higher interest (Cova 1996).

The success of negotiation, then, is directly linked to the quality of communication it is based on (Stacey 2003). Pursuing this quest for quality, purpose-related communication can become what Schmidt called a 'programme of competence to solve problems, which lends acting and communicating of company members commonly accepted sense' (2004, 195). Otherwise, when identities are protected in orthodox concepts of corporate identity, distortion (Deetz 1995) is likely to happen.

Giving up on a one-way managerial identity process, however, does not necessarily mean to lose control of the company's communication offerings. While stakeholders insist on being involved in the creation of identities, actively engaging in negotiation gives companies 'the ability to have as great a control as is possible and, maybe more importantly, the only possibility to maintain livelihood in the complex, fluid, and highly dynamic postmodern markets' (Christensen, Torp et al. 2005, 165).

9 Organising by linking decisions and actions

This Chapter focuses on analysing Strand 2 of the revised framework, i.e. aspects of 'organising by linking decisions and actions'. Apart from relating Strand 2 back to the overall framework for analysis, Table 10 also lists the concrete research questions for analysing this Strand of interrelations between strategy and communication processes.

Table 10. Focal points for analysis of Strand 2 – Organising by linking decisions and actions

Generic codes	Descriptors for Strands of interrelation between strategy and communication processes
S1 Coordinating	Coordinating the company around dynamic purposes
S2 Organising	Organising by linking decisions and actions
S3 Facilitating	Facilitating implementation and change processes
S4 Leveraging	Leveraging the competitive position and distinctive competencies
Research question related to stocktaking of themes [Thematic analysis]	
Which themes with regards to organising processes did corporate communication discourse reveal?	
Research question related to construction of themes [Discourse analysis]	
How did corporate communication discourse constitute organisation in the concrete case? How was it constituted by other modes of organising?	

The previous Chapter dealt with a high level of complexity in a fairly unstructured set of discourse fragments focusing on 'Coordinating the company around dynamic purposes'. The analysis of the discourse related to 'organising by linking decisions and actions' revealed a clearer picture from the outset. First of all, this had to do with the fact that Intech – both on corporation and business unit levels – had developed and implemented a dedicated communication programme to accompany the implementation of the Intech management system, following one clear objective: to turn decisions – in this case the launch of the Intech management system – into action. As the taxonomy will show, many discourse fragments were clustered around individual elements of the related communication programme. Second, this Strand of interrelation between communication and strategy was one of the core issues the interviewees had addressed in the open-ended interviews. Therefore, themes emerging from these interviews provided a good structure for thematic analysis and also suggested relevant issues for the later discourse analysis.

9.1 Developing a taxonomy

So-called 'company calendars' were developed at both Intech corporation and business unit in order to structure and coordinate a top-down infiltration of the Intech management system into the company. These calendars included key dates for planning and decision-making as well as the accompanying corporate communication activities. In chart format, they were presented at employee events and in company publications in order to create awareness of ongoing activities.

A significant amount of corporate communication discourse had evolved around this calendar, its implementation and execution. Consequently, the themes that emerged as discourse fragments clustered in individual codes during the analysis process in ATLAS.ti could rather easily be understood in the context of this calendar.

Three generic themes emerged from this process of clustering individual quotations into consistent topics: (1) discourse related to 'cascading' information on the Intech management system down through the hierarchies to all members of the company, (2) discourse focusing on the 'modes of decision-making' while implementing the Intech management system, and (3) discourse showing evidence of 'sense-making' processes of company members while consuming (Schmidt 2004) the information provided through the cascade.

9.1.1 Cascading

Discourse around cascading can be broken down into five sub-themes. The majority of quotations related to sub-themes concentrated on discourse covering a detailed analysis of how 'top-down communication' emerged (75 quotations). According to the company calendar, the process of cascading embraced two steps. Step one involved creating 'awareness' for the Intech management system (13 quotations), step two the sharing of 'best-practice' examples of implementation on common communication platforms (17 quotations). In the course of cascading information into the company, a minor discussion evolved around 'similarity', e.g. in terms of joint and consistent wording, this information should share (8 quotations).

Finally, a sub-theme evolved around the communication 'tools' that were used for cascading the information (40 quotations).

9.1.2 Modes of decision-making

This generic theme was broken down and clustered into four concrete modes of decision-making used at Intech: (1) 'signalling' willingness to contribute to the Intech management system was a rather common behaviour of managers while making decisions (17 quotations); (2) another behaviour which occurred was merely 'showing initiative' rather than implementing new structures (4 quotations); (3) also 'referring to' factors external to the situation, e.g. changes in the market environment, were quite commonly applied in order to justify decisions (23 quotations); and (4) several managers simply took an 'opportunistic approach' to decision-making, i.e. they decided based on political considerations (14 quotations).

Table 11. Taxonomy for Strand 2 – Organising by linking decisions and action

Domain [Section]	Generic themes [Section]	Sub-themes	Recurrence [No. of quotations]
S2 Organising [9.2]	Cascading [9.2.1]	Top-down communication	75
		Awareness	13
		Best-practice	17
		Similarity	8
		Tools	40
	Modes of decision-making [9.4.1]	Signalling	17
		Showing initiative	4
		Referring to	23
		Opportunistic approach	14
	Sense-making [9.2.2]	Creating meaning	67
		Dialogue	31
		Credibility	11
		Concerns	7
		Management processes	29
Total			304

9.1.3 Sense-making

The generic theme of sense-making consisted of general processes of 'creating meaning', including the different approaches company members used to make sense of decisions and actions (67 quotations), discourse around how to use 'dialogue' rather than top-down cascaded information in the course of implementing the Intech management system (31 quotations), 'credibility' (11 quotations) as well as personal 'concerns' (7 quotations) as important factors influencing the process of sense-making (11 quotations). Also 'management processes' directly related to the company calendar formed a significant part of the discourse (29 quotations).

The complete taxonomy for Strand 2 is summarised in Table 11.

9.2 Thematic analysis

Thematic analysis follows the aim of filtering the most relevant themes out of the taxonomy and to give an overview of key elements constructing the discourse. In analysing Strand 2, repetition was a relevant filter criterion.

As has been shown in Chapter 6 (analysis), open-ended interviews formed part of data collection, specifically in order to obtain reflections on the initial framework during the observation period. Whereas that had not revealed any discourse with regards to business concept and identity (Strand 1), regular discussions evolved around Strand 2. Themes that came up repeatedly in these open-ended interviews were related to cascading information on the Intech management system down into the company as well as the ongoing processes of sense-making in the company. Thematic analysis, therefore, narrows the overall taxonomy down to these two discourses.

These two discourses also, from a theoretical viewpoint, cover a core theme of viewing communication as a mode of organising – i.e. turning decisions into action. Taylor, Cooren et al. (1996, 5), rather colloquially, termed this challenge as 'getting people to do and think what you want them to do and think'. In a definition of strategy not only as 'where to go', but also as 'how to get there' (Eisenhardt 2001, 85), it also becomes clear that this discourse, at the same time, covers a key dimension of strategy.

9.2.1 Cascading communication

Launching cascade processes to communicate new strategies and management systems into a company seems to be a generally accepted management practice, though success at local levels is generally seen as very diverse (Soderberg and Björkman 2003, 160-163). Underlying the idea of cascading is the concept of 'information processing' – again a container approach to communication. The understanding is 'that if the same contextual (or given) information is always supplied to make sense of a given expression, then presumably the same information can be assumed to have been communicated' (Taylor 1993, 84). The intended function of information cascades, implemented in the form of communication programmes, can be seen as control 'by specifying a standard rating procedure and attaching organizational awards and penalties to it' and coordination, i.e. 'fulfilling the need for interdepartmental predictability' (1993, 87). In that sense, cascading is probably one of the core principles advanced by an orthodox corporate communication theory.

The taxonomy demonstrates that the communication cascade played an important role in corporate communication discourse at Intech. It does not reveal, however, that certain challenges were associated with that cascade in practice. An Intech strategist who was interviewed regularly during the observation period repeated the challenges several times. In an interview in June 2004 he framed his concerns in the following way:

'I think that we indeed do have a communication problem. I think we reasonably arrived where we wanted to get on top management level, i.e. business unit heads, division heads. But if we go further down the line, there are considerable deficits. The role which is intended for middle management, the cascaded communication of our idea, this is not looked after in our sense. We thought that middle management is going to communicate down the cascade, and that doesn't happen this way. Amongst others, the reason is that no basic materials have been provided. This will be caught up on now, which means some standard presentation slides with pre-defined gaps, which can be filled individually, permanently, globally applicable.'
(Intech strategy manager) [80:18]

This statement contains several themes which can also be found in the taxonomy: the top-down process which is initiated at top management level intended to move down the organisational hierarchy level by level; creating awareness for the Intech management system, but also positioning it more concretely by best-practice examples in a local context. Communication tools, like presentations, are intended to transfer knowledge objects between sender and receiver. Additionally, however, the strategist detects the communication problem that information flow stops right after top management.

At the same time, within Intech business unit the need for a cascade was discussed heavily, both among corporate communication managers and with the management team. On that occasion, one of Intech's general managers made the point that a communication cascade in many cases may not even be sensible, e.g. if the information can alternatively be transferred through company media:

'OK, I do not want to deny that there are certain kinds of information where we need a cascade to implement them in the organisation. For example, this is the case for planning topics. This, for me is the classic example where I need to communicate to all employees, and where the question is relevant what this means for me personally. There I can see this immediately. But with most kinds of content we have delivered so far, I do not see that there is implementation necessary.'
(General manager, Intech business unit) [40:18]

The manager here makes the point that a decision should be made with regards to the right channel, based on the content of each theme – and that not all information should automatically be cascaded down the line to each employee. This argument is in line with Larkin and Larkin (1994) who had argued that communicating information through company media can even de-motivate managers to pass information on to employees who can also read these in the company media. Yet, throughout this discussion the container metaphor of information is maintained by which it is possible to exactly distribute information to recipients who then will create the intended meaning from it.

The general two-step communication strategy – first, creating awareness for the Intech management system, second, supplying best-practice examples – was explained in an e-mail, sent from Intech's central corporate communication department to all communication managers in May 2004:

'On April 28th and 29th members of [top management] met to discuss the status of the three [Intech] company programs during their quarterly review meeting here in Germany. This session marked the beginning of the second phase of our [Intech] management system communications efforts. The first phase – beginning with the [Intech] business conference in October…, and culminating with regional meetings in February and March – was designed to introduce the company to the fundamentals of [IMS]. Our task now is to strengthen our employees' and managers' commitment to the implementation of the [company] programs through individual initiatives and projects.'
(E-Mail to Intech communication managers) [73:3]

While a clear separation of two phases of communication is made, also the purpose of communication is re-enforced at the end of the discourse fragment with regards to strengthening commitment to the new management system.

Meanwhile, a rather extensive discourse had developed among communicators on both corporation and business unit levels with regards to the question of which are the most suitable communication tools and instruments to support and lubricate the cascade throughout the company. The common-sense argument was, as illustrated here in an interview section with one of Intech's communication managers, that there should always be a target-group specific mix of media:

'You will always need a mixture of several instruments. This has to do with the fact that we get target groups which are clustered differently everywhere. We have the ones which hesitate, the over-motivated ones, and the ones which are principally rejecting. And still all these people communicate, whether we are there or not. If we send out messages through one channel only, you will never reach everybody. Therefore, there will always be different means of communication.'
(Intech communicator) [73:3]

The various discourse fragments on cascading information into the company displayed the variety of opinions held on this topic throughout Intech. On the one hand, each opinion, in some way referred to the container model of communication, i.e. was constructed using orthodox views of communication. On the other, each discourse fragment revealed aspects that the cascade was not working as intended.

Coupled with this discourse around the cascade processes, there was a second stream of discourse focusing on the question of how company members made sense of the information that was pushed through the media and the cascade.

9.2.2 Sense-making

The discourse around sense-making is illustrated by a fewer set of examples because most arguments were summarised in the two positions which the strategy and communication managers took over in the course of the interviews throughout the year. Similar arguments, occasionally complemented by additional themes mentioned in the taxonomy, occurred on Intech business unit level between strategy and communication managers as well as during discussions between members which formed part of the body of discourse at corporation and business unit level.

The Intech strategy manager, in the same interview quoted in the subsection above, took a position that the Intech management system needs to be broken down in a rather strict way to local levels of the company in order to become meaningful:

'[The Intech management system] needs to become more and more concrete moving down the line ... You do not need to understand everything fully at the lowest level, but you have to know what your own role in the system is. What we had imagined has not really happened yet. Personally, I continuously make this experience when presenting at [internal management] seminars and asking all the time: 'What do you know about the [IMS]?' Generally, there are just a few who answer, so, the message doesn't really get through. Although, in this specific case, you can easily play the ball back and say that you are the future leaders, and if you don't care about this you are at the wrong place here. It is also their responsibility. There we still have some work to do. So far, management has played the major

role. It should now be communicated through to all employees. ... This is not easy. There are only very few people which understand [the IMS] completely and can also model it in a way that it is represented 100 percent in presentations. These are always the same people and they have 100,000 other things to do.'
(Intech strategy manager) [80:19]

Following the information processing concept (Kreps 1990), the manager argues that it is necessary to break information on the Intech management system down to every employee in order to create meaning for each member of the company. According to Kieser (2002), such approaches of rationalising information refer back to Max Weber. In Weber's theory, providing and gathering information was seen as a prerequisite for understanding and appropriate decision-making.

At the same time, the active search for information as well as the active contribution of information are interpreted as signs to the company that a manager is behaving in a suitable way (Feldman and March 1981). The Intech management system was partly built on such assumptions, e.g. in that it incentivized contributions of managers presenting at training programmes.

An alternative view is provided from a corporate communication manager at Intech corporation who, too, was interviewed regularly throughout the observation period. His position was that breaking the Intech management system down through all levels of hierarchy, should not necessarily be an aim for communication. The following statement was made in an interview in November 2004:

'Of course, it is not really surprising that intensity [of knowledge about the Intech management system] somehow decreases down the line. We have to think now what the aim is. Do we have the aim that the cascade reaches down to every employee on a production line, so that everybody can praise the basic elements of the [IMS]? Or is this not a reasonable aim? I would say this is not a reasonable aim. Right, management needs to know the systematics of the [IMS]. Depending on ramifications, what counts is that the employee knows these parts of the [IMS] which really are relevant and decisive for his work, and to which he can contribute somehow, right? And this does not necessarily mean that this person can pray that there is an [IMS] which contains three company programs, there is a certain number of initiatives, there is a committee structure, there are supporting resources, and so forth. This person does not have to be able to paint the full model, this is a silly imagination.'
(Intech communication manager) [87:7]

In contrast to the strategy manager quoted above, the communication manager states that it is not necessary to break the full Intech management system down to everybody in the company in order to facilitate meaning creation – although he follows the same aim as the strategy manager, i.e. to put each individual member of the company into the position to make sense of his/her personal contribution to the IMS. Rather than proposing a view that this meaning creation should happen based on the full range of information available to everybody, he suggests that a selective approach is sufficient, i.e. information can be limited 'to the extent that they help us understand, interpret, and predict phenomena' (Kreps 1990, 27).

Similar positions were also uttered by the communication manager's colleagues on Intech business unit levels at several meetings throughout the year.

Again, a container metaphor of communication and knowledge creation prevails. Similar to the discourse on cascading, the metaphor is interpreted differently by different persons – however, without providing a conclusion with regards to how the challenge can be fixed.

'Getting people to do what you want them to do', remains the challenge. Taylor, Cooren et al. who framed that sentence in 1996 (5), also provided a communicational model for explaining how cascading and sensemaking can work considering alternative theories. This model will form the basis for the following review of the orthodox model.

9.3 Communicational review of organising

The notion that communication forms a core component of organising processes has long been put forward by management gurus like Drucker (1974) and Handy (1992; 1994). Drucker, in particular, alluded to a surfeit of communication media applied in managed communication a long time ago. 'The noise level has gone up so fast that no one can listen any more to all that babble about communication. But there is less and less communicating' (1974, 390). The point had been made above already: communication, in Drucker's terms, surpasses information processing. It is based on perception by the recipient, influenced by expectations and interrelated with the logic of information by giving it meaning. Additionally, all managed communication is charged with an intention 'to get something across', and, therefore, always some sort of propaganda (1974, 394).

Another point which Drucker made early on, is that 'downward communication cannot work' (1974, 396). The problem with this view of communication is that it assumes that the uttering individual communicates, not the recipient. A lot of thought has been given to the question of how the sender can be improved as a communicator. 'But all one can communicate downwards are commands', writes Drucker. This statement is, by the way, completely in line with the statement of Intech business unit's general manager above when he made the point that planning processes should be cascaded rather than it is information which needs interpretation. Also 'more and better' communication, often prescribed by orthodox corporate communication theory does not solve the problem. It puts an increasing amount of data into circulation, but not necessarily meaningful information which can only be achieved by effective communication. Drucker's suggestion is for managers to stimulate purposeful upward communication, based on management by objectives. The task for management to create a ground for functioning communication, therefore, is to skilfully 'frame' communication (Deetz, Tracy et al. 2000), starting out with the subordinate's views.

9.3.1 Taylor's 'communicational basis of the organization'

James Taylor and connected scholars have provided several contributions to an alternative theory for explaining processes in the sense of this Chapter, i.e. for 'Organising by linking decisions and actions'. Communication is viewed as a core managerial process in a large, complex company (Taylor 1993; Taylor, Cooren et al. 1996; Cooren 1999; Taylor 1999; Heaton and Taylor 2002; Taylor 2002; Robichaud, Giroux et al. 2004). The key concepts of this theory are laid down in Taylor, Cooren et al.'s 'Communicational basis of organization' (1996). Their main concern is to view the properties of a company, e.g. organisational structures, performance, mechanisms of coordination and control, not as activities as such, but as socially constructed, interpretive processes. In fact, communication is the core of these interpretive processes. Again, communication plays a twofold role: on the one hand 'as a more or less shared understanding', on the other 'as a dynamic play out of relationships' (1996, 4).

Viewed from this perspective the aim of 'getting people to do and think what you want them to do and think' which is taken as a given in most management theories and strategy schools (Mintzberg 1979; Mintzberg 1994) becomes a complex and communicational task.

Taylor's theory is based on a distinction of two modalities of communication (1993): 'conversation' which is always situation-specific, constantly generated by interaction, and 'text' with fixed properties across situations. The decoding of both conversation and text, however, according to this theory happens in the individuals' minds, within a context of internal conversation (Taylor 1993, 92): 'information is a property of conversation, texts are merely data.' The interpretive processes mentioned above, then, happen in an ongoing translation from one modality to another in which context is essential.

Based on Weick's (1979) loosely coupled aspects of organisation, Taylor continues to apply and extend the notion of ongoing translations between conversation and text to the level of complex companies. In this analysis, Mintzberg's (1979) requirements for structuring a company – division of labour and coordination – are interpreted communicationally – namely as 'performance' ('what is to be done?') and 'belief' ('how is it to be done?').

The question then is how company actions can be explained in this ongoing social construction of meaning (Hosking and Haslam 1997) and how division of labour and coordination can happen in the managers' intended way, given a high level of complexity of texts, conversations and contexts in a large company.

In situations of one-on-one supervision, this can be achieved by recognizing the kind of work which has to be done and getting company members to accept their tasks and mandates. Transferred to the level of a whole company, however, this situation needs to be compared with acts of speech (illocution) and effect (perlocution), because an immediate feedback loop is not given.

A company as such, though, cannot speak. It is always individuals which act as speakers for the company, even not knowing whether this individual 'is correctly presenting the principal' (Taylor, Cooren et al. 1996, 22). The crucial point, then, is, whether the speaker's voice is accepted as legitimate by the company members or not.

Taylor, Cooren et al. expand their theory by six 'degrees of separation' in which this company-wide acceptance in the sense of 'meaning which endures' can be achieved in a network of successive conversations (1996, 23-25).

First degree

This degree of separation occurs, for example, in the situation of direct supervision mentioned above, when text is used to produce an intended effect.

Second degree

In this degree of separation, conversations are turned into a 'narrative representation' of them, i.e. company members who are not the immediate agents start to interpret the original intention. This interpreted intention is launched into new conversations.

Third degree

The third degree of separation contains 'transcription of the text onto a permanent or semi-permanent medium permitting storage and hence temporal and physical removal from the original communication event.' Presence of initiator and interpreter is not required any more. Minutes of a meeting are an example.

Fourth degree

In this degree of separation a 'specialized media-specific language' is developed, represented in specialised media. This separation, for example, was heavily used for the implementation of the Intech management system, when specific company publications were produced using IMS-specific terminology. Generalization is one result, but, at the same time, the original intentions by that degree of separation have become almost non-recoverable (Hodge and Kress 1988).

Fifth degree

This degree of separation represents the stage when physical frames and designs appear. Much of the elements referred to as symbolic management in Chapter 8 analysing Strand 1 of the reference framework could be subsumed here. Also for the Intech management system, a specific brand name and logo was used. 'At this point, conversation has mutated from the entirely local and specific to the entirely global and generic (Taylor, Cooren et al. 1996, 25).

Sixth degree

The sixth degree of separation covers publication, dissemination, broadcasting – the basis for 'standardization'.

Considering these six degrees of separation, 'voice' is a necessary condition for a strategic issues or themes to become turned into action, i.e. an individual authorized to speak in the company's and issue's name. Voice cannot only be viewed as a starting point for getting the chain of separation going. It is also the crucial aspect in that it cannot simply be assigned to somebody, but it needs to be achieved by somebody in a process of authorization in the company (Taylor, Cooren et al. 1996, 26).

Another common academic term for this authorization is 'legitimacy' which Suchman (1995, 574) defined as 'a generalized perception or assumption that the actions of an entity are desirable, proper, or appropriate within some socially constructed system of norms, values, beliefs, and definitions.'

Who aspires to become a 'voice' of the company, following Taylor, Cooren et al.'s theory, must produce a text and get it validated within the company. This process involves networking, which in Taylor, Cooren et al.'s (1996) model is part of the higher degrees of separation. This is primarily a political process, manifested – or 'fixated' in the authors' words – in the communication products representing fifth and sixth degree of separation. The acceptance of these products, in the end, becomes 'the concrete proof of the legitimacy of management itself' (1996, 27).

The separation from first to sixth degree is not a one-way route, because this alone does not yet create action. Text from sixth degree of separation, again needs to be reinterpreted somewhere in the company in terms of the first degree of separation to become effective, and so on.

9.3.2 Contributions from strategy theory

Strategy theory adds further aspects to Taylor, Cooren et al.'s communicational view in that it provides further insight into the communicational aspects of decision-making.

Decisions and actions, generally, are viewed as core elements of the strategy process (Chakravarthy and White 2002). Instead of rational information gathering and information processing – the orthodox view of decision making – an increasing number of scholars argue that many other modes of decision making are predominant, e.g. politically-driven mode, process-oriented modes, or even anarchic mode (Choo 2002). Given the complexity of processes decisions are involved in, Andersen (2000) introduces the notion of decisions as paradox: only questions which, in principle, are undecidable, may be decided. If an answer can be found by analysis, it is not a matter of decision.

Not many strategy scholars have reflected on the communicational aspects of decision-making in particular. Hendry (2000), drawing on Brunsson (1982), defines strategic decision-making as part of organisational discourse and communication. According to Hendry, decisions are always manifested in discourse: 'the decision which matters is that which is communicated' (2000, 964).

Kieser (1998) reviewed processes of organising and decision-making from a social constructionist perspective, and – similar to Taylor, Cooren et al. (1996) – came to the conclusion that organisational rules and decisions need to undergo a process of interpretation before they can be transformed into action. In order to achieve a sufficient level of agreement in the interpretations necessary for common action, company members need to communicate continuously (Kieser 1998; Kieser, Hegele et al. 1998). These scholars stress the importance of face-to-face communication as part of the overall process, and also point to the performative character of such interpretation processes, because rules and decisions can also be modified while being interpreted. At the same time, they claim that some form of written fixation is necessary – again in line with Taylor, Cooren et al.'s communicational theory. Communication, then, as a core process of organising and strategizing accounts for the gradual manufacturing of organisation (Kieser 1998). In other words, the company is continuously constructed in communication – with the consequence that managers are not simply in control: instead, 'managers are "in control" and "not in control" at the same time' (Streatfield 2001, 91). Decision-making, from a strategy point of view, then also becomes a communicative process operating in specific organisational contexts (Fulop, Linstead et al. 2004).

9.4 Discourse analysis

Having examined the theory, the challenge is now to refer back to some of the outcomes of the implementation of the Intech management system and explain them from the communicational viewpoint of organising which has been developed above. The sequence of themes corresponds with the six degrees of separation introduced above. Subsection 1 covers 1st and 2nd degrees of separations, i.e. the way decisions are made and communicated in face-to-face modes. Subsection 2 focuses on 3rd and 4th degree by giving insight into the processes of networking decisions at Intech. And Subsection 3 sheds light on how communication instruments like magazines, newsletters and events were used to embed the Intech management system into the company (5th and 6th degree).

9.4.1 To decide or not to decide

Considering orthodox communication and strategy theories, one would expect managers to leverage their formal power, take rational and straightforward decisions and communicate them to their subordinates. In the reality, however, rationality of decisions is often the exception. This is what seminal studies of Brunsson (1982) and Jackall (1988) have shown, and this is also what the discourse at Intech revealed.

A large number of discourse fragments supporting this notion were collected during the observation period. One of the most obvious was the following when a communication manager at Intech's May 2004 peer meeting among communicators formulated his view on how decisions are taken at Intech. He commented on a presentation slide which showed the organisational structure of one of the company programmes:

'Is it possible to make a comment? From my perspective, when I look at this chart, this is a typical [Intech] approach, right? You have a problem, and the first thing is not to define who is now responsible to solve the problem, the first thing is to set up a committee. So, the council is in one sense responsible, but it is not acting as a responsible person, because [member of the management board] has a lot of other things to do still. We get people to handle the problem in their second responsibility, then we get the business units involved, and then we have from each business unit two people involved in this, excellent, two people who now can discuss who is responsible in their business unit. And then they have another approach as managers. This means, managers maybe get training as project managers within [Intech], and then all these people will discuss these things for two and a half years...'
(Communication manager) [75:16]

This discourse fragment was taken from a discussion following a presentation by one of the general managers of the Intech management system. The communication manager starts his argument with a set of questions which he uses to trigger the assumption that the presented approach is typical for Intech: committees are founded in order to avoid loading responsibilities on the shoulders of individual managers. He continues to elaborate that the manager who heads the committee does so in a part-time responsibility, representatives of each business unit are involved – again it is two of each business unit, in order to avoid individual responsibilities, the speaker suggests.

The manager who voices his opinion here generalizes that one of the consequences that individual responsibilities are avoided is that members of the committee will rather discuss who is responsible than decide or install a training session on project management in order to formally qualify committee members to manage their job. But, finally, the speaker resigns and concludes that the committee – rather than deciding – will continue to discuss for a long time.

Implicitly, the manager proposes that committees are primarily founded to reduce risk and to evade responsibility for individual managers. In other words, the intention of forming committees can be alternatively be interpreted as 'to restrain an organization from action which could be regarded as risky' (Brunsson 1982, 57). Jackall refers to 'decision paralysis' as a consequence of strategies to avoid risk (1988, 78).

Managers at Intech practiced other modes of avoiding decisions which are probably common behaviour. Rather than keeping away from decisions completely, practices of 'looking up and looking around' (Jackall 1988, 79) were applied to come to decisions. Such decisions often end up as implicit decisions which are not even explicitly voiced.

One of these practices involved 'signalling' (see taxonomy) that one intends to contribute to overall Intech activities rather than taking an explicit decision to implement the activity. A manager of Intech business unit gave an example of this mode of 'looking up' at the business conference in December 2003 when, in a summarising discussion, he made the following statement:

'So, without mentioning it all the time, we were talking about the [Intech] management system. And what we talked about is very much in line with what we heard at the [Intech] business conference. So, we have got to show that we are very much part of [Intech]. We cannot be a captive company without [Intech]. The [Intech] life is very much what we think and what we believe. I am enthused because of the presentations I have seen. They gave truth to what I have been trying to explain to you.'
(General manager, Intech business unit) [16:2]

The point that the Intech management system was intended to launch new mandatory programs for each of the business units is undermined in the first and second sentence. Rather than taking the decision to implement the management system, the manager explains that what had been said before fitted the Intech management system already. This, he suggests, as the reason for 'looking up', stresses the captive role and demonstrates participation in the management system. In doing so, he also 'looks around' by referring to the business concept, i.e. a factor external to the decisions – again, a processes which can be viewed as fairly common in reasoning decisions (Brunsson 1982).

One more example for looking up and looking around goes back to a feature in Intech business unit's employee magazine which in December 2003, on the occasion of the launch of the Intech management system, was published in the form of a special issue focusing on this launch. There, one of Intech's managers was quoted the following way:

'I think it is important that we approach this issue with a lot of our own initiative. Our goal should be to identify the needs of our customer [Intech] even before it has formulated these. Only when we fulfil this requirement will we be able to position ourselves as a valuable service provider within [Intech].'
(Intech business unit manager) [15:18]

This example illustrates the sub-theme of 'showing initiative' in the taxonomy – a mode of 'looking up' to Intech corporation 'with a lot of own initiative'. The purpose for showing this initiative is derived from the structure of the company: Intech business unit is defined as part of Intech corporation. As such, it needs to position itself in the Intech conglomerate, and one way of doing so is to actively participate in company initiatives.

These two examples of how decisions were treated at Intech as well as the other modes of decision-making that were laid out in the taxonomy showed that decisions rarely followed a rational mode in the sense of a conscious choice between several alternatives.

Brunsson (1982) showed some time ago that this 'irrationality' in decision-making is common in many companies. Mintzberg, Waters et al. (1990) argued that managers often seek to avoid making decisions and that, therefore, decisions often rather unfold than are explicitly made at one point in time. Such behaviour, culminating in decision-making paralysis, has been confirmed in several studies until recently (Fulop, Linstead et al. 2004).

Scholars which have dealt with these irrationalities of decision-making, generally point to the importance of the actions resulting from decisions (Brunsson 1985; Mintzberg, Waters et al. 1990; Taylor, Cooren et al. 1996; Fulop, Linstead et al. 2004). This leads back to the 3rd and 4th degrees of separation mentioned above, i.e. aspects of legitimising decisions, which had been detected as a particularly important precondition for decision-based action.

9.4.2 Facilitating the legitimisation process

It is an important aspect that the data collected throughout the observation period did not include any discourse fragments which gave evidence that the Intech management system was actually being legitimised. Partly, it may be the case that such processes had been included in earlier steps of the management process at Intech and the researcher may have started his observation period after the decision to implement the IMS had been made already. Another reason may be that corporate communication during the observation period was not involved in legitimisation processes, so that the researcher did not have access to such legitimising discourse. Alternatively, it may be that the legitimisation process did not happen at all on a wider basis.

The latter option appeals to be likely. As far as company documents on the Intech management system revealed, mainly external drivers – like a low market capitalisation of Intech compared with its competitors or like entering a new phase of company development – were put forward by Intech top management in order to rationalise the new management system. The general manager in charge of the launch of the management system used the following wording at Intech's business conference in October

2003 when the management system was officially launched in the presence of the top managers of the company:

'While we used a rather opportunistic and, granted, rather rudimentary approach in the past, we have now decided on a unified and systematic approach. [The former programme] was exactly the right move at the time – at the end of 2000. We were considerably distanced from competitor benchmarks. It was therefore necessary to define the most critical themes for eliminating the worst deficits, in order to get the company closer overall to the competitive margins. Although we still have problems in some parts of the company, overall we are now close to the competitive level and are now entering the phase of permanent optimization. To achieve this, a systematic approach of implementation is far more suitable and more enduring than what we once had.'
(Intech general manager) [54:44]

The general manager, right in the first sentence of this discourse fragment made clear that a 'decision' was made on a 'unified' approach. The persons who made the decision are not named in the fragment, but talking about 'we' it is clear from the context that he referred to the members of Intech's management board and the strategy department. Hints with regards to legitimisation processes in a wider context are not given.

The wording chosen suggests rational considerations behind the most critical themes that were 'defined' in order to overcome deficits. Efficiency and effectiveness in achieving performance criteria is the logic followed, based on a rational model of decision-making behind the Intech management system (Fulop, Linstead et al. 2004, 469).

The same general manager took a stand with respect to the implementation of the Intech management system in the management magazine issued on the occasion of the same business conference:

[Editor]: What is the [IMS] about?
[Manager]: The [Intech] management system is a vehicle for implementing our strategy. As the name says, it's about taking a systemic approach to things. All of the components of the system are conceptually and chronologically coordinated as well as logically linked to each other.
[Editor]: What are these components?
[Manager]: First, the [IMS] contains clearly defined and organized company topics coordinated in a logical progression. These topics need to be publicized throughout the company so that everyone knows their primary focus. Second, a consistent corporate calendar ensures all planning, decision-making, reporting and communications in the business units, regions and corporate units is carried out to a common content baseline and a common schedule. … Third, it is up to managers and employees – qualified and motivated by incentives – to implement corporate strategy. A cascading committee structure keeps things running smoothly.
(Intech management magazine) [55:20]

The statements again embody a rather rational approach to strategy and decision-making. In the first answer, the Intech management system is positioned as a vehicle to implement strategy. With that, the intention to create action – by implementing the management system – is stressed. An assertion follows that the term 'system' was consciously chosen and that all components follow the logic of a system.

The reply to the second question points towards the logic of implementation which was pursued by the manager. Rather than initiating a legitimisation process, the topics should be 'publicized' within Intech – following the logic of information gathering and information processing (Choo 2002). The corporate calendar, as had been discussed above, again in a very assertive style, is presented as the component which 'ensures all planning in the business units, regions and corporate units'. Finally, control mechanisms are embedded in order to 'qualify and motivate' managers and employees to implement the management system. Control mechanisms in that sense had been introduced in Brunsson's (1985) and Jackall's (1988) companies as well, and are a common approach according to rational strategy models (Fulop, Linstead et al. 2004).

This leads to a specific kind of control mechanism which was termed as 'blame time' by Jackall. By blame time he meant the practice of hurting people publicly in large companies. In these companies, the image of an individual plays a major role. Therefore, blame time can be understood as 'posing the most serious sort of threat' (1988, 85). One of the company strategy managers in November gave an example of blame time which was intended to happen at quarterly review meetings between management board and business unit heads:

'For him [new member of the management board], it is a huge matter to let each business unit report what it actually does. In fact, not only in a general way that each division praises itself, but he has very simple systematics. He says: "Right, we have the champions' league, midfield, and candidates for improvement. There are these three clusters probably in each business unit, therefore, everybody can report specifically for his business unit what the three core levers are for further improvement. ... These are the best-practice days which are locked up for this year already, 2005, for all business units.
(Intech strategy manager) [106:22]

A type of blame time, in this case, was applied under the cover of best-practice days by publicly sorting managers and their business units into one of three performance-related categories. Although this kind of meeting provides a formal arena for discussing and legitimising strategy, due to the execution of hierarchical power in public, most managers will react by applying defensive strategies in order not 'to be caught in the wrong place at the wrong time' (Jackall 1988, 88-90). As other discourse fragments have shown, at Intech a common business unit practice was to polish presentations for such purposes, apply some of the decision-making modes explained above, and keep the presentation as uncritical as possible.

Also discourse among corporate communication professionals revealed little evidence of actual legitimisation processes. One of the few examples is the following discourse fragment. It was taken from another peer meeting among corporate communication managers in April 2004 when a head offices representative explained the strategy for spreading information on the Intech management system company-wide:

'And this is also important for the business units: It must be made clear to the manager that he or she cannot get away by not communicating to the employees. They must know that the information is available on a public platform, fermenting. On the other hand, I need to ask how I can support the communication between manager and employee, which is per se the best. And implementing a slight delay in time is a rather easy way to do this. This gives the manager the time to know what is relevant and, also, to catch up with deficits.'
(Intech communication manager) [65:8]

First of all, the manager refers to the business unit as the decentralised unit required to increase accountability of their managers in terms of exerting control in a hierarchical sense (Lindkvist and Llewelyn 2003). He continues to stress the need for direct communication between manager and employee and proposes a privileged early access to information for managers as one solution to this problem. This would correspond to Schmidt's (2004) notion of viewing company media as offerings to communicate. The term 'fermenting' which was used, points to the fact that the information is processed somehow and also changed while publicly available. However, even if the communication process between manager and employee starts, it is not necessarily ensured that the communication objective has been achieved at the individual management level.

Particularly critically received on business unit levels was the fact that – in the absence of a legitimisation phase – business units were viewed as responsible for the implementation. One business unit communication manager made this point on one of the cross-business unit meetings in May 2004 when the implementation of the Intech management system was discussed:

'I think this [Intech] management system is a rather complicated story. The centre understood roughly 15 years ago that we could not continue like that. And since that time there were initiatives, work groups, circles and so on, to push vertical projects, horizontal projects, sectoral projects, and so on, but nothing happens. Then somebody had the idea…, who said that we have all these things already, let us draw a nice box around it, and structure it in a way that everything makes sense. … Let us call it [Intech] management system now. This needs to be carried

into all business units. They are now in charge of implementing it somehow. But what they really want is that these business units earn money, and that they get their costs down, and so on. Now, there is just nobody who says how this exactly has to happen.'
(Business unit communication manager) [41:38]

This manager confirms the impression that the Intech management system in the business units was understood as a central initiative, not necessarily owned by the business units. Having been with the company for several years, he ranks the IMS among preceding projects and initiatives and interprets it just as another attempt from the head offices to re-structure a well-known problem, namely to increase profitability. He directly addresses, however, the interface between centre and business unit where a gap of accountability opens up.

Research has been conducted on the question of which strategies managers apply to adopt new organisational practices. Kostova and Roth found that ceremonial adoption of practices, i.e. 'formal adoption of a practice on the part of a recipient unit's employees for legitimacy reasons' (2002, 220), regularly occurs in decentralised units of companies where central forces to implement a practice are high, but the level of understanding and interpretation in decentralised units is low. This kind of reaction is exactly what Taylor, Cooren et al. (1996) predicted in cases where communication legitimisation is absent.

In order to reach adoption in these cases, companies, according to Castaner and Ketokivi (2004), use a variety of mechanisms such as rules, monetary incentives, authority or structural changes. These authors, however, also highlight the integrative nature of participatory processes. Some concrete suggestions of how these can be implemented in practice are proposed below in the final section of this Chapter.

9.4.3 Re-evaluating conduit tools

The integrative power of communication plays a crucial role in processes leading from decisions to action and strategy implementation (Zerfaß 1996). According to Taylor, Cooren et al. (1996), company media play an important role in the fixation of decisions in the organisation. Integrative power of communication, however, can be different – depending on whether communication happens between present persons or between actors separated through time and space (Zerfaß 1996, 288). In the first case, communication can be based on common forms of social interaction. The actors can work together on a solution for a question. In the second case, however, social integration remains restricted to mediated processes. In

Schmidt's (2004) words, company media can provide offerings for information production in the minds of company members, but they cannot enforce it.

Inherent in the move from personal to mediated communication is an increased degree of separation from the original intention, because company members involved, purely via company media, are not able to judge the full account of the original intention any more (Zerfaß 1996, 214). Instead, they have to trust that the assessments made in the media are reliable. Schmidt sees company members as autonomous in constructing their meaning from media. Therefore, he argues that it is unlikely to be able to influence company members purely through company media, unless the media get the company members themselves to initiate actions in the sense of provider of the information.

Communication managers at Intech were aware of the support role company media play. In a meeting in May 2004, one of the Intech communication managers explained the role of the newly launched management magazine as follows:

'Sometimes you are trusted in advance, sometimes not. But we wanted to get confirmed, and had hoped that we are not wrong with our ideas. It was good luck that we concentrated the launch of the new media on [the business conference], and it was a lucky coincidence that we had this launch of the [Intech management system] there. Based on [the conference], it was possible to make sure that it was the top 500 people who come back with some sort of information to their managers, and they knew that the information these top people have is going to be important.'
(Intech communication manager) [65:6]

The manager, in the first sentence, confirms that trust cannot be assumed at the outset when distributing a company medium. He also states that it was important to launch the medium in the context of the business conference so that the 'offering' of information, at least for the top managers, was put in the concrete context of the launch of the Intech management system. And, probably, for many of the managers who subsequently took the magazine back into their units, the publication was indeed seen as a useful tool to be passed on into the organisation. This happened at Intech business unit, for example. Also, the specialised IMS terminology was depicted in the magazine, generic features of the Intech management system were portrayed, and the inventors of the management system interviewed. Therefore, this issue of the magazine corresponds to 5th and 6th degrees of separation in Taylor, Cooren et al.'s (1996) framework.

The second issue of the management magazine was launched at the end of April 2004, six months after the launch of the management system. Having analysed the discourse fragments above, the following discourse fragment did not reflect the problematic legitimisation process of the IMS which was, in reality, happening in the business units at that time. The editorial team had interviewed the manager in charge of the organisational committee for the Intech management system:

[Editor]: ...You are organizing "Best Practice Days" with the Business units and visiting the regional conferences. What is your impression of the implementation of the company programs? Are there any uncertainties?
[Manager]: Not a trace. On the contrary, the business units and regions are addressing the issues more than ever. The business units in particular have quickly taken stock of their activities and assessed them with respect to the [company programs] and their initiatives.
(Management Edition 2) [21:8]

By the time that issue of the magazine appeared, most managers had built their own opinion on the management system based on the information they had. The business unit manager quoted above, for example, who had explained his view of the management in a fairly critical way, would probably not have trusted a statement as positive and sweeping as the one which was printed in the magazine.

These two examples highlighted some of the problems inherent in a very media-focused, top-down communication campaign accompanying the launch of a complex issue like the Intech management system. Several more topics with regards to the application of company media were discussed among communication professionals at Intech corporation and business unit levels. These concentrated mainly on the right mix and prioritization of media to be applied and the depth of information on the Intech management system that should be provided on various levels of the hierarchy.

Displaying further examples would have reconfirmed the problems resulting from a media-focused communication strategy, rather than revealing new aspects of the discussion. In the sense of Jäger (2001; 2004) who suggested that discourse analysis reaches completeness after the first appearance of a new aspect, therefore, repetitive aspects are not followed up further in this study.

9.5 Theorising

The analyses conducted in the previous Sections allow an in-depth explanation of the communicational processes occurring as part of Strand 2 – i.e. 'Organising by linking decisions and action'. Like in Chapter 8, this explanation will form the basis for defining the contribution of Strand 2 towards an alternative theory of corporate communication.

In order to put the following discussion into context, first, Strand 2 is highlighted in the reference framework (see Figure 9).

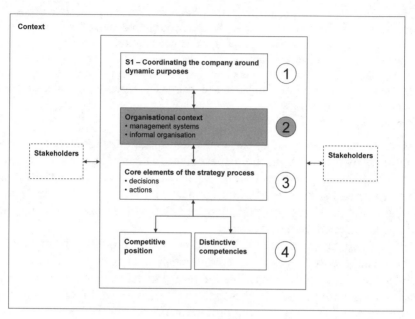

Fig. 9. Referring back to Strand 2 in the reference framework

Analysis of Strand 2 focused on the following set of research questions which were summarised in Table 10: One question setting the focal point for thematic analysis: 'Which themes with regards to organising processes did corporate communication discourse reveal?'; and two questions related to discourse analysis: 'How did corporate communication discourse consti-tute organisation in the concrete case? And how was it constituted by other modes of organising?'

In summary, the analysis of Strand 2 of the reference framework has re-vealed that orthodox corporate communication theory and practice only focus on a very small sector of communication processes related to organ-ising in general, and decision making in particular. Concentrating on mainly mediated processes supporting the communication of allegedly ra-tional decisions left important parts of the sense-making processes at In-tech unmanaged.

Analysis yielded that this concerns particularly communication proc-esses which are crucial for transforming strategy into action, i.e. the link between making the actual decision and its fixation via company media. Strategists and general managers saw their role at Intech particularly in preparing and making the decisions.

The role allocated to corporate communication – broadly summarised – was to report and broadcast the decisions to members of the company, i.e. to facilitate a support process like proposed according to orthodox theory. This process was addressed to both middle managers and employees.

The Intech management system, however, was decided and elaborated upon within the rows of top management. Then, a logically timed communication cascade was established, leveraging all internal media-like publications, intranet, e-mails and events.

Throughout the observation period interviewees detected that there is a communication problem linked to processes of creating meaning around the decision to implement the Intech management system. In most cases this was described in a way that the cascade stopped immediately after top management. Additionally, several discourse fragments showed a rather low level of acceptance of the system among middle managers – although a concrete reason or solution was not mentioned by any of the participants.

Taylor, Cooren et al.'s (1996) six degrees of separation helped to shed light on the missing link between decisions and actions, i.e. a process of legitimising decisions. From a social constructionist viewpoint, this is – at least in large and complex companies – a precondition for getting people to do and think what you want them to do and think.

Therefore, as a result of this analysis, three interrelated communication and strategy processes for linking decisions to actions are suggested in Figure 10: (1) the actual processes of decision-making which can be either rational or – more probably – irrational, (2) the facilitation of a legitimisation process of decisions in the company, which includes creating voice for decisions and leading decisions through processes of networking, and (3) the credible fixation of decisions in company media, i.e. the part of corporate communication which is already known from orthodox corporate communication theory and practice.

This summary illustration covers and structures the results of thematic and discourse analysis: (1) Thematic analysis focused on replying to the research question of which themes covered organising processes, whereas (2) discourse analysis concentrated on the question of how corporate communication discourse constituted and was constituted by organising processes (see Table 10). Two of the three generic themes identified in thematic analysis, were adopted in Figure 10 right away, namely the themes of 'decision-making' and 'sense-making'. The third theme – i.e. 'cascading' – was replaced by and split into 'legitimisation' and 'fixation'. This change resulted from the above discussion which concentrated on the problems associated with cascade processes. The findings of discourse analysis, i.e. the modes of how corporate communication discourse contributed to organising, are summarised in the explanations of the three boxes – i.e. rational and irrational modes of decision-making, creating voice and social networking as modes of legitimisation, and maintaining credibility and use of company media as modes of fixation.

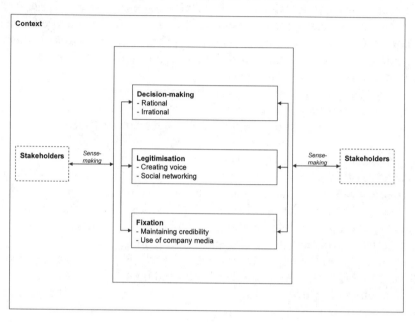

Fig. 10. Review of Strand 2 – Organising by linking decisions and actions

Following the steps proposed in Section 8.5, Strand 2 is now adapted in the reference framework. This step is illustrated in Figure 11.

This summary is not intended to question the fact that managers simply can take decisions and execute them. It is maintained that decisions are necessary prior conditions for action (Mintzberg, Waters et al. 1990). In line with Taylor, Cooren et al. (1996), it is, however, argued, that a straight-forward decision-action process works mainly in one-on-one situations. When it comes to implementing large-scale programmes affecting big companies, action cannot simply be expected throughout the company after the decisions had been made and broadcast via company media.

Based on the analysis, an alternative approach requiring three alternative fields of action for effective communication and strategy implementation are proposed in the concluding paragraphs. These have not yet been addressed in orthodox theory.

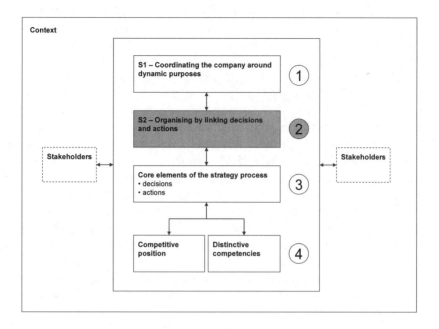

Fig. 11. Adapting Strand 2 in the reference framework

9.5.1 Giving decisions voice

The Intech case and others (Brunsson 1985; Jackall 1988) have shown that managers often decide irrationally rather than through rational processes. In consequence, many decisions are not as obvious and easily detectable as rational decision-making theory suggests. In combination with the fact that a company cannot speak in its own name, but only managers or employees can perform acts of speech (Taylor, Cooren et al. 1996, 22), this makes the situation even more complex. 'Voice' (1996, 26) is necessary in order to get the authorization process for the speaker going. Company members need to 'recognize' a speaker before that speaker can effectively advocate a decision. Corporate communication in many cases is the 'owner' of the platforms that are suitable for giving voice to decisions and various speakers in the company. These platforms can be used to present actors and their positions, rather than purely informing about existing decisions. This is in line with Brunsson (1990) who made the point that decisions must be clearly visible to the stakeholders before they can act as legitimising devices.

The challenge and the critical point in this is that, given the existing information overload, selecting mechanisms will have to be applied in order to prioritise voices that receive access to these platforms. This is part of the political character of legitimisation and authorization processes, as has been stated by Taylor, Cooren et al. (1996).

Handy (1992) has argued that, due to their political constitution, all management processes of a company should be based on a normative model which also respects the communicational nature of organisations. His suggestion is to implement a federal framework, putting forward the notion that authority must be earned from those over whom it is exercised is realised. 'Federalism properly understood is not so much a political structure or system as it is a way of life' (Handy 1992, 60).

Federalism is defined as a way to organize social processes by breaking them down into small units, based on a high level of autonomy of each unit, including rights, competences, and legitimacy (Münch and Meerwaldt 2002, 3). However, this autonomy is always paired with a certain level of unity. Cooperative federalism means that originally autonomous decision-makers decide to solve these tasks together, which make a collaboration of several levels of decision takers necessary. There is an elaborated body of literature on pros and cons of federalism available[31]. The important point is, however, that a company needs to take a decision to implement these structures in order to work effectively according to them (Handy 1992;

---

[31] See e.g. Münch, U. and K. Meerwaldt (2002).

Arguments pro federalism are: Democratic values can be realized in a federal structure due to its higher level of participation than in Unitarianism. Due to subsidiarity each individual has the opportunity to participate. Federalism creates a climate for innovation and experimentation in the decentralised units. A federal system minimizes concentration of power – horizontally (different functions) and vertically (e.g. regions vs. corporate). Federalism creates competition among participants. Due to decentralisation and the broad base of managers there are hardly any management problems to be solved. A high level of continuity and reliability is reached, leading to a high level of stability of the system. Federalism strengthens democracy by promoting autonomy etc. A federal structure promotes intellectual, cultural and social diversity. Because power is decentralised, there is also a variety of media and information sources.

Arguments against federalism are: Equality is not ensured among the different decentralised units. Decision-making can be seen as difficult. Some see changes hard to implement because of the shared agreement which has to be achieved before. Activities of the top decision makers are not necessarily transparent because individuals do not know the exact processes of decision-making. Responsibilities are not always clear. Costs for coordinating the activities can be high. Infrastructures which are created by one decentralised unit can be used by the others as well (spill-over-effect) which can keep other units from investing as well.

Dearlove 2002)[32]. This is clearly not a task for solely corporate communication managers, but for an interdisciplinary approach in companies, including – besides corporate communication – at least general and middle management as well as strategy functions. Corporate communication should have a vital interest participate in such communicational decisions and perhaps be an active driver to bring such decisions on the agenda of management boards.

9.5.2 Facilitating the legitimisation process

Decisions should be used as a rationale to produce dialogue and communication (Brunsson 1990) – rather than a rational process which in all cases automatically produces the intended outcomes. As has been argued in the analysis sections, a 'networking test' (Taylor, Cooren et al. 1996, 27) needs to be passed by both speaker and the speaker's text in order to transform the text into a fact of the company – and, therefore, to generate action. 'A network is a grouping of organization members who engage in patterned interaction' (Kreps 1990, 221).

Networking among peers – in the following referred to as 'peer communication' – intended to build collective intuition, can be an effective way to facilitate networking tests (Eisenhardt 2001; Lindkvist and Llewelyn 2003). This has to work by a two-way form of communication which, in turn, means that communication can also fail, and that failure can also impede further decisions (Baecker 2000).

Following a participative management approach – in the sense of the hypothesis that the more peer groups participate in decision-making, the more likely they are to develop an appreciation for the problems of the company (Kreps 1990) – is a precondition for successfully establishing peer-to-peer communication. Again, peer communication can easily be implemented in federal management systems similar to the one proposed above.

Network theory and network communication have provided insight into how these processes of authorization can be initiated and managed (Barbasi 2002; Tuomi 2002; Cheney, Christensen et al. 2004). Communities of practice (Wenger 1998) and strategic communities (Kodama 2005) have proven as effective concepts and tools to bring peers together, based

---

[32] A further and more in-depth discussion of federalism as a principle of organising companies leads into political theory and breaks the limits of this study. For readers who want to gain a more in-depth insight into implications of federalism for management theory and practice it is referred back to Handy (1992; 2002).

on negotiated relationships in order to create strategic thinking in an ongoing communicative and collaborative process.

Corporate communication managers will need to become familiar with these kinds of communicational toolsets and have to develop concrete modes for applying these in company contexts in order to do justice to their role as facilitators of the legitimisation process of decisions. Both mutual accountability (Wenger 1998, 84) and an emergent formation and implementation of business concepts and management systems (Kodama 2005, 28) can be achieved through its practical and consequent application.

9.5.3 From cascading to using the performative capacity of communication

Another important finding of the analysis was that the six degrees of separation, and, respectively, associated decision-making, legitimisation and fixation processes summarised in this conclusion, do not necessarily happen in a timely order, but act in a constantly interrelated way (Taylor, Cooren et al. 1996). Consequently, the inefficiencies detected in the cascading process at Intech also lead to the conclusion that the performative capacity of communication tools and instruments applied can be improved by adhering to the notion of addressing all three processes in parallel (Quirke 2000, 176).

It can be argued that this extended focus of communication would further increase the information overload which has been addressed and criticized several times before (Tsoukas 2001).

Against this context, it is clear that companies only have a limited ability and willingness to assimilate decisions and derive actions (Quirke 2000). The suggested solution, therefore, is not necessarily to expand the amount of corporate communication, but to shift resources from 'fixation' of decisions – by publishing them in company media, organising events, and maintaining a large amount of communication channels – towards the other two dimensions of the legitimisation process, i.e. giving voice to decisions and, particularly, facilitating the legitimisation process.

A 'more selective coordinated use and greater linkage' between communication channels can be an approach to increase the performative capacity of communication (Quirke 2000, 176). In the Intech case, this point gains particular importance given the fact that due to the matrix structure of the company many of the headquarters' communication channels are mirrored at business unit and regional levels so that central information is multiplied even further in subsequent processes of publishing.

Without changing the amount of official information, a shift of focus towards broader communication activities would contribute to leveraging the performance of corporate communication.

10 Facilitating implementation and change processes

Analysis in this Chapter moves on to Strand 3 of the reference framework, i.e. aspects of 'facilitating implementation and change processes'. In addition to the generic code and descriptor assigned to the Strand, Table 12 highlights the specific research questions which go back to Chapter 4.

Table 12. Focal points for analysis of Strand 3 – Facilitating implementation and change processes

Generic codes	Descriptors for Strands of interrelation between strategy and communication processes
S1 Coordinating	Coordinating the company around dynamic purposes
S2 Organising	Organising by linking decisions and actions
S3 Facilitating	Facilitating implementation and change processes
S4 Leveraging	Leveraging the competitive position and distinctive competencies
Research question related to stocktaking of themes [Thematic analysis]	
Which themes covered discourse focusing on implementation and change?	
Research question related to construction of themes [Discourse analysis]	
How did corporate communication discourse unfold its performative capacity in these processes?	

Analysing the processes of innovation and transformation at Intech leads to another core aspect of the communicational approach to organising. Communication is no longer seen as a tool enabling information exchange – as the orthodox view would have suggested.

Instead, communication is viewed as constitutive and performative, and, therefore, also changing a company's reality (Heracleous and Barrett 2001).

Orthodox management theory, driven by assumptions like 'stability, routine and order' (Tsoukas and Chia 2002, 567) treated company change as something exceptional, as a project that needs to be planned and executed. Following the communicational approach, change is seen as 'the normal condition of organizational life'. Communication, in the sense of discourse, is an integral part of this condition. The aim of this Chapter is to analyse how corporate communication shaped the change processes associated with the launch of the Intech management system.

10.1 Developing a taxonomy

Following the communicational approach of this study, coding, which resulted in a related taxonomy (see Table 13), was conducted with the aim of clustering ongoing change-related themes rather than trying to define a one-way process for conducting change programmes.

Three ongoing themes of discourse were identified throughout the observation period: (1) discourse related to the 'implementation' of the Intech management system, (2) discourse covering the challenge of 'initiating change' at Intech, mainly covering the question of how the change processes necessary to implement the Intech management system started, and (3) discourse summarising 'perceptions' of different facets of change.

10.1.1 Implementation

Three sub-themes emerged throughout the observation period covering aspects of the implementation of the Intech management system. The majority of discourse fragments of this generic theme focused around the purpose of the Intech management system which can be described as 'implementing strategy' (21 quotations). Another sub-theme related to implementation focused on the question of whether there is a certain lifetime associated with the IMS as a change programme or whether it should be interpreted as a continuous program. The code 'lifetime and continuity' (5 quotations) was associated to this sub-theme. Finally, a set of discourse had evolved around the role of 'collaboration' during implementation (11 quotations).

10.1.2 Initiating change

The majority of change-related discourse during the observation period covered the question of how change processes were initiated at Intech. Discourse related to the generic theme spread into four sub-themes: (1) discourse around who or what drives change, i.e. 'change drivers' (30 quotations), (2) immediate 'expectations' with regards to change which were mentioned by various stakeholders (21 quotations), (3) discourse related to a 'lack of consequences' which several participants viewed as a factor impeding the initiation of change (18 quotations), and (4) discourse explaining various levels of 'management commitment' which – depending on level of commitment – was seen as either supporting or impeding the initiation of change (26 quotations).

10.1.3 Perceptions

Change was perceived in multiple ways by the participants, which can be clustered in the following way: (1) first of all, discourse evolved around the question of whether the Intech management system actually follows the 'purpose of change' (23 quotations), (2) 'organisational change' was quoted by several participants as the most prominent appearance of change at Intech (6 quotations), (3) 'continuity and change' was the duality put forward by top management towards the end of the observation period in order to balance between change and implementation aspects of the IMS (10 quotations), (4) 'change and innovation' were also penetrated as a single duality (10 quotations), and (5) the final cluster emerged around discourse focusing on change necessary to achieve the company goal of growth, coded 'change and growth' (8 quotations).

A full taxonomy of themes is displayed in Table 13.

Table 13. Taxonomy for Strand 3 – Facilitating implementation and change processes

Domain [Section]	Generic themes [Section]	Sub-themes	Recurrence [No. of quotations]
S3 Facilitating [10.2]	Implementation [10.2.1/ 10.2.2]	Implementing strategy	21
		Lifetime and continuity	5
		Collaboration	11
	Initiating change [10.2.1/ 10.2.2]	Change drivers	30
		Expectations	21
		Lack of consequences	18
		Management commitment	26
	Perceptions [10.2.3]	Purpose of change	23
		Organisational change	6
		Continuity and change	10
		Change and innovation	10
		Change and growth	8
Total			189

10.2 Thematic analysis

In contrast to Strand 2, where a pre-determined cascaded communication was launched in order to link decisions and actions at Intech, there was no specific change programme set in place in order to implement the Intech management system. Change was still intended to happen – but not in an orthodox way, e.g. based on a change management project. Instead, top management from the outset expected change to happen as an ongoing process. The general manager in charge of the launch of the Intech management system explained his view in the following way:

[Communication manager]: 'Why is there no programme on cultural change?'
[General manager]: 'We did not include a specific cultural change programme. We did that on purpose. Personally, I am convinced that cultural changes are extremely important. But cultural change cannot be enforced, and you cannot say that I want to have cultural change in the company. This is an automatic mechanism. If we change the way we manage the company we automatically change the culture of the company. In consequence, we cannot have a programme on cultural change. Cultural change has to be a logical consequence when you do things right. But we need cultural change, I agree.'
(Meeting of communication managers) [60:9]

The discourse fragment was taken from a discussion between general manager and communication managers in December 2003 right after the management system had been launched at the Intech business conference. The manager states that cultural change is intended, but that he sees it as an automatic mechanism which happens when the way the company is managed changes. The specific problem associated with this was explained as part of Strand 2. Viewing change as an ongoing mechanism, generally speaking, matches the view of theorists supporting the communicational view of a company (Heracleous and Barrett 2001; Tsoukas and Chia 2002). A communicational position, however, goes further in that communication processes, in particular, are viewed as shaping change.

This performative view will be applied to further explain some of the themes which emerged from the taxonomy. To start with, one discourse fragment per generic theme will be drawn upon in order to explain the communicational aspects of each theme. As in the earlier Chapters, later sections will focus on summarising theoretical contributions from a communicational review of communication, in order to then move on to re-examine these theories as part of discourse analysis. This will, finally, head to suggestions for an alternative communication theory.

10.2.1 Multiple worldviews

As the statement of the general manager showed, ongoing change was obviously intended as a consequence of the launch of the IMS. He had addressed change in the way the company is managed as well as cultural change. Throughout the discourse related to the implementation of the management system, however, different understandings of change became apparent at different units of the company.

The following conversation gives an example of these understandings. The discourse fragment was part of a discussion between a communication manager and a human resources manager who jointly attended a meeting of communication managers in May 2004:

[Communication manager – CM]: ...you state that the function of the [IMS] is about achieving real change. Do you view the [IMS] is a change program?

[Human resources manager – HRM]: My personal view is that the [IMS] should work towards change...

CM: ...but change to where?

HRM: To participate in the big picture to create value across the business units. And we have the discussion on how to incentivize people across the business units. How do we reward people to come and participate in these programs?

CM: I have another view on the [IMS]... My opinion is, that now, at the beginning of the [IMS]..., a consolidation process starts in the heads of the managers. During the last years we have changed, now we lead it over to a clear system. Therefore, for me the goal is not to organize change, because that has already been done now.

HRM: I do not disagree, I just think this is a very big, global organisational thing. Therefore, the aim is now to create a common understanding across all the business units.

CM: I agree that there is now a way back to the horizontal. But I do not agree that we are now in a place where we have to tell our people that we have to change. (Meeting notes) [94:4]

This dialogue reflects the multiple worldviews which seem common when explaining change in companies from both practical and theoretical viewpoints. Van de Ven and Poole (1995) identified about 20 different theories explaining processes of change. They clustered these theories into four schools of thought: life-cycle theory, teleological theory, dialectical theory and evolutionary theory.

The communication manager's position in this dialogue can best be described as supporting a life-cycle view of change. He views change as happening in different developmental phases of the company, moving from change which had happened during the last years to consolidation happening now through the implementation of the Intech management system. The human resources manager, instead, supports a rather teleological view on change by making the point that the Intech management system also defines an envisioned end state, namely to create value across the business units.

The general manager who was quoted in the introductory paragraph, probably held a third position which is close to evolutionary theory: he viewed change as an ongoing process, emerging based on new modes of managing the company.

These are only a few examples in which three managers held three different worldviews of change. The discourse fragments clustered under the 'implementation' theme revealed several further positions which are also reflected in the identified sub-themes. In these sub-themes questions like "To which end does the IMS initiate change?" (teleological worldview), "Within which time do the company programs need to be implemented?" (life-cycle worldview), or "How should change be achieved?" (dialectical worldview) were brought up.

This leads to the conclusion that several worldviews co-existed at Intech. Considering the discursive character and communicational aspects of change (Heracleous and Barrett 2001), a complex web of communication with regards to the implementation of the Intech management system resulted.

10.2.2 Multiple expectations

In the Intech case, the multiplicity of communicated worldviews also resulted in multiple expectations that members of the company developed. These expectations included various views on the question of how change processes were initiated. The set of discourse fragments covering these expectations was summarised in the 'initiating change' theme.

One example of discourse resulted from an interview with an Intech communication manager in which the researcher had referred to a statement of a strategy manager. This manager had made the point that change related to the IMS is, for example, initiated through organisational changes, i.e. changing company structures and reporting lines.

[Researcher]: Some people at [Intech] see organisational change as an important change driver.
[Communication manager]: Yes, I would always say that there are concrete examples like [a new central company unit which was established]. But I would also say that it is not primarily a question of changing the organisation. [Organisational changes], for example, are not at all obvious when it comes to the business units, where I must sharpen the mindset of people, that collaboration is designed and incentivized differently through the IMS, without questioning the organisation. At

[Intech] everybody likes to think first that this means changing the organisation. Instead, we must change the attention first that it is the market or the customers that demand a new identity or appearance. And where the collaboration works, we do not necessarily have to change the organisation.
(Interview) [81:13]

In the context of multiple expectations, structural changes are often viewed as among the most concrete modifications expected from planned and episodic change programmes (Linstead and Linstead 2004). This was also the case at Intech, where various company members attached expectations to this kind of obvious change. Another obvious set of expectations, for example, was attached to the company programme on 'global competitiveness' which many company members – and external stakeholders – linked to the immediate effect that more and more jobs would be moved away from Germany to low-cost countries. Many of these immediate effects were seen as highly context-sensitive (Pettigrew 1987), but mostly linked to a teleological worldview: people tried to estimate what possible outcomes are, given the end towards which the Intech management system works.

The communication manager rather seemed to have expected evolutionary change of ongoing processes, e.g. in the form of collaboration with customers. Reading the theory behind the Intech management system, evolutionary change can indeed be assumed as one of the intentions of top management. Strengthened horizontal collaboration across various company units, for example, was one of the rationales for implementing the IMS.

Evolutionary change, however, was not necessarily expected by company members involved in the ongoing change at Intech. As the taxonomy revealed, they rather expected highly committed managers talking about a vision where the IMS is going to lead the company. They had expected clearly identifiable drivers of change, and they also expected clear consequences to be drawn by management in cases where company members did not act conforming to the principles established by the new management system.

10.2.3 Multiple perceptions

The taxonomy also revealed a wide variety of perceptions linked to change associated with the Intech management system. Issues perceived primarily by company members focused – as expected – on organisational change. Also changes in the way of conducting business were perceived. This is mirrored by themes such as 'change and innovation' or 'change and growth' in the taxonomy. Change was not perceived in the form of a re-invention of business processes, however. This is reflected in a duality of 'continuity and change' in the respective sub-theme.

A manager at Intech business unit expressed his perceptions in the following way. This discourse fragment was taken from a discussion on the effects of the IMS for Intech business unit in July 2004:

'[The IMS] has an impact on how we [implement change] and I think it has an impact on the speed at which we can do it. What we want to do is think line with the context of what [Intech] wants to do. The good news is that I think we are absolutely allowed to do it. You only have to think of how you can put [your activities] into context with, say, the customer focus initiative... It is about wrapping the organisation entirely around the customer. And we are doing that by recognizing that you have to change the people and you have to get the approach to the people, you have to be able to change the approach to the customer. So, yes, the [Intech management system] is having an impact on us. Sometimes it is very helpful like the customer focus initiative. Sometimes it can get in the way of what you actually want to go out and achieve.'
(Intech business unit manager) [100:17]

This manager understood the IMS very much in the way in which it was meant by the general manager in the introductory discourse fragment: as an intended change in the way of managing business leading to ongoing cultural change – i.e. an enforcement of customer focus and an increase in customer attention, in this case. He perceives and uses freedom with regards to the concrete implementation of the IMS for his unit, e.g. by implementing teleological follow-on change measures (he mentions, for example, that he changed team members in order to initiate change towards the customer).

It cannot be concluded, however, that change was perceived that way in every case of the organisation. In fact, the majority of discourse fragments of the generic theme were assigned to the sub-theme covering the discussion of whether the IMS actually follows the 'purpose of change'. This leads one to assume that many company members rather struggled with perceiving change related to the IMS.

This is a phenomenon which has extensively been covered in change theory (Feldman 2000; Heracleous and Barrett 2001; Tsoukas and Chia 2002). According to these studies, change in ongoing processes is often much more difficult to detect by company members than substantive changes. 'Perception ... has its limits. There are differences so small we cannot detect; or we may have become accustomed to the new state of affairs before our senses could tell us that it is new' (Tsoukas and Chia 2002, 572). In Feldman's words, 'organizational routines have a great potential for change even though they are often perceived, even defined, as un-changing' (Feldman 2000).

Thematic analysis itself has not yet revealed reasons why this is the case from a communicational perspective. The aim of the following theoretical review is to shed light on that question.

10.3 Communicational review of change communication

In the orthodox tradition, corporate communication management in chang-ing times focuses on concepts like clarity of message in order to avoid am-biguity, reliability of communication processes, and the notion of ex-change processes in order to ensure participation. Also, it aims for a symbiosis of cognitive and emotional processes through focusing on face-to-face communication (Mast 2002, 395). The overarching idea is to avoid uncertainty. In summary, communication is viewed as a management in-strument following the aim of making change as bearable or tolerable as possible by trying to play down fear which is seen as the major emotional driver for company members in change situations.

A communicational perspective, in contrast, helps to shed a significantly different light on change. First of all, change is not seen as a project or situation, but as an emerging process – happening continuously, based on varying level of enforcement from management. Second, communication is not seen as a tool which helps companies to avoid consequences of change. Instead, communication takes a performative role in change, by actively contributing to and shaping change.

The orthodox view that 'the key roles communication plays are provid-ing and obtaining information, creating understanding, and building own-ership' (Ford and Ford 1995, 542), therefore, needs to be reviewed, or, at least, extended. A communicational view of change implies several aspects which are not covered in the orthodox/rational view. The aspects relevant for explaining the mode of corporate communication are brought together now.

10.3.1 Continuity and change

Thematic analysis has shown that, based on multiple worldviews of change, multiple expectations with regards to change were created at In-tech. This, in turn, led to multiple perceptions, including the perception that the Intech management system did not change the company at all. This shows that perception has its limits, particularly when it comes to perceiving change which happens gradually and over a long time. Individuals' experience is limited in duration and in terms of scope. This can be illustrated by the example that company members at Intech were able to perceive new organisational structures, but they did not perceive change in the general approach of the company towards customers.

The reason for this may be that, from a synoptic viewpoint, reality often appears as rather stable, whereas, if viewed from a more detailed perspective many little changes happen. Tsoukas and Chia illustrated this on the basis of an acrobat (2002, 572):

'For example, at a certain level of analysis (or logical type) – that of the body – the statement "the acrobat maintains her balance" is true, as is also true the statement "the acrobat constantly adjusts her posture," but at another level of analysis – that of the parts of the body. The apparent stability of the acrobat does not preclude change; on the contrary it presupposes it.'

Considering this example, it becomes clear that apparently stable concepts and routines are in fact situated in 'ongoing accomplishments' (Feldman 2000, 613) – and, therefore, keep changing. Feldman suggests that due to these inherent dynamics both 'change can be more ordinary – and … routines can be more extraordinary – than they are often portrayed' (2000, 626). Communication and discourse become major performative activities in this course of change (Heracleous and Barrett 2001).

Tsoukas and Chia (2002, 572) conclude that 'both "synoptic" and "performative" accounts of organizational change are necessary', i.e. "what stays stable" and "what changes" should become clear at the same time. This is also in line with the 'ideal organization' Weick and Quinn (1999) proposed. Successful companies do not rely on either episodic or continuous change. Weick and Quinn, instead, suggest 'both that change starts with failures and that change never starts because it never stops' (1999, 381). At Intech, this notion, for example, was inherent in the discourse around 'continuity and change'.

10.3.2 Towards a communicational model of change

How can, from a social constructionist viewpoint, change communication become effective? Cheney, Christensen et al. (2004, 328) pointed to the variety of research and practical advice, but concluded that solutions for change communication problems always need to be found depending on the specific context and occasion. Also Linstead and Linstead (2004) analysed a huge variety of change concepts and theories, without being able to conclude on one suitable model. Their advice is the same as Cheney and Christensen's: to embark with one conceptual framework as a guide and then continue to carefully consider how change evolves. Therefore, this advice will be followed in the discourse analysis following this section.

In order to identify a suitable framework for further analysing change associated with the Intech management system the following criteria were used: (1) the framework has to support a discursive research methodology, (2) it should view communication from a communicational viewpoint, and (3) it should have been successfully applied to explain the intended change processes in a large company.

A concept mathching these criteria was Ford and Ford's (1995) framework which has been referred to in various management studies since then (Grant, Keenoy et al. 2001; Doolin 2003).

According to Ford and Ford, 'to produce intentional change ... requires that some intended result, state, or condition that does not already exist must be brought into existence' (Ford and Ford 1995). As stated by the general manager in the introductory paragraph, the intended change during the implementation of the Intech management system focused on the way the company is managed. Additionally, cultural change was expected to happen and, therefore, also considered as intended.

Ford and Ford's (1995; Ford, Ford et al. 2002) model of change, in line with social constructionist thinking, views change as both communication-based and communication-driven, i.e. communication is seen as one of the performative modes mentioned above by Feldman (2000).

The authors propose four different types of conversations[33] as key in producing change: initiative, understanding, performance and closure (Ford and Ford 1995, 545-552).

Initiative

Initiative communication intends to create awareness for what should be done, focusing on assertions, directives or declarations. It can use synoptic or performative arguments, mostly related to aspects of context. In this sense, intentional change generally emerges after a claim for change has been made. Clearly, this type of communication involved 'issue selling' in terms of shaping 'an organization's investment of time and attention' (Dutton, Ashford et al. 2001).

---

[33] Conversation in Ford and Ford's model includes 'what is said' as well as 'what is done in correlation with what is said' (Ford and Ford 1995: 545), i.e. symbols, artifacts and other products of corporate communication. Their own focus is, however, on verbal interaction. Therefore, the terms 'communication' or 'corporate communication' are continuously used where Ford and Ford applied the term 'conversation'.

Understanding

This type of communication aims to create understanding of change processes. It entails dialogue about rationale, context, and meaning for change. Ashkenas and Jick (1992), based on their study at General Electric (GE), judged such an 'organizational dialogue' at the heart of the change process. It includes collaboration focusing on concrete business issues – and, for GE, meant also to 'learn to talk effectively and constructively' (1992, 271). Ensuring full collaboration has successfully been practiced in other case studies, too, e.g. at Alcatel Standard Electrica in Europe (Chakravarthy 1996).

Performance

The aim of this type of communication is to produce a specific result. Ford and Ford highlight that at this stage of the conversation it is crucial for all participants to be clear about the 'conditions of satisfaction' (1995, 549) among all participants. This includes high levels of liability towards fulfilling the performance agreements for all parties involved.

Closure

In this type of communication, claims are made that the change is complete, including 'some form of acknowledgement conveyed in assertions, expressives and declarations (1995, 551).

Ford and Ford point towards the importance of managing transitions from one type of communication to the next. Particularly to make the transition from understanding to performance in order to create concrete action steps and accountabilities. Instead, relying purely on conversations for understanding can lead change initiatives to a breakdown – as does 'lack of rigor' of the managers who apply to conversations of breakdown (1995).

10.3.3 Communication as a strategic practice

As in the preceding Chapters, research in the field of strategy is used to enrich the communicational view at the specific Strand of interrelation between strategy and communication.

It is with regard to change processes, where the prevailing literature following the practice paradigm in strategy research can be particularly helpful. As had been argued in the initial Chapters, this strand of strategy research primarily aims to explain how managers perform the work of strategy (Whittington 1996; Hendry 2000; Whittington 2001; Jarzabkowski 2003; Jarzabkowski 2004). Symbolic practices, as applied in orthodox corporate communication, also explicitly form part of this discourse (Knights and Morgan 1991; Heracleous and Barrett 2001) – and the possible role of communication is viewed as both a help or hindrance to the enactment of a strategy (Dunford and Jones 2000; Hardy, Palmer et al. 2000).

To a much stronger extent than Ford and Ford's model suggests, these studies propose that managers 'cannot simply produce a discourse to suit their immediate needs and, instead, must locate their discursive activities within a meaningful context if they are to shape and construct action' (Hardy, Palmer et al. 2000, 1228).

This leads back to the discussion of context in Chapter 7. According to Jarzabkowski's (2003) framework, corporate communication acts as a mediator between management as actors, collective structures and strategic activities. The view of communication as a mediator in change processes is fully shared by Ford and Ford (1995). As Jarzabkowski's research had revealed, this mediation can be used to work towards two ends: constructing continuity through aligning actors, collective structures and activity, but also towards constructing dynamics of change 'by surfacing and mediating between contradictions' (2003, 48). To which ends this operated at Intech, will be one of the key questions of the following related discourse analysis.

10.4 Discourse analysis

Discourse analysis, as indicated earlier, is now based on Ford and Ford's (1995) framework in order to analyse in more depth how corporate communication discourse at Intech influenced change. As argued in thematic analysis, this model should be analysed with a focus on context and the nature of change underlying the implementation of the management system at Intech (Cheney, Christensen et al. 2004). Jarzabkowski's (2003) framework for strategic practices and Weick and Quinn's (1999) typology of episodic and continuous change will be used as elements structuring these two aspects.

In Ford and Ford's sense, one consistent stream of discourse was selected for analysis, covering all four types of communication, i.e. initiative, understanding, performance and closure. All four discourse segments were taken from publications or other documentations of Intech describing and explaining the launch of the Intech management system.

10.4.1 Initiative

Intech's CEO formulated his view 'on what could or should be done' (Ford and Ford 1995, 546) in an editorial statement which was published in the first issue of a new management magazine which was handed out to all participants on the first Intech business conference in October 2003. This was the initiative statement for the IMS:

'The main topics at the [Intech business conference] in 2003 were the operational issues crucial to implementing our strategy and the fundamental principles that govern the way we run our company. At that event, the [Intech management system, IMS] was launched. Its purpose is to provide a suitable framework for aligning our longer-term goals with the resources and mechanisms needed to achieve them. The [IMS] is enabling us to [move on] to the next level. What are the defining elements of this new level? First, the [IMS] is now a binding system, company-wide. ... Second, the [IMS] is enabling us to systematize the levels on which we collaborate and to synchronize the processes in the company to a far greater extent than before. ... Third, besides continuing to optimize vertical cooperation, we are now placing equal emphasis on optimising horizontal cooperation... It is now up to each and every one of us to help set the [IMS] in motion, to establish it within the company, and to leverage this excellent management instrument into greater market strength. In what has been a turbulent business environment, we have demonstrated that [Intech] is a robust and solid company. Let us build on this foundation together to become – and remain – a world-class company.
(Intech CEO quoted in management magazine) [55:21]

In the introductory sentences of this statement, the CEO uses a similar logic to the general manager quoted earlier on in this Chapter. The IMS is not positioned as a change programme, but as a system which defines the way the company is managed or 'run'. The intention behind the IMS, however, is to link goals to resources and, in consequence, to change the company to 'the next level'. This way of arguing links the management system to continuous change (by linking existing elements according to a new logic) and episodic change (heaving Intech to a new level).

In the subsequent sentences, elements of this new level are listed: first, the IMS becomes a 'binding system', which can be interpreted as the "call" for change demanded by Ford and Ford (1995, 546); the IMS is, second, intended to 'systematize' and 'synchronize' what is happening in the company, i.e. the IMS can also be interpreted as a sense-making device; and, third, the company moves on towards putting vertical collaboration (synoptic element) and horizontal collaboration (performative element) on one level. Again, notions of episodic and continuous, as well as synoptic and performative change are mixed. This supports the multiplicity and complexity of change perspectives at Intech which were identified in thematic analysis, too.

The "call" for change, which was clearly made in the elements defining the new level, is then, however, somehow undermined by a statement with low commitment. The CEO says that implementing the IMS 'is now up to each and every one of us'. Shifting responsibilities away from the speaker has been identified as rather common, but also weakening the performative impact of communication in change processes (Ashkenas and Jick 1992; Ford and Ford 1995).

In his conclusion, the CEO draws on business context in order to re-enforce the notion of synoptic and performative elements of change at the same time by referring to the foundation of the company as both 'to become' and 'to remain'.

This initiative communication has to be viewed as the beginning of an issue-selling approach (Dutton, Ashford et al. 2001) rather than an immediate reaction to a crisis or other drivers for change. Issue selling 'affects the allocation of management attention' (2001, 717), inviting consideration of issues by a wide range of recipients rather than enforcing it immediately.

10.4.2 Understanding

In Dutton, Ashford et al.'s (2001) account, issue selling involves modesty in how to mobilize change in that it leaves the efforts to actually change behaviour to those below top management, i.e. middle management. When an issue selling approach is chosen, change happens from below, in local conversations, whereas activities from top management remain 'complementary' (2001, 732). Therefore, issue selling may involve other forms of understanding than suggested by Ford and Ford (1995), whose focus was on clearly defined conditions of satisfaction for change. In an issue selling approach, top management can only define structures within which this happens, such as reporting procedures, decision-making committees.

The change process observed at Intech very much confirms Dutton, Ashford et al.'s (2001) findings in that it is managers on decentralised levels who realize change. A communication manager at Intech, who was heavily involved in developing messages for the issue-selling approach, explained the ongoing change processes in an interview as follows:

'There are different attitudes to [how change is understood]. One can, of course, say that we are not yet in the leading group of companies worldwide, where we need to get in terms of profitability margins. And this is bound to be true for half of the company. Unfortunately, only one half of all business units has

achieved sufficient profitability margins yet, while the other half has not yet achieved this. In those cases it is not even clear how this can happen quickly. Therefore, the [IMS] office rather urges… the need for change …We say that one half of all business units signal that it works, and this half should provide an incentive for the others to move in the same direction. In our opinion, we do not need to argue in terms of cultural change, this is too threatening for employees. Instead we rather need to say that it is necessary to change, but there are already examples which show that all this works already within [Intech].
(Intech communication manager) [96:14]

This statement, again, reveals aspects of both episodic change – happening in business units which do not yet fulfil their profitability margins – and continuous change – in the second half of business units which do not need to change for profitability reasons. That puts interventions from the centre in the context of profitability of each business unit. Top management, represented by the IMS office, pays particular attention to those business units which need to catch up in terms of financial performance.

At the same time, there is no need for change signalled to the business units which fulfilled their margins already. Instead, these business units were used in the sense of 'best practice' for the other business units. They are referred to as examples of who implemented the IMS successfully.

In the middle of the discourse fragment the manager also draws attention to the point that, given the varying need for change in different business units, it does not necessarily make sense to refer to a general need for changing all of Intech. In light of this statement, also the complex construction of change explained by the Intech CEO during the initiating communication starts to turn out as a conscious attempt to understand the thought patterns of those who execute change afterwards – decentralised, in each business unit, depending on target achievement in local context.

Following the issue selling approach, a great deal of 'understanding' needs to be made happen at local levels in the company. This was supported by the approach to define 'conditions of satisfaction' (Ford and Ford 1995, 548) mainly in terms of performance goals for each business unit, but not as part of the Intech management system. It can be concluded that change was intended to happen locally.

Dutton, Ashford et al. (2001) proposed that an issue selling approach also requires local skills to facilitate the understanding process in order to get the local change going. This aspect was not part of the original plans for the Intech management system. The following subsection will give further insight into whether this influenced the performance of change at Intech.

10.4.3 Performance

Performance communication, according to Ford and Ford (1995, 549) intends to lead understanding over to action. In this sense, it appears as a similar communication task as identified in the analysis of Strand 2: to lead decisions over to actions through communication. Decisions stand for immediate forces to act for a specific person or group of persons. In the issue selling approach, however, action is delegated to middle management – and middle managers need to convince their teams to execute the task.

The communication manager who was quoted in subsection 2, said with regards to performance:

'What surprised us is that there is currently no real correlation between [IMS] communication and success of the business unit. One reason for this is probably that many successful business units have practiced elements of the [IMS] for years already, and that the [IMS] is made up of elements which promise success. That is always the claim [of successful business units], and we can also hear it from the comments of their CEOs, for example. They say that their units have practiced the [IMS] for a long time already. Therefore, they are successful – without having named it [IMS]. … If there are other business units that are appreciating that they need to think about [IMS] elements in a more focused way now, these are also the ones which communicate very much about these elements. There is, for me, at the moment, no clear correlation between [IMS] communication and success. But this can actually be explained from the history of each business unit, and from the history of the [IMS] itself.
(Intech communication manager) [96:13]

This discourse fragment, indeed, reads like an episode continuing the 'understanding' phase. Ford and Ford's (1995) argument that there is a sequence between understanding and performance communication is opposed by the communication manager. Viewed from a global Intech viewpoint, having communicated the IMS extensively, was not directly linked to a consistent success story of the company in terms of performance.

Instead, differentiation between successful and failing business units was seen as necessary. He explains that successful business units claim to have implemented and practiced what the IMS proposes already – and that, along this line, top management uses this as an argument to sell the implementation of the Intech management system to the failing business units as a recipe for success.

While successful business units see no need to communicate the IMS – i.e. something which they have, in their eyes, practiced already, and which is now simply re-labelled – the failing business units indeed communicate about the IMS, its elements and how they can work for the specific business unit. In consequence, at that stage of the process it was particularly the failing business units who consistently communicated the management system.

Referring to structure and concrete context reveals the explanation from the manager's point of view. How rigorously these performance communications were conducted at the various business units cannot be concluded from this study. An analysis at the level of a failing business unit would have been necessary. The Intech business unit which was part of the study fulfilled its performance goals – and, supporting the quoted manager's logic, did not conduct IMS-related performance communication.

The manager's observation that not all failing business units had – despite a significant amount of communication related to the IMS – returned to the route of success, gives rise to suspicion that performance communication was not everywhere conducted in the sense of Ford and Ford (1995).

Similar to Dutton, Ashford et al. (2001), Ashkenas and Jick (1992) emphasized the crucial role of organisational dialogue in putting strategy into action. At General Electric, this necessary action was elaborated during two to three day events with top management participation and at decentralised locations. According to their summary (1992, 269-270), the following characteristics of these events were particularly effective: focus on concrete business processes rather than 'junk word'; multifunctional and multilevel participation; small-group brainstorming; plenary decision-making sessions in the form of town meetings; and concrete follow-ups.

10.4.4 Closure

In Ford and Ford's (1995) model, communication for closure plays an important role. Considering a wider definition of change, including episodic and continuous change, 'closure' of change seems to become unrealistic, due to its ongoing elements. Companies need to be capable of 'continuous adaptation' (Weick and Quinn 1999, 366).

As the following statement documents, also top management at Intech interpreted change as an ongoing requirement. The discourse fragment needs to be seen in a sequence with the CEO's statement used to analyse initiating communication. The following fragment was again taken from his editorial statement in the management magazine, this time in the October 2004 issue, i.e. one year after the launch of the IMS:

'Continuity and change affect the most fundamental questions our company must answer. In which business areas do we want to be active? Do we stand a chance in global competition when it comes to innovation? How are we doing in terms of customer focus and customer responsiveness? Do we really always un-

derstand what it means to be a global business? Are we giving our employees and colleagues enough opportunities to develop and grow and to contribute to our company's success? ... These are the critical questions that must be answered, especially now, when we are undergoing a change in leadership. To these questions, we have persuasive answers that this company's management stands behind. We need continuity in our basic attitudes; yet we must be relentless in our efforts to shape change!'
(Intech CEO [98:16]

A few months before the business conference, a change of the CEO had been announced – a forthcoming episodic change in top management, which had been discussed and planned within Intech for quite some time. Handing over from to the new CEO was planned for January 2005, three months after the business conference.

The retiring CEO, at that business conference shaped the motto of 'continuity and change'. This can be interpreted as the continued elaboration of the analogy 'to become – and to remain' used the year before (see above). This duality was penetrated on many occasions. A few weeks after the business conference the CEO, at the annual press conference, said that 'Continuity and Change is the phrase that best expresses our fundamental characteristics' [104:11]. By that time, continuity and change had become a motto to define the core of the company.

In the above discourse fragment, the CEO uses that motto in a fashion to make sense of the core challenges for the company rather than stating the closure of change. This indicates that one year after the launch of the management system elements of continuous change were stressed (Weick and Quinn 1999). Many elements of Intech's context were addressed in the questions of the CEO, ranging from structures to strategies, including the company programs of the Intech management system; from external market developments to cultural issues of the company. A closure of change according to Ford and Ford's (1995) notion, however, was not evident.

This discourse analysis has shown that in the case of Intech change communication had emerged in a much more complex way than suggested in Ford and Ford's (1995) model, although elements of all four proposed phases had been covered. In the concluding Section of this Chapter, a model of change communication is suggested which considers additional elements, as identified in the above analysis.

10.5 Theorising

Again, the three steps proposed in Section 8.5 are now carried out in order to adapt Strand 3, based on the findings of the analyses conducted in this

Chapter: (1) Strand 3 is highlighted in the extant version of the reference framework, (2) a revised illustration of Strand 3 is developed summarising the contribution of this Strand towards an alternative theory of corporate communication, and (3) the extant framework is adapted.

Figure 12 highlights Strand 3 – 'Facilitating implementation and change processes' – as part of the reference framework which was drawn upon for the analysis.

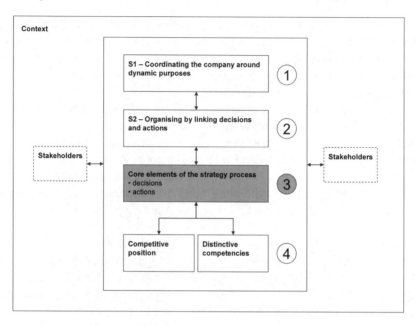

Fig. 12. Referring back to Strand 3 in the reference framework

According to Table 12, thematic analysis focused on the following research question: 'Which themes covered discourse focusing implementation and change processes?' In addition, discourse analysis concentrated on the question: 'How did corporate communication discourse unfold its performative capacity in these processes?'

Having analysed the Intech case in terms of these questions, enriched the picture of Strand 3 with regards to both the reference framework and the communication theories applied throughout the analyses.

In Ford and Ford's (1995) model, for example, intended change was seen as hand in hand with episodic change. The case of Intech showed that this does not necessarily have to be the case. Instead, at Intech episodic and continuous change happened at the same time – and, based on the interpretation of the CEO's statements, it was most probably intended that way.

Additionally, the context in which change happened played a major role. This brought change and its interpretation down to the level of individual business units within Intech. The performance of each business unit was one of the criteria which lead to the interpretation of either episodic or continuous change. Also the various structural elements of the Intech management system, e.g. committees and reporting lines, played an important role in this process.

Finally, not only top management was acting, but an issue selling approach was put in place in an attempt to shift responsibilities for action to middle management – and middle management, at decentralised levels in the company, suddenly became core actors in change.

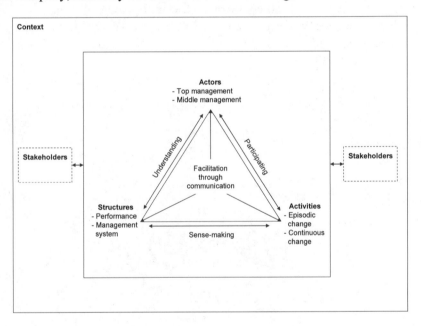

Fig. 13. Review of Strand 3 – Facilitating implementation and change processes

The analysis revealed several constituents of the change process at Intech that were each interrelated through corporate communication discourse. From a more generic viewpoint, this leads back to Jarzabkowski's (2003) activity theory-based framework for strategic practices. That framework was comprised of top management team actors, collective structures and strategic activity.

As argued above, corporate communication is one of the strategic practices within organisations. Constituents identified in the analysis matched those identified by Jarzabkowski (2003) in terms of actors (top management and middle management), structures (e.g. performance and elements of the Intech management system) and strategic activity (in this case both episodic and continuous change). In Figure 13, Jarzabkowski's original framework is adapted in order to illustrate findings of the Intech case and, based on that, to suggest a communicational model of change.

As this framework shows, viewing corporate communication as a strategic practice facilitating change, leads away from the orthodox view, defining corporate communication as merely an instrument to avoid uncertainty in change processes. Instead, it sheds light on corporate communication as an important practice helping to trigger change which is happening through the activities of all company members. Episodic change as well as continuous change can result from these activities. The general conclusion is that all communicational acts have the potential to change ongoing processes (Hosking 2004).

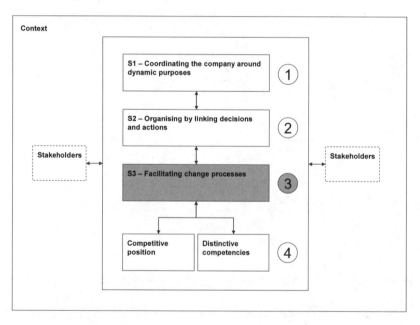

Fig. 14. Adapting Strand 3 in the reference framework

One more reference needs to be made from Figure 13 back to the original research questions as posted in Table 12. According to that list, thematic analysis focused on identifying themes related to implementation and change processes. In the respective taxonomy (see Table 13), three generic themes were listed, namely the themes of 'implementation', 'initiating change', and 'perceptions'. These themes were not literally adopted in Figure 13. This decision was made in order retain the general structure of Jarzabkowski's (2003) framework. Nevertheless, the generic themes are represented in the concepts of 'actors', 'structures', and 'change'. 'Implementation', for example, was based on the 'structures' of the Intech Management System, 'initiating change' was heavily driven by the 'actors', and 'perceptions' related to the mode of 'change', i.e. whether change was perceived as episodic change or continuous change. The results of discourse analysis, in Figure 13 are represented by the modes of 'understanding', 'participating', and 'sense-making' which had throughout the analyses been identified as key modes in which corporate communication discourse unfolded its performative capacity in implementation and change processes.

In order to complete step 3 in the process of revising the framework, Strand 3 is adapted in Figure 14.

As in the preceding Chapters, the above conclusions draw attention to some of the concrete implications for an alternative view on communicating change within the field of corporate communication theory and practice. In the above framework, these are illustrated through the arrows linking the three constituents.

10.5.1 Understanding intention and structures

Discourse analysis showed that – particularly when following an issue-selling approach – it is important to have top and middle management's intentions in mind as well as the structures that are going to be influenced, before crafting change-related corporate communication activities. In Dutton, Ashford et al.'s words, change 'can only be accomplished if it is based on an understanding of the thought patterns of those who are "working" the context' (Dutton, Ashford et al. 2001, 733).

'Substantive communication' was identified as an important issue in identity work (Strand 1 of the reference framework) – and it remains important for facilitating implementation and change. First, communication managers need to deeply understand structural issues, such as, in the Intech case, the Intech management system and the current performance of decentralised units in the company. Second, communication mangers also have to understand the roles of top and middle management. In the case of Intech, following the issue selling approach, top management set the parameters in which the change happens, e.g. through incentives and reporting structures. Third, communication managers also need to understand how actions and structures are interrelated in the company. Theoretically, they can be characterised 'both as automatic responses and as accomplishments which have to be worked at continually' (Costello 2000, 147). At Intech, these parameters contributed to patterns of change emerging at the local level and it also moved middle management into the role to actually implementing episodic change where necessary.

Given the complex structures of many, particularly larger, companies, this also makes it necessary for corporate communication to act at a local level rather than using a 'watering can' approach. Tsoukas and Chia put it the following way (2002, 578):

'Change programs are made to work and, insofar as this happens, they are locally adapted, improvised, and elaborated by human agents; institutionalized categories are imaginatively extended when put into action.'

In this sense, the company with its actors and structures needs to be deeply understood before the possibilities communication opens up can be taken up in concrete corporate communication activities. This approach leads to 'richly connected communication systems' which are found at successful companies (Weick and Quinn 1999, 371).

10.5.2 Ensuring full participation

'Full participation' (Chakravarthy 1996, 536) is a practice which has been proposed by several scholars as a valuable concept. It follows a communicational proposition, but it is not a concept which can be viewed as commonly applied. Its value is seen in particularly moving attention to processes in that participants get voice. Practices developed from a participative approach 'will accordingly depend on how the members understand the current situation and what they see as desirable solutions for the future organization' (Levin 2004, 73). Levin contrasts this to approaches involving external consultants. In that sense, participation can be viewed as an approach inviting members of a company to construct their own practices. This, according to Levin, can also have a positive effect on the acceptance of change: 'If employees participate in the design process, then the results do not need to be implemented, simply because implementation is integrated into the change process itself' (2004, 73).

However, this theory has remained an abstract concept and application in daily communicational and strategic practices is difficult. Depending on the approach to change, participation can either happen at top management level (Chakravarthy 1996), middle management level (Dutton, Ashford et al. 2001), or involving all employees (Levin 2004).

Instead of creating passive opposition – which is often the case when following the avoidance strategies suggested by orthodox corporate communication – a participatory approach actively integrates all stakeholders involved in change. This goes beyond pure information, two-way communication or 'cooption' (Chakravarthy 1996, 536) in that it means 'participating in direct interaction with other people' (Stacey 2003, 416).

Hosking (2004) argues that change needs to leverage multiplicity of voice rather than suppress it in an attempt to achieve 'consensus'. The orientation of participation moves to an equal inclusion of all voices rather than generating any common-sense solution. In this, the aim is not to reconstruct a problematic world. Instead, leveraging on the performative capacity of communication implicates a shift to possibilities as an ongoing quality of change work should happen, i.e. to show participants how to deal with ongoing change. In concrete ways, this kind of participation can be created in conferences, 'mutual gains bargaining', meetings and other platforms (Levin 2004, 78-82). The outcome of participation, then, is shared understanding.

10.5.3 Focus on sense-making

As the Intech case has shown, it is crucial to ensure that change is embedded in the deep structures of the company and that employees on all organisational levels can make sense of what is going on in the company over time. As various discourse fragments have shown, in many cases, particularly when following the issue selling approach, change needs to be enacted at decentral levels in the organizational structure.

'Making change from below requires specific types of practical knowledge and skills' (Dutton, Ashford et al. 2001, 732). One of the core skills necessary is communicational: 'learning how to talk effectively and constructively with each other – across functional and status boundaries' (Ashkenas and Jick 1992, 271).

Apart from the skills explained in Chapter 9 when it came to sense-making during decision-making processes, particularly story-telling approaches have been used successfully in communicational change processes (Larsen 2000; Hough and White 2001; Bryant and Cox 2004). Stories have been used in order to help individuals make sense of ongoing change processes (Bryant and Cox 2004), and also to explain changing company identities and cultures (Larsen 2000). It is, therefore, proposed that story-telling can additionally be applied by corporate communication professionals in communicational change processes.

In summary, it remains crucial to focus on the full triangle presented in Figure 13 when communicating for the purpose of change. Managers need to be recognized as key actors, structures can be considered as a general framework for change, and activities by all company members influence the style of change. Communicational processes of understanding, participating and sense-making constitute the performative capacity of corporate communication in this model.

11 Leveraging competitive position and distinctive competencies

This Chapter completes the series of analyses by focusing on Strand 4 of the interrelations between strategy and communication processes, i.e. leveraging the competitive position and distinctive competencies. In addition to the generic code and descriptor used throughout the study, Table 14 highlights the specific set of research questions guiding both thematic and discourse analyses throughout this Chapter.

Table 14. Focal points for analysis of Strand 4 – Leveraging the competitive position and distinctive competencies

Generic codes	Descriptors for Strands of interrelation between strategy and communication processes
S1 Coordinating	Coordinating the company around dynamic purposes
S2 Organising	Organising by linking decisions and actions
S3 Facilitating	Facilitating implementation and change processes
S4 Leveraging	Leveraging the competitive position and distinctive competencies
Research question related to stocktaking of themes [Thematic analysis]	
Which themes were covered by corporate communication discourse relating to competitive position and distinctive competencies?	
Research question related to construction of themes [Discourse analysis]	
How did corporate communication discourse contribute to the constitution of competitive position and distinctive competencies? How was it formed by these?	

Strand 4 of the reference framework launches two new concepts: (1) the concept of competitive position, and (2) the concept of distinctive competencies.

The notion of competitive position, derived from the positioning school (Porter 1980; Porter 1985), comprises the approach that a company gains its competitive advantage from its position in the industry, sustained by barriers to entry and barriers to mobility. The company's activities determine its position in the marketplace and, ultimately, its profitability. Preferred strategies are differentiation focus or cost leadership.

The notion of distinctive competencies is derived from the resource-based strategy approach (Prahalad and Hamel 1990; Grant 1995; Müller-

Stewens and Lechner 2001). According to this view, the company consists of a bundle of resources, some of which are rare, valuable, difficult to imitate and substitute, i.e. distinctive competencies.

Both competitive position and distinctive capabilities theories are divided, lacking a dynamic perspective. Instead of linking both theories, a 'chicken-and-egg problem' (Cuervo-Cazurra 2003, 20) has been created: competitive positioning scholars argue that the resource-based view neglects the environment, and scholars supporting the resource-based view argue that purely focusing on the competitive position treats the company as a black box.

Competitive positioning and distinctive competencies concepts, however, fit to an orthodox corporate communication theory. Particularly marketing communication builds on concepts like differentiation or core values (Buttle 1995). Following the conduit metaphor, many of these orthodox theories, however, preferably focus on how to make use of a company's positioning and competencies in order to create awareness (Varey 2002), e.g. in advertising, rather than also considering the performative view of communicational practice. Instead, according to orthodox theories, communication 'instruments', 'techniques' or 'programmes' play a major role in transporting positioning and competencies to the target audiences (Grunig and Hunt 1984; Cutlip, Center et al. 1985; Grunig and Dozier 1992; Hunt and Grunig 1994; Dozier, Grunig et al. 1995).

Leveraging the performative capacity of communication

'Leveraging' as used in this study goes further in that it is intended to include and analyse the performative capacity of corporate communication as well. It is argued that performative communication influences both strategic position and distinctive capabilities.

Rindova and Fombrun (1999), in an attempt to integrate positioning and resources (competencies), have proposed a 'competitive terrain' of strategic interaction or practices in which competitive advantage emerges. In two dimensions, company ('the firm') and environment ('the organizational field'), as well as 'material resources' (e.g. financial or human resources) and 'human interpretations' (e.g. through communicational acts) are drawn together.

Rindova and Fombrun view competitive advantage as an outcome of interaction within this strategic landscape in that 'it develops as firms and constituents strategically target each other in the material and interpretative domains' (1999, 701). Several corporate communication processes are part of this. Product differentiation, reputation and identity which are terms taken from Rindova and Fombrun's landscape have been analysed above.

Also in the field of competence-based studies, dynamic views drawing on constructionist theories have developed (Teece, Pisano et al. 2000). They advance the argument that the competitive advantage of companies lies with its managerial and organisational processes, its present position and the paths available to it. Dynamic capabilities[34] of a firm relate to the company's ability to continuously reconfigure distinctive competencies in these processes. Resources and competencies need to be seen as social constructs which enable and facilitate strategy development – and constrain it at the same time. Again, communication is a key process in driving dynamic capabilities towards 'core competencies' (Hamel and Prahalad 1992) which are fundamental to the company's performance – e.g. in managing customer relationships.

Leveraging position and competencies through genres

As argued above, in the orthodox view, particularly marketing communication deals with processes of leveraging positioning and competencies through mainstream communication channels like advertising. These channels not only nourish a large proportion of the communication industry (Buttle 1995), they are also mainly driven by a one-way and container notion of communication in the sense of transporting information from the company to its customers (Elliott 2004). These channels have been fundamentally criticized for being costly and inefficient (Christensen and Cheney 2000; Gladwell 2002). Another critique included that marketing communication contributes to 'the colonization of discourse by promotion' (Fairclough 1993, 142).

In the course of the following analysis, therefore, the aim was not to identify the set of communication vehicles used to simply transform the message from the company to customers and other stakeholders. Instead, the analysis intended to reveal communicational processes which had emerged in the Intech case – in the sense of a social constructionist worldview – and to analyse how these processes helped to leverage competitive position and distinctive competencies.

Yates and Orlikowski (1992; Orlikowski and Yates 1994; Yates and Orlikowski 2002) have proposed the term 'genre'[35] to identify a 'typified

---

[34] Literature uses the terms 'capability' and 'competence' interchangeably (Hamel and Prahalad 1992).

[35] The term 'genre' is also used in discourse analysis (see, for example Fairclough (2003)). In that context, 'genre analysis' identifies aspects of discourse analysis focusing on questions how a text contributes to social action. Although this analysis also focuses on the performative capacity of communication, the use of the term 'genre' is different from the one suggested in the above definition.

communicative action invoked in response to a recurrent situation' (1992, 301). The recurrent situation covers history and nature of practices as well as the media applied in communicative action so that genres are a category of social events which go far beyond a pure consideration of communication instruments. Individual genres are marked by 'substance' – themes expressed in communication – and 'form' – observable features of communication. They are enacted through 'genre rules' which link substance and form to recurrent situations (1992, 302). Substance, form and genre rules are going to be analysed now.

11.1 Developing a taxonomy

Following the above definition of genre, the coding process for developing the taxonomy did not focus purely on the identification of communication instruments in order to leverage competitive position and distinctive competencies, but on communicational action which was similar in terms of substance, form and rules. An additional criterion for coding was that individual discourse fragments were related to either positioning or competencies of Intech.

Two, in themselves consistent streams of discourse, were identified that were clustered under terms that are commonly known already: (1) issue communication, i.e. discourse in which companies seek to define and communicate topics of concern (Hill 1992) and (2) branding, i.e. the 'systematically planned and implemented process of crafting and maintaining a favourable reputation of the company' (van Riel 2001, 12).

11.1.1 Issue communication

Discourse related to issue communication, in the Intech case consisted of three sub-themes. First of all, communication practices revealed that many issues were closely related to Intech's competencies, specifically the knowledge available at Intech. This sub-theme was termed 'knowledge as competence' (13 quotations). The majority of issue communication-related discourse was assigned to 'definitions of issues' (39 quotations). This sub-theme covered ways of how to define issues which are suitable for corporate communication purposes. Finally, discourse evolved around the question of how the company's 'story and messages' were used in terms of issue communication (10 quotations).

11.1.2 Branding[36]

Leveraging position and competencies also played an immediate role in branding-related discourse. Relevant fragments were assigned to the 'branding as leveraging' sub-theme (33 quotations). One core question addressed in this discourse covered the alignment of the Intech corporation and business unit levels of competencies in the leveraging process. Another sub-theme summed up discourse fragments on how Intech's 'competitive position' (24 quotations) and 'distinctive competencies' (27 quotations) were reflected in the brand. Finally, a limited number of discourse fragments (5 quotations) were assembled around the question of which and how 'resources' should be allocated for branding.

The resulting taxonomy is displayed in Table 15.

Table 15. Taxonomy for Strand 4 – Leveraging the competitive position and distinctive competencies

Domain [Section]	Generic themes [Section]	Sub-themes	Recurrence [No. of quotations]
S4 Leveraging [11.2]	Issue communication [11.2.1]	Knowledge as competence	13
		Definitions of issues	39
		Story and messages	10
	Branding [11.2.2]	Branding as leveraging	33
		Competitive position	24
		Competencies	27
		Resources	5
Total			151

11.2 Thematic analysis

This taxonomy provides a stocktaking of generic genres applied in leveraging position and competencies. The analysis so far revealed that issue communication and branding were two generic genres applied at Intech.

According to Röttger (2001), it is important to distinguish two views of issue management: first, the notion developed by orthodox communication scholars that issue communication needs to be applied in order to prevent crises, and second, the concept developed from management theory that issue management focuses on the relationship management between a com-

---

[36] The terms brand and reputation are used interchangeably as suggested by Kitchen (2004).

pany and its stakeholders. Kuhn (1997) developed the following working definition which comes close to the way issue communication was treated at Intech and which will be used subsequently. Kuhn refers to issue management as 'the particular sort of public discourse in which organizations seek to "define" issues, or topics of concern, as well as to influence public argument about issues in a way favourable of the organization' (1997, 189). He also put forward the notion of issue management as a 'genre' of corporate communication, i.e. accounting for similarities among its characteristics and execution.

Such a communicational definition has not yet been proposed for branding. Instead, a large variety of definitions circulate, mostly located in marketing theory, ranging from logo-based definitions, to viewing a brand as an identity system, from defining branding as image work to focusing on brand personality (Louro and Cunha 2001). A summary of the current state was provided by Knox and Bickerton (2003, 1013), by proposing the following definition: 'A corporate brand is the visual, verbal and behavioural expression of an organisation's unique business model.'

To start with, this study proposes to view branding, too, as a genre of corporate communication rather than an instrument, because all three criteria applied above – substance, form and rules – were met in the Intech case. Additionally, previous research has suggested that there is a coherent set of organisational processes associated with branding (Einwiller and Will 2002; Davies, Chun et al. 2003; Kitchen 2004). In orthodox theory, for example, a company's position and its competencies are widely accepted as substantive elements of a brand, and advertising has become a common form of brand discourse (Fairclough 1993), whereas differentiation is one of the rules branding generally follows. In consequence, the genres of corporate communication discourse are consistently referred to as issue communication and branding throughout this study.

Thematic analysis focuses on substance and form (Yates and Orlikowski 1992; Orlikowski and Yates 1994) of these two genres at Intech. For illustration, two examples were taken from each stream of discourse, covering the most prominent aspects of substance and form.

11.2.1 Issue communication

As Heath (1994; 1997; 2002) and Kuhn (1997) have proposed, issue communication – in its orthodox form – is applied as a rhetoric game and often follows the logic of a strategic vision the company wants to advance.

Implementing the Intech management system and advocating related issues in the public domain was the primary strategic intention at Intech during the observation period. Corporate communication, in consequence, subordinated communication themes to one of the three company programmes of the IMS. In the course of the year, the company programmes received a kind of headline function for a set of concrete issues that were put forward to various stakeholders, e.g. journalists, analysts, managers in the company, or the works council.

In terms of substance, this discourse, therefore, was executed rather consistently. In most cases presentations were commenced with an overview of the financial situation, based on the overall directive to "Go for profit and growth". The three company programs, then, were put forward as key issues driving the company.

While the company programmes on innovation and customer focus were of rather informative character for most stakeholders, a significantly controversial discourse – both within Intech and in the external public – had developed around the global competitiveness programme. This had to do with the fact that innovation and customer focus were primarily intended to create action from management (see Chapter 10). Global competitiveness, however, affected various stakeholders. In the German public it was embedded in a continuous discussion around the competitiveness of Germany as an industry location. For employees and works councils it meant a discourse around offshoring and shifting workplaces to low-cost countries. For analysts it involved the question of whether these measures would help Intech to increase profitability, and so on.

Given this diverse context, communicating the global competitiveness programme repeatedly occurred as a point of discussion in the interviews with strategy and communication managers. The following discourse fragment was taken from an interview with a strategy manager in June 2004:

[Researcher]: Global competitiveness in Germany got a rather negative touch.
[Strategy manager]: This, in the public, definitely is the programme with the strongest impact. You can find it everywhere. If the works council says "Let us talk about the [Intech management system], and we ask "Who should present?" of course it is always [the head of the global competitiveness programme]. This is the thought-provoking topic. The rest can be knocked off. I experienced this recently at a works council meeting. This happens quickly. The council member said: "Customer focus and innovation, we don't need to talk about this. We support this, as long as all this happens in Germany, too. Let's talk about the rest." No question, it is always communicated nicely that this has to happen. The two other programs, everybody agrees, are important. But it is about the interplay of many parts. You cannot have a look at one thing in isolation. This is the escape function for [the head of the global competitiveness programme] – to say "OK, I am this, but the [Intech management system] is more." He never says low-cost, he always says customers, making use of know-how, a huge reservoir of experts, and so on.

He is simply trying to leave this strong focus on workplaces in Germany in order to broaden the discussion.
(Interview) [80:11]

The strategy manager confirms that there are varying degrees of stakeholder interest in the three programmes. He also illustrates that there is interest from stakeholders to discuss the burning issues, and, that rhetoric plays an important role in this discourse as suggested by Heath (1994; 1997; 2002) and Kuhn (1997).

Global competitiveness issues also played a role in interviews with communication managers. The following discourse fragment was recorded in the same week as the interview with the above strategy manager in June 2004:

[Researcher]: The issue innovation can be seen as a topic to get out of the way of global competitiveness.
[Communication manager]: In Germany, this is the problem, and in other high-cost countries, rather than in other regions. We have to avoid one topic, offshoring, which is the risk behind the global competitiveness program, but which in the end is only one part of the program. There are important other parts which do not have this touch. Although in corporate communication these issues get overlaid. This is a communication issue, but the program is much wider... There is also the question what to do with the contents of the global competitiveness program. We use it in speeches also to demonstrate that it does not show the full beauty of the program if you focus on one aspect purely. On the other hand, it is necessary to align the value chains, and the program cannot simply be hidden. But we do not only focus on offshoring.
(Interview) [81:8]

In this discourse fragment, the communication manager lays out the struggle with the issue of global competitiveness. In his view, it is an ongoing balancing act between avoiding the offshoring issue – the aspect which, however, is of public interest – and actively pushing the other elements of the global competitiveness programme.

Overall, the two fragments confirm the substantive characteristics of the issue communication genre as advanced by Kuhn (1997, 197-202) and as manifested in the global competitiveness issue: (1) There is a concrete subject, i.e. 'challenges' to which the issue refers. In the case of Intech these challenges are documented in the Intech management system; (2) an 'appeal' is made in the issue-related discourse, which, in the Intech case is already inherent in the programme's name. The appeal is to keep Intech competitive in global business; (3) 'evidence' is presented to create a sense of urgency. One kind of evidence which was continuously put forward in the global competitiveness discourse related to cost differences between high- and low-cost countries, giving specific examples comparing Germany with Eastern European as well as Asian countries; (4) a 'solution' is presented. The rhetoric solutions used at Intech directly result from the above examples. The Intech management system was presented as 'more than' global competitiveness, and global competitiveness is 'more than' offshoring. Another option was to use the argument that ensuring Intech's competitiveness will also secure its long-term presence in Germany, including support for Germany as a business location.

The Intech case also provided evidence for the second set of genre rules identified by Kuhn (1997, 199) which identify the company's intention to link issues to company image. This approach was frequently applied at Intech business unit, where the corporate communication department proactively monitored issues related to corporate financing, produced studies to identify and explain relevant trends and used these in Intech business unit's corporate communication work, i.e. media relations, customer workshops etc.

The following discourse fragment was taken from one of the sessions which were held at Intech business unit to identify issues in July 2004. A communication manager explained the approach as follows:

'If we put aside the challenge to be exciting, essentially, one of the challenges is that we need to extend beyond being a captive funder. And we have to be careful that we don't end up being so high in the sky. We might have coverage high in the sky, but people still don't understand what we do and what we are about. At some point you have got to come to a point where it connects and people do understand what we are about. And the dimensions, I think, we have to agree upon. But, otherwise, I think we could fairly easily find ourselves in that kind of space where we are commenting about things and people don't really understand why. They are quite interested in what we comment on, but they don't really understand what we do, you know, where our specialisms lie.'
(Intech business unit communication manager) [42:12]

What becomes apparent again is the rhetorical intention behind creating these issues: a link to the identity of the company is intended by connecting the issue to 'what we are about' (see Chapter 8). By making this claim, the manager underlines the need to link issues to concrete competencies (Grant 1995; Teece, Pisano et al. 2000), and, therefore, to the business concept.

The approach chosen by Intech business unit was to identify 'performance gaps' (Heath 1997, 361), which are very close to the business. Identifying performance gaps, i.e. gaps between expectations and what happened in the market, and docking corporate communication activities to it, is another rule of the issue communication genre, following various strategies like 'ingratiation' (aiming for approval by displaying positive action), 'presenting itself as effective and in control', 'factual distortion and denial' (claiming that accusations are false), 'apology and acknowledgement', and 'justification' of strategic practices (Kuhn 1997, 200). Motives at Intech business unit were closely related to ingratiation and displaying effectiveness by illustrating that Intech business unit provides alternative financing solutions that are in the interest of business and society.

11.2.2 Branding

Rather extensive discourse emerged on branding during the observation period – both at Intech corporation and business unit. In this thematic analysis, too, a focus will be put on substance, form and rules of this discourse.

In terms of substance the following discourse fragment reveals some of the core themes and motives which were discussed during the corporate branding process at Intech business unit. It is a summary statement of one of the corporate communication managers during a meeting of communication managers at Intech business unit in March 2004:

'Let's have a look at how we can achieve [our branding] objectives. On the one hand, the challenge is to create awareness which puts [IBU] in a position to be perceived as the default financial services provider. On the other hand, also to underpin it with the competencies we are aiming for in financial services business. I think it has to be a kind of dual approach. We have to do some fairly concrete branding activities to directly increase the awareness, and to underpin it with a strong media relations strategy which focuses on these national and international media. To support the brand in the most effective way, we need to have a look at the various communication instruments.'
(Intech business unit communication manager) [27:8]

The manager, first of all, refers to increasing awareness of Intech business unit, which is seen as one of the common modes of leveraging the brand in a wide range of theories (Urde 1999; Louro and Cunha 2001). The second set of modes refers to Intech business unit's competencies, i.e. elements of the resource-based strategy view (Grant 1995), which need to underpin the concrete themes used in the branding process.

This provides a link to both strategy and issue communication, because in this case branding is applied as a means to increase awareness, i.e. to strengthen the positioning, and to transfer competencies into the market.

With regards to the form of the branding genre, the conclusion corresponds to issue communication, i.e. again a variety of communication tools and instruments were applied to communicate the brand to various stakeholders. This variety extended from print and online advertising via customer workshops to media relations. As the manager mentioned above, some branding activities were also combined with an issue approach, particularly media relations activities.

Some of the rules applied in the branding process at Intech result from the next discourse fragment. It represents an extract of a presentation which an Intech communication manager held at an international meeting of communication managers in May 2004. The purpose of the presentation was to announce the idea of a new global branding campaign which should be launched the following fiscal year:

'Why do we need a worldwide campaign for [Intech]? What is our common approach? Why should we start now? What does the process look like? And, what are the commitments we can make today? What we take from the whole day here at [conference location] is that a strong brand image can foster our growth strategy. We can position ourselves as a technology leader. We can influence the relevant set which will lead hopefully to a better purchase situation. We can generate competitive advantage. We can help all the businesses to realize price premiums which will help to increase profits. And we will increase, at the bottom line, the company value. On the growth side, we can establish sufficient awareness, we will win customers and projects because they know us, we can further strengthen our overall position, also in co-operation. It is also very important to have a solid company value when we talk about joint ventures. Just to keep in mind the [brand measuring model] which you all know…'
(Intech communication manager) [74:13]

Various motives and rules for the branding process at Intech are contained in this fragment, and the manager lists them in his rhetoric questions at the beginning of the presentation. The purpose he puts forward for the campaign is to strengthen the competitive position of Intech in key markets. The associated rule is that, by strengthening the position, branding helps to support profits, which in turn leads to an increased company value. Additionally, strengthening the brand, the rule follows, will support business growth, because increased awareness will build new relationships with customers.

This discourse follows in many aspects the 'adaptive paradigm' proposed by Louro and Cunha (2001) as one of the four branding paradigms apparent in common marketing literature. According to the adaptive paradigm, customers are viewed as the core constructors of brand meaning (Aaker 1996). Customers are also viewed as the key drivers of company performance, and brand performance is often measured along the customer value chain combining short- and long-term measures (which was also the case in the brand measuring model addressed above). Outside-in processes are important to ensure customer satisfaction.

In addition, Louro and Cunha (2003) identified the product, projective and relational paradigms. Characteristics of the product paradigm are a focus on products and positions, following a planned strategy approach. The projective paradigm is partly apparent at Intech business unit in the aspect that brands are used as 'focal platforms for articulating and implementing an organization's strategic intent' (Louro and Cunha 2001, 860). It is characterized by a strong focus on resources. Finally, in the relational paradigm (Fournier 1998), brands are viewed as personalities, evolving in interactions between brands, companies and customers.

In a detailed analysis Knox and Bickerton (2003, 1006-1011) identified altogether six 'conventions' determining the substance, form and rules of corporate branding which were fairly consistent with the substance of discourse found at Intech business unit: (1) 'brand context' comprising vision, image, culture and competitive landscape, (2) 'brand construction' by combining inside-out and outside-in approaches, (3) 'brand confirmation' by articulating the corporate brand proposition, (4) 'brand consistency' by applying the brand consistently throughout individual corporate communication measures, (5) 'brand continuity' as the link to and implementation of the brand into relevant business processes, and (6) 'brand conditioning' in a continuous monitoring and alignment process to ensure distinctiveness of the corporate brand.

11.3 Communicational review of genres

Having identified some of the key elements of the issue communication and branding genres, this Section focuses on a social constructionist review of the identified patterns which will then be used as a basis for the subsequent discourse analysis.

11.3.1 Issue communication

Thematic analysis has shown that issues need to be seen as simultaneously strategic and communicational, substantive and symbolic (Cheney and Christensen 2001). A rhetorical view of issues dominated discourse at both Intech corporation and business unit. This, however, has not revealed the performative qualities of issue communication as a strategic practice.

In contrast to orthodox models of issue management (Wartick and Heugens 2003), little academic work has been done to explicitly advance a social constructionist theory of issue management. A theoretical basis on the question of how issues are enacted was proposed by Dutton, Fahey et al. (1983) with a focus on issue creation, and Weick (1988) with a focus on issue construction during situations of crisis. In a summary of existing stakeholder research, Pajunen and Näsi (2005) proposed a model for constructing stakeholder relationships as consisting of four elements: players (the company and its stakeholders), strategies (used by the company to influence stakeholders and by stakeholders to influence the company), rules (moral underpinnings of the relations) and arenas (internal and external context of stakeholder relationships).

Additionally, Heugens (2003), in an attempt to integrate strategy and communication approaches into issue management, provided results on a study addressing the question of how companies construct issues that are viewed as effectively influencing outcomes of organisational activities.

Comparing the results of all four studies, it becomes quite apparent that there are significant overlaps in the conclusions of how issues are constructed. They are summarised in the following paragraphs. Common to all these views is that discourse (i.e. communication in the sense of this study) forms and structures issues as well as the context in which issues take place (Dutton, Fahey et al. 1983; Weick 1988).

Issues as a process unfolding over time

Dutton and Fahey et al. (1983, 310) advanced the notion that issues are constructed by all participants in a continuous process of interpretation ('recursiveness'). Participants organise data gained on issues into meaningful concepts in the interplay of indicative and deductive modes of sensemaking (retroductivity), and then interact with others to check and revise their interpretations (heterarchy). Issues are continuously changing, and communication practices contributing to this process need to be aware of and sensitive to this, e.g. through continuously checking processes of issue construction. Issue communication, from that viewpoint, rather opens opportunities for discussion rather than contributes to a transfer of facts (BOAG 2000).

Issues constructed in interaction

All participants in issue communication processes have the opportunity to contribute to issue formation (Pajunen and Näsi 2005). All four studies, therefore, advance that both companies and stakeholders play a crucial role in issues discourse. The pragmatic consideration of companies is 'to uncover the true positions and interests of these outside parties, for the purpose of incorporating them into corporate decision-making processes' (Heugens 2003, 13). Stakeholders, in turn can apply withholding strategies, i.e. discontinue the provision of resources directly or indirectly, for example through manipulating the flow of resources (Frooman 1999).

Several authors, however, have pointed to the situation that power between company and stakeholders is in many cases not equally distributed (Knights and Morgan 1990; Deetz 1992; Deetz 1995). Discourse serves to form and structure issues in interaction between the players, each applying their strategies.

Issues shaped in multi-voiced processes

In accordance with Weick (1988), social constructionists have advanced the notion that opinion multiplicity should be promoted rather than avoided (Knights and Morgan 1991). The suggestion is that purely more communication does not generate the intended results (Healey 1997). Instead, multi-voiced communication is necessary to ensure that the performative capacity of communication is used, e.g. in terms of releasing learning processes or even necessary strategy adaptations (Deetz and Brown 2004; Lehtimäki and Kujala 2005). Again, a concept of 'full participation' seems necessary, because applying discourse theory and social constructionism also heads to the realization that 'diverse group participation will lead to better decisions than are currently being made' (Deetz 1995, 6). Barry and Elmes (1997, 444) proposed that strategic practices should be 'more concerned with surfacing, legitimising, and juxtaposing differing organizational stories'. And, in proposing a multi-voiced strategy process, Smircich and Stubbart (1985, 730) made the point that strategy should move from a planning and decision-making focus to providing a 'vision to account for the streams of events and actions that occur – a universe in which organizational events and experiences take on meaning.' Based on the results of the analysis so far, this could also provide a useful perspective for corporate communication viewed as a strategic practice.

Shaping competencies by communicating issues

According to Gibbons (2002, 10), social constructionism influences the competency-based view of the company altogether in four ways: (1) competencies are an outcome of social action, (2) competencies are reflected in structures of the company, (3) competencies influence strategic practices through interpretive schemes, resources and norms (i.e. modalities), and (4) strategic practices reproduce or influence the company's structures through these modalities.

This means, if discourse shapes issues, it also shapes a company's competencies (Grant 1996; Teece, Pisano et al. 2000) – and, in turn, a company's competencies also influence its issue communication. This matches the motives of companies, because learning and developing competencies is clearly one of the motives of companies in the issue communication process (Heugens 2003). It also brings competencies into issue communication as a common process (Heath 1994; 1997).

In the ongoing issue communication process, this involves drilling down to the bottom line of issues in order to understand its recursiveness and fluidity (Dutton, Fahey et al. 1983). At the same time, it means increasing the awareness of issues and competencies in the company as well as trying to develop strategies for how to introduce these competencies into the issue communication process.

11.3.2 Branding

In the four brand management paradigms proposed by Louro and Cunha (2001), Fournier's (1998) relational paradigm comes closest to the alternative social constructionist view put forward in this study. While the merits of this approach are based on the launch of the notion of an active role of customers and the view of branding as an ongoing process, it has also been criticized for considering only a few of the aspects relevant from a constructionist viewpoint.

Bengtsson (2003) made the point that brands cannot necessarily be 'humanized' in the way a relational paradigm suggests. His question is whether brands, managed by managers, really qualify as a relationship partner in the actual sense of human relationship theory.

Marketing-based approaches to branding have also been criticized for being 'undersocialized, behavioralist, functionalist and managerialist' (Kärreman 2002, 4-6): undersocialized because a marketing approach does not give insight in the social construction of brands; behavioralist due to its 'notions of stimulus-response, conditionings, and positive reinforcement'; functionalist because of the assumption that brands exist in an objective sense and that, therefore, it is possible to determine its impact and effects; managerialist because 'what is good for management may not automatically be good for everybody else'.

Despite comprehensive critiques of orthodox approaches, a social constructionist theory of branding was not advanced by Kärreman or other critical scholars. Therefore, the following paragraphs attempt to compile aspects of such a communicational perspective on branding.

Branding as a strategic practice

Varey and Karklins (2001, 40) suggested that 'a corporate brand is a dynamic formation that binds together and reflects the corporation with all its constituting elements, systems, and subsystems'. This definition corresponds with Jarzabkowski's (2003) definition of a strategic practice as shared activity between actors, collective social structures and the practical activities. Viewing branding as a strategic and, at the same time, communicational practice leads to an understanding that branding needs to be defined as one of the mediating processes between various elements of context. This mediating function is not limited to the relationship between company and customers, but involves all stakeholders, inside and outside of the company. In other words, 'the brand is a strategic platform for interplay with the target group and thus is not limited to being an unconditional response to what at any moment is demanded by customers' (Urde 1999, 130).

Branding as advancing key symbols

Branding means communicating certain 'key symbols' (Kärreman 2002) to stakeholders, e.g. brand values in the case of Intech. These key symbols link to the strategy perspective on branding by providing the opportunity to focus on core competencies and values of the company (Urde 1999; Urde 2001). The underlying idea is to propose core elements of the company, its products, services and people to the customer. An additional aspect is to provide meaning around certain reference points internally for employees. 'Informants think it is important, sometimes obsess over its meaning, respond emotionally to it, and its usage and meaning is formally monitored, pruned and developed' (Kärreman 2002, 15-16). As a key symbol the brand summarises what the company stands for, highlights these aspects and provides opportunities for identification with the company. Even more, a strong corporate brand acts like a 'beacon in the fog', and it works 'because it expresses the values and/or sources of desire that attract key stakeholders to the organisation and encourages them to feel a sense of belonging to it' (Hatch and Schultz 2003, 1046).

An important concept in this is the notion of 'brand integrity' (Urde 1999) or 'authenticity' (Moore 2003), because 'many of the problems that undermine brands come from within organizations' (Urde 1999, 131) – i.e. incoherent communication, exaggerated focus on positioning, unclear values and responsibilities, lack of top management passion for the brand.

Branding as understanding what counts

Most orthodox branding theories and strategies take it for granted that there is external interest for branding programmes and campaigns. This is not a given following the social constructionist approach. 'More of the same won't work', concludes Moore (2003, 112). The stakeholders themselves have the option to decide whether they perceive the message or not.

The concept of auto-communication – i.e. 'self-referential acts of communication through which senders relate *to their own messages*' (Cheney, Christensen et al. 2004, 131) – was introduced in Chapter 1, and it expresses the risk that companies simply over-value brand and identity issues and communication without considering whether their brand indeed is important for their stakeholders. With growing critique of brands in general (Ind 2003) this needs to be increasingly questioned.

With regards to product branding this issue has been addressed by so called 'guerrilla-marketers' (Gladwell 2002; Godin 2003), who propose word-of-mouth communication as one solution. Following the social constructionist notion, a standard solution to this challenge cannot be proposed. Again, as in Chapter 10, it has to become increasingly the task of managers to understand the social constructs of the specific brand in detail in order to find out which rules apply in the local context (Urde 1999). Digging into the brand and analysing the importance of messages, not only its credibility (as is common in mainstream marketing research programmes) can be a way forward (Cheney and Christensen 2001).

11.4 Discourse analysis

In the following section, based on this communicational review, discourse analysis is used to shed light on the question of how these communicational forces of issue communication and branding were enacted in the concrete Intech case.

11.4.1 Constructing issues

It has been argued above that stakeholders and competencies play an important role in the process of issue communication. The following discourse fragment is an example for how Intech brought its competencies into the relationships with shareholders. The fragment was taken from the speech of a general manager at the Intech business conference in October 2003:

'Fortunately we withstood the recommendations – sometimes they were also formulated as demands – to dismantle the company and limit our activities to the areas of information and communications and industrial automation. The magic formula – you might recall – was "focusing." We by far do not cover the entire field of electrical engineering and electronics. But we have achieved a balance

with our six business areas that helps us better master industry crises than is the case with specialists. But one thing is also clear: We must continue to ban cross-subsidies among our businesses. Naturally it can happen now and then that individual businesses run into trouble. And we certainly won't lose our nerves in such moments and sell or close them. But these businesses must then come up with a convincing plan and carry it out with full consequences in order to secure their future. The general rule for every business is: EVA[37] must be positive!'
(Intech general manager) [54:39]

Discourse represented in this text, first of all, reflects recursive interaction between Intech and its shareholders. With satisfaction, the manager at the beginning confesses that Intech consciously withstood the recommendations of analysts to focus its activities. He not only uses this expressive statement, but also applies speech acts which had been detected by Palmer, King et al. (2004) in their analysis of General Electric's shareholder discourse: (1) assertions that not all proposals of the shareholders were withstood, but that the general principle of shareholder value has even been enforced, and (2) commissions that cross-subsidies will be banned and that convincing plans and executions will be demanded in order to ensure shareholder value. Altogether, this confirms that issues – in this case the portfolio of the company – were constructed in interaction with shareholders, and that this happened in a multi-voiced process in which Intech stuck to some of its principles, i.e. to keep a balance between focus and diversification.

The latter aspect also validates the theory that competencies were negotiated in the process. Intech brought its competence to manage a complex conglomerate successfully into the negotiation, whereas it learned from the negotiations that it is necessary to fulfil shareholder value demands at the same time. The latter included the necessity to develop the competence to create and manage shareholder value within Intech in the long run.

An Intech communication manager, in an interview in August 2004, made the point that real participation in multi-voiced processes had paid off for Intech in other cases as well. He referred back to the issue of global competitiveness which had led to a general discussion around the competitiveness of Germany as an industry location. Reflecting on media coverage, he explained Intech management's stance as follows:

'And also the efforts of [Intech] to change labour conditions in Germany were absorbed strongly. This is the topic which leads to a strong identification with [Intech]. And also the success became clear that [Intech] was the first big company to negotiate a new collective wage agreement. ... This is highly interesting. My conclusion is that the topic global competitiveness was placed positively in the media,

---

[37] EVA = economic value-added.

because [Intech] now is considered to be the leader for establishing work conditions in Germany which have proved successful internationally... However, it was not [the CEO] himself, but an article in the Financial Times, where the topic really became public. [Intech] then picked it up, and defended it, and [board member in charge of human resources] played the internal part towards the employees, and the works council. This was a good combination on top management level, and that is why the media took possession of it. The topic had been in the media many times before, but [Intech] launched the proposal to increase working hours without adjusting wages. Same wages, but more work, this was the key.'
(Intech communication manager) [96:17]

The manager at the beginning states that it was Intech driving the issue, i.e. it was an approach proactively driven by the company, not a crisis scenario (Weick 1988). He immediately adds that picking up the issue proactively can support identification with the company and the issue. The manager repeats that Intech drove this issue actively and was the first company to start negotiations of new collective wage agreements in Germany.

The tactic was to use an article which appeared in a daily national newspaper and, based on this, to approach the works council[38] and start negotiations. The paratactic grammatical relation chosen by the manager indicates that this process was viewed as socially constructed.

In parallel to negotiations with the works council, Intech launched the proposal to increase working hours without adjusting wages, which was a new aspect in a rather fruitless discussion in the media at that time. In consequence the media followed up on that idea and recognized it as a solution to keep the work places which had been at disposal in Germany. The works councils agreed to this proposal. Both parties had achieved their core goals and a solution was found which could be applied for other German companies as well.

A deeper analysis of this specific case would be necessary in order to conclude whether this process fulfilled the criteria for participation put forward by critical scholars such as Deetz (1995). It shows, however, that negotiation based on an issue communication process had contributed to the construction of an urgent problem of strategic significance for many stakeholders. Schüz (2001, 82) made the point that 'the ability to negotiate interests is an elementary and vital means for getting from others what you desire yourself', but that at the same time negotiation does not work without legitimisation processes involving all stakeholders. Negotiation, there-

---

[38] Works councils in German companies are statutory representatives of employees in order to ensure worker participation in a company's decision-making processes. For a detailed description, see Zerfaß (1996).

fore, should aim for maximizing opportunities and minimizing risks for all participants at the same time.

Schüz (2001) proposes that responsible action of company and stake-holders is necessary to achieve this intended outcome. It happens if company and stakeholders appear as trustworthy to each other, i.e. if the gap between claim and reality of participants is minimized.

On the company's side, therefore, it is not sufficient to produce corporate responsibility reports (Clark 2000; Vehkaperä 2005), but to create a context for the whole company to act in a responsible and reliable way (Schüz 2001). This includes the implementation of communicational principles throughout the company, e.g. in stakeholder relationships, managerial decision-making, corporate governance, business conduct guidelines and their execution, etc. (Smith 2004).

11.4.2 Deconstructing the brand

In the thematic analysis of branding discourse in the above section a communication manager was quoted who advocated the 'adaptive paradigm' (Louro and Cunha 2001) of the Intech brand. In contrast, the manager in the conversation at Intech business unit had put a projective view on the brand.

According to a social constructionist worldview in which structure and content of a brand shapes and is continuously shaped by discourse and interaction (Weick 1979), it is not surprising that elements of different paradigms of a brand turn up in a single company.

Corporate communication managers at Intech, together with external consultants, had collected and analysed various views of different stake-holders during the observation period. The aim was to identify the core of the Intech brand and its key characteristics. The result of this process was a so-called 'brand charter' which was published as a printed brochure as well as online on the Internet. The following discourse fragment represents an excerpt of this charter, downloaded form the Internet in January 2005:

Brand charter
The brand is nothing other than the personality of the [Intech] corporation. Just like the human personality, it is the sum of all our talents, of all our abilities and all of our characteristics. And it therefore offers the basis for the relationship between [Intech] and a wide range of target groups as our customers, our investors, the general public and of course our employees…
Brand core
Our brand core is made up of the basic principles of our corporate strategy and the abilities described in our corporate principles. It describes the fundamental ideas behind our strong personality. It makes [Intech] an architect of modern global so-

ciety. A creative force that shapes structures and develops networks.

Ever since the founding of the company over 150 years ago, [Intech] has directed its thinking well beyond geographical borders. With this kind of history, it's no wonder that the company today has a special sensitivity to the most diverse world cultures. And it's no wonder that [Intech] makes use of this knowledge with all of its senses. Through our global network of more than 400,000 employees, knowledge, experience and values can be shared and put into effective use all over the world. This gives us an extraordinary advantage for developing and shaping a steady series of new markets in new regions. In this way, [Intech] makes its own contribution to a world in which resources are limited, but possibilities are not.

There's no recipe for success when it comes to developing new concepts or innovative product ideas. Only those who think big know that it's rarely the most direct and seemingly fastest and simplest route that leads to an exceptional solution. In its role as architect, [Intech] has the strength and flexibility to afford to take some intellectual detours now and then, on the road to new and creative destinations.

[Intech] makes space for personalities. No matter of we're developing new products or new services - at the centre of all considerations is always the human being with its individual needs. Every solution from the house of [Intech]is therefore so conceived that it supports the potential of every individual and helps people to live together harmoniously.

This discourse fragment is particularly interesting because it reveals a third brand paradigm immediately in the first paragraph: the relational brand paradigm, i.e. defining the brand as a personality which maintains relationships (Fournier 1998). Fournier, however, defined the brand as primarily in interaction with customers, whereas in the Intech brand charter the stakeholder view is extended to investors, the general public and employees. Also, the brand charter links the brand to the competencies of the company, which is an aspect of the resource-base strategy view (Broadfoot, Deetz et al. 2004). All these statements are made in a rather assertive style, not leaving room for further interpretation.

The link to strategy is re-enforced in the second paragraph which introduces the concept of brand core as a point of reference to core competencies and values (Urde 1999; Urde 2001), based on which the personality of Intech as an 'architect of modern global society' emerges.

The following paragraphs try to explain the concept behind this personality, and consequently, also use the name 'Intech' to identify the person 'Intech' who directs its thinking, has sensitivity, shares values etc. The text refers to history and geographical presence as important elements of context in which the personality of Intech emerges. Also, Intech's huge network of resources and competencies is put forward as a characteristic, which provides the company with advantages in a world which is itself characterized by limited resources. The notion to focus on possibilities rather than restrictions has been put forward as a constructionist concept (BOAG 2000), and corresponds with the view represented in this book.

In the subsequent paragraph, the concept of innovation is presented as an element of the brand core. It is not explained as a straightforward process. Instead, 'intellectual detours' are necessary and are afforded by Intech to come to creative solutions. The paragraph contains a straightforward admission that in the process of innovation a 'recipe for success' is not available. Instead, innovations need to be constructed individually.

Finally, Intech is explained as a person that is not dominating but that opens spaces for other personalities. The human being is put into the centre of consideration.

Overall, the metaphor of Intech as an 'architect' which is advanced in this brand charter, and many of the statements analysed above, propose the conclusion that Intech itself can be viewed as a 'constructionist entity' – constructing the social world around it, and, at the same time, constructed by the stakeholders interacting with it.

A critical aspect remains, however, as put forward in the communicational review of branding as to whether the brand really can be understood as a separate person (Bengtsson 2003) or whether it should rather be viewed as a mediator in relationships between real persons, i.e. actors on behalf of the company and stakeholders (Hosking and Haslam 1997; Varey and Karklins 2001). The crucial relationship is between the individual or the media representing the brand and the stakeholder interacting with this individual or medium. Only if this actor on behalf of the company behaves coherently with the brand personality brand integrity can be achieved (Urde 1999).

11.5 Theorising

This section completes the series of four sections in which the contribution of each Strand of interrelations between strategy and communication processes is defined. Comparable with Chapters 8 to 10, the contribution is derived in a three-step process: (1) Strand 4 is referred back to in the reference framework, (2) an additional figure is proposed in reply to the specific research questions relevant for Strand 4, and (3) the Strand is adapted in the framework.

First, Figure 15 highlights Strand 4 – 'leveraging the competitive position and distinctive competencies' – in the reference framework.

As outlined above, a specific set of research questions was applied throughout the analyses in this Chapter in order to gain further insight into the interrelated strategy and communication processes which constituted corporate communication discourse focusing on Strand 4 on the reference framework. The research question guiding thematic analysis was: 'Which themes were covered by corporate communication discourse relating to competitive position and distinctive competencies?' Discourse analysis focused on these research questions: 'How did corporate communication discourse contribute to the constitution of competitive position and distinctive competencies? How was it formed by these?'

Thematic analysis showed that, in the Intech case, issue communication and branding were two communicational practices that linked to the strategy concepts of competitive position and distinctive competencies. More specifically, both issue communication and branding were proposed to be viewed as genres of corporate communication, sharing to a great extent consistency in terms of content and execution throughout the observation period. In contrast to orthodox communication instruments, which follow the conduit metaphor of communication, the genres of issue communication and branding are applied in communicational terms, i.e. they both shape and are shaped by position and competencies in an ongoing process.

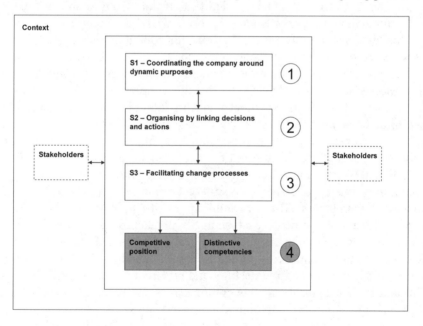

Fig. 15. Referring back to Strand 4 in the reference framework

The communicational review has, in addition, pointed towards the importance of the complete spectrum of stakeholders in this process – as full participants in multi-voiced issue communication processes as well as in advancing key symbols in branding exercises. As related discourse analysis showed, stakeholder participation is particularly important in developing solutions for critical problems. Stakeholder attention is, however, not guaranteed, particularly in orthodox branding situations in which brand integrity cannot be taken as a given. Considering and understanding processes of constructing brand personality – in the Intech case even literally by constructing Intech as an 'architect of modern global society' – were identified as crucial.

Einwiller, Prykop et al. (2003) proposed that issue communication can support branding by drawing attention to aspects of the brand which are relevant from stakeholders' viewpoints and by providing established internally linked strategy and communication processes which brand managers can hook on to. In turn, it is argued now that branding can also contribute to this relationship by focusing attention on 'key symbols', i.e. characteristics and values of the company which need to be applied by issue managers in their negotiation processes with stakeholders in order to maintain integrity. Additionally, if issue management is viewed in its 'proactive' (Einwiller, Prykop et al. 2003) mode, it can benefit from established external communication channels and platforms which are continuously fed in the branding process. These can be used for combining issues with brand personality in order to increase its relevance for stakeholders.

The genres of issue communication and branding were identified as both influencing and being influenced by Intech's competitive positioning and – even more – its distinctive competencies. In addition, both issue communication and branding need to be viewed as 'married' to the strategic concepts of competitive position and distinctive competencies. This relationship was repeatedly focused on in the above analysis stages. They are not only linked in communicational terms, however. They are also linked by a common purpose: to create competitive advantage, simply to be 'more successful than others' (Rindova and Fombrun 1999, 704).

The concept of competitive advantage has been proposed individually as a purpose for each component, e.g. by Halal (2000) and Heugens (2001) for issue communication, by Urde (1999) for branding, by Porter (1980; Porter 1985) for competitive position and by Grant (1995) as well as Cool, Costa et al. (2002) for distinctive competencies. It has not been recognized as a linking pin between all four components, however. Based on the Intech case, competitive advantage needs to be viewed as the rationale behind the notion of 'leveraging' which had been proposed in the context of the original framework. In line with Rindova and Fombrun (1999, 705), it is concluded 'that the development of competitive advantage is an interactive process' in which processes of influencing are relevant.

Nahapiet and Ghoshal (1998) detected a similar link between market variables and forms of organisation. They proposed the term and concept of 'organizational advantage' to express that the conception of advantage lies not only in market variables, but also in forms of organisation. Having defined communication as one mode of organising, the term 'organisational advantage' is adopted for the purpose of this study.

The full network of relationships between all four components is illustrated in Figure 16.

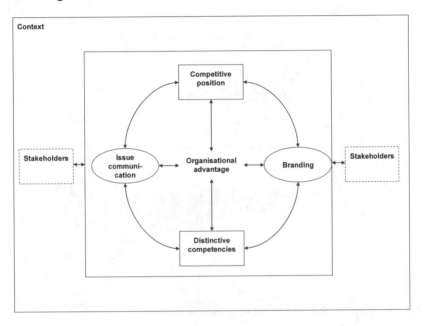

Fig. 16. Review of Strand 4 – Leveraging the competitive position and distinctive competencies

This figure represents step two in the three-step process for adapting the framework, i.e. it summarises the contribution of Strand 4 towards an alternative corporate communication theory. Thematic analysis focused on the research question of which themes were covered by corporate communication discourse relating to competitive position and distinctive competencies. In the taxonomy (see Table 15), the following generic themes were identified: 'issue communication' and 'branding'. Both themes were adopted in Figure 16. In addition, discourse analysis concentrated on revealing how corporate communication discourse shaped and was shaped by the constitution of competitive position and distinctive competencies. The various forms of shaping and being shaped, including the crucial role of stakeholders in this, were referred to above – and are symbolised by the network format of illustration. 'Organisational advantage', as the ultimate outcome of the relations in this network, was put in the centre of Figure 22.

In a third step, illustrated in Figure 17, the revised version of Strand 4 is adapted in the reference framework.

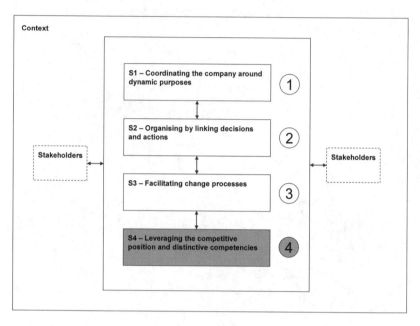

Fig. 17. Adapting Strand 4 in the reference framework

In the following additional features of an alternative theory of corporate communication are proposed in the concluding part of this Chapter.

11.5.1 Stakeholders as sources of competence

Prahalad and Ramaswamy (2000) suggested the concept that managers should regard customers as a source of competence – but that, at the same time, these customers can become competitors through an increasing degree of transparency which results from this knowledge exchange. A similar concept of 'market-based strategic communication' was proposed by D'Aprix (1996) in an attempt to increase employees' knowledge of the marketplace.

Constructionist work suggests that companies who deal successfully with knowledge exchange solve these challenges in specific practices (Kogut and Zander 1996; Orlikowski 2002). Some of the practices relevant in processes of knowledge creation are of communicational nature. Kogut and Zander (1996), for example, found that shared identity supports knowledge creation in practice, because shared identity structures discourse, coordination and learning. A shared brand, for example, can fulfil similar functions (Urde 1999; Kärreman 2002). Similarly, in Orlikowski's (2002) study the importance of identity in knowledge creation was highlighted. Additionally, Orlikowski found that the practice of face-to-face communication played a key role in facilitating knowledge-creation.

In consequence, both branding and issue communication genres can and should be applied to integrate stakeholders in processes of knowledge creation.

11.5.2 Creating communicational platforms

It has been argued that participation should be implemented as a principle of issue communication in order to improve effectiveness, decisions and commitment to the company. What matters, however, is the form of participation, not just its existence. Success of participation is linked to the quality of communication (Cheney, Mumby et al. 1997). Deetz and Brown (2004) criticize orthodox approaches to participation in exactly that aspect:

'As companies imported liberal democratic conceptions in their development of participation plans, much of the focus has been on developing forums. Whether these are low engagement sites like suggestion boxes or more engaged forms like cross-functional teams or Board of Director membership, they have been often justified and marked principally by giving people a chance to have a say.'
(Deetz and Brown 2004, 179)

This chance to have a say, the mere expression of ideas, however, is not sufficient to achieve communicational participation. Instead of focusing on expression of personal experience, the focus should be put on joint development of ideas and solutions (Deetz and Brown 2004, 180). In ongoing construction processes, communication needs to focus on the ongoing production of possibilities (Weick 1988). According to Deetz and Brown, this involves, for example, greater diversity in participants. Also Chakravarthy (1996) had made that point. Apart from diversity, also the content of participation needs to shift from mere expression to the deconstruction of how meanings were created. Deetz and Brown's notion proposes that participation should focus on clarifying how meaning in specific cases is produced and reproduced. Collaboration in that sense also needs to lead to more pur-

poseful conclusions by focusing 'on the reaching of a common understanding and mutual commitment to a decision by focusing on the ends to be
achieved rather than the preferred means of achievement or present positions' (Deetz and Brown 2004, 186).

Based on the above analysis of issue communication discourse, it has already been suggested that diversity can lead to better decisions. The extension of that notion is to develop the issue communication genre into a platform which itself is structured according to constructionist principles. In
that, rules of issue communication (and respectively branding) should be
applied in a sense that both issue communication and branding function as
ongoing processes producing and reproducing meaning in continuous
form.

III Integration of findings

In Part II, the analysis of each of the four Strands of interrelations between strategy and communication practices was completed. Part III concentrates on an integration of the individual findings into an extended, integrated framework of alternative corporate communication, and it summarises the contributions gained from this study.

In order to get to the integrative framework, in Chapter 12, at first, interdiscursivities of management practices at Intech are analysed and structured. This analysis results in seven Propositions. The interdiscursivities put forward in these Propositions form the basis for Figure 25 in which the integrated framework of alternative corporate communication is presented. This framework can be viewed as the core contribution of this study to corporate communication theory.

From Section 5 of Chapter 12 onwards, the contribution is considered in more detail. In the course of this, orthodox corporate communication theory is (1) recontextualised (see Table 15), (2) the use-value of the findings is evaluated more precisely, and (3) the relevance of the findings for practitioners is discussed. This corresponds with Gergen and Thatchenkery's (2001, 164-167) three requirements for closing the gap from a social constructionist viewpoint.

The methodological review which closes this study deals with issues of quality of the generalisations and completeness of the analyses conducted. Suggestions for further research conclude the study.

12 Key conclusions

This study focuses on theory-building. Throughout Chapters 8 to 11, the gap between orthodox corporate communication theory and management theories considering the linguistic and practice turns in social theory was explored in detail. The analysis of each of the four Strands of interrelations between strategy and communication processes resulted in the conclusion that there are significant gaps between applying orthodox corporate communication theory and following such alternative theories.

In Chapter 12, these individual findings are integrated into a new framework and evaluated against the three aspects of purpose which were defined in Chapter 2.

12.1 Summary of initial findings

Sections 5 of Chapters 8 to 11 provided answers to the individual research questions, and core aspects of the gap between orthodox and alternative corporate communication theory were highlighted. These gaps were identified based on thematic and discourse analyses. Before starting the process of integrating these findings into an alternative corporate communication theory, some key aspects of the gaps are briefly summarised.

12.1.1 Gaps identified from the analysis of Strand 1

Section 8.5 summarised the key contributions of the analysis of corporate communication discourse as part of coordinating the company around dynamic purposes. Based on this summary, an alternative corporate communication theory needs to consider: (1) a demand for understanding the complexity of the field: according to this finding, communication is not an unproblematic solution to crises of purpose and identity (Cheney and Christensen 2001); instead, in many cases communication is part of the identity problem if treated as a one-way managerial process; one conclusion was that container forms of communication need to be viewed as communication offerings rather than purely a means of transporting information to various stakeholders; (2) a plea for more substance in corporate communication: instead of substantive communication, symbolic communication (Alvesson 1990) has evolved as a straightforward solution to manage communication, covering a large proportion of today's communication industry; in business reality, however, symbolic and substantive management always go hand in hand, i.e. identity work cannot be done without substantive underpinning work; this, rather than a strong focus on symbolic communication, allows for a meaningful discourse on the purpose of a company in a concrete and local business context; and (3) a need for taking identity negotiation seriously: the aspect of negotiating identity becomes particularly relevant in companies with multiple identities (Larson and Pepper 2003); understood as communication offerings rather than means of transportation, corporate communication products – e.g. newsletters – need to be viewed as being part of the negotiating process rather than functioning as a means of transporting information from sender to recipient.

12.1.2 Gaps identified from the analysis of Strand 2

In Section 9.5, the results of analysing corporate communication discourse as part of organising processes were summarised. According to this, the communicational turn in corporate communication puts focus on: (1) giving decisions voice: many decisions are made in irrational modes; therefore, they are not easily detectable; nevertheless, these decisions need to be given voice in order to initiate processes of sense-making; selecting mechanisms will have to be applied in order to prioritise voices; Handy (1992) made the point that a normative model is necessary for conducting this process of prioritising, which can, for example, be based on a federalist approach; (2) providing sufficient focus on facilitating the legitimisation process: decisions should be used as a rationale for creating peer-to-peer communication (Brunsson 1990); this was identified as a necessary component for building collective intuition; network theory provides further insight into processes of authorization which, for example, happen in communities of practice; and (3) a shift from focus on cascading to leveraging the performative capacity of communication: the six degrees of separation analysed do not necessarily happen in a timely order, but act in a constantly interrelated way; in order to be able to leverage the performative capacity of communication, organising processes need to be addressed in parallel.

12.1.3 Gaps identified from the analysis of Strand 3

Corporate communication discourse also unfolded performative capacity as part of implementation and change processes. According to the findings summarised in Section 10.5, an alternative corporate communication theory should consider: (1) the need for understanding intention and structures: particularly when following an issue-selling approach, such as in the case of Intech, it is important to be aware of top and middle management's intentions as well as the various elements of structure that are going to be influenced, before crafting communication activities; in this, substantive communication remains key; (2) that it is necessary to ensure full participation: instead of creating passive opposition, a participatory approach actively integrates all stakeholders involved in change; multiplicity needs to be leveraged rather than suppressed in an attempt to achieve an imaginary consensus (Hosking 2004); and (3) a strong focus on sense-making: it is crucial to ensure that change is embedded in the deep structures of the company and to recognise that employees on all organisational levels can make sense of what is going on in the company over time; corporate communication discourse, therefore, needs to involve the multiple types of conversations proposed by Ford and Ford (1995).

12.1.4 Gaps identified from the analysis of Strand 4

At Intech, corporate communication discourse also played an important role when it came to processes of leveraging the company's competitive position and distinctive competencies. Findings summarised in Section 11.5 lead to a view that a communicational turn in corporate communication theory should: (1) regard stakeholders as sources of competence: according to alternative management theories, customers, employees and other stakeholders are viewed as sources of competence (D'Aprix 1996; Prahalad and Ramaswamy 2000); an identity and a brand which are shared between a company and its stakeholders can support knowledge creation in practice, because shared identity and brand contribute to structuring discourse, coordination and learning (Kogut and Zander 1996; Urde 1999); (2) focus on creating communicational platforms: what matters, is the form of participation and multi-voiced processes, not their existence; instead of focusing on expression of personal experience – as is the case in many extant corporate communication platforms – the focus should be put on joint development of ideas and solutions (Deetz and Brown 2004); this involves diversity in participants.

12.2 Interdiscursivity of management practices

Whereas the above summary highlighted aspects of the performative capacity of communication within each of the four Strands of the reference framework, an alternative corporate communication theory needs to go further. In addition to the individual view on each Strand, the question is whether and how these Strands interrelate.

The phenomenon that management practices happen in interrelated modes, even within a singular company, has been addressed for some time. Pettigrew (1992) described it the following way:

> 'The analysis of any single process occurs not just in a nested context but also alongside other processes... Such an analysis moves the researcher away from theories of individual causes towards theorizing about a constellation of forces shaping the character of the process and perhaps explaining differences in outcome.'
> (Pettigrew 1992, 8-9)

Therefore, Pettigrew (1992) suggests that strategy should generally be viewed as a multi-level process. This can happen by conducting context-sensitive analysis – like in the previous Chapters.

In discursive and communicational theories the relations between several texts are also referred to as 'intertextuality' (Allen 2000). This term was first introduced by Kristeva (1967) defining that each text is multi-voiced in the sense that it relates to statements that have been made earlier. Intertextuality is identifiable on many levels, reaching from very general to very concrete relations (Auer 1999). Intertextuality on the general level, for example, contains the relation between discourse fragments which are embedded into an overall theme or discourse.

The communicational view applied in this study was characterized as 'conceptualizing organization as a communicative process' (Taylor 1999). This means that the company is situated in 'infinite intercourse' (Cheney and Tompkins 1988). Attention is drawn to multiple discourses occurring in the company as a 'fluid entity situated within the broader cultural economy of intertextual activity' (Taylor 1999, 65).

This leads to a specific type of intertextuality: one which is 'concerned with a dynamic of contingent discourses and contexts, not merely contiguous ones' (Orr 2003, 43). This type of intertextuality has been referred to as 'interdiscursivity' (Fairclough 1993) and is characterized by voices of various interests competing for authority and legitimisation (Taylor 1999).

Taylor used this concept of interdiscursivity for theorizing relationships between different cultures in a company setting, based on the assumption that interdiscursivities occurred 'when the frames and routines of "membering" in one culture draw on those of another, creating a condition in which cultural spheres are joined through the instrumentality of social action' (1999, 62-63).

Analogously, interdiscursivity for the following integrative analysis was supposed when discourse of one or more Strands of interrelation between strategy and communication practices drew on discourse of one or more of the other Strands. In this sense, a web of interrelations between Strand 1 to 4 of the original framework was assumed (see Figure 18[39]).

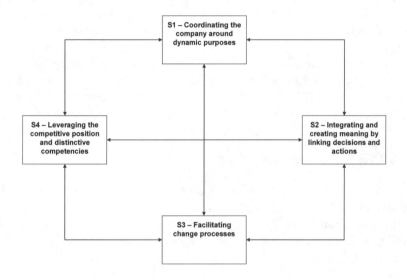

Fig. 18. Interrelations between strategy and communication practices

12.3 Interdiscursivity in the Intech case

Interdiscursivity covers a wide range of possibilities (Fairclough 1992). Broich and Pfister (1985, 31-47) listed a whole range of 'marks' pointing to interdiscursivity in texts, ranging from direct reference to the other text and various forms of quotations to footnotes. Interdiscursivity can also ap-

---

[39] This Figure is proposed purely for illustration purposes. It is not relevant in the process of gradually adapting the conceptual framework.

pear in actions of participants or it can be established by referring to a whole group of texts, i.e. discourses. Another option is that interdiscursivity simply occurs in re-appearing core themes in different discourses.

The aim of this Chapter is to summarise and integrate communicational practices which were already analysed in previous Chapters. Therefore, interdiscursivity analysis at this stage is going to focus on a high level examination of 'the forces guiding affiliation between discourses' (Taylor 1999, 62). Reference points are the four Strands of interrelations between strategy and communication practices. The concrete intention is, first, to identify practices which occur as part of more than one of the identified Strands, and, second, to extract rules that shed light on how these Strands of interrelations influence each other in terms of rules governing the interdiscursivity.

Each of the interdiscursivities is summarised in a proposition in the form of 'measurable constructs' (Eisenhardt 1989, 547) or 'moderatum generalizations' (Williams 2002) which have been concluded from the theory-building process and which can be tested in further research.

12.3.1 Recurrent practices

A closer look at the conclusions of each of the previous Chapters yields that there are several processes recurring in the analysis of more than one of the four Strands. These are summarised in the following paragraphs as guiding principles of an alternative theory of corporate communication based on the Intech case.

Implementation of stakeholder thinking

Conclusions from the analysis of all four Strands suggest that developing a sense of 'stakeholder thinking' (Näsi 1995) helps to embed communication practices in context. This goes beyond treating stakeholders as 'target groups' – the term frequently used in orthodox corporate communication theory – and means to understand the communicational aspects in the interaction with stakeholders, i.e. that stakeholders are not only consumers of information, but active participants in an interaction with members of the company, both contributing to and constraining communication practices. An example analysed at Intech were processes of auto-communication (Cheney, Christensen et al. 2004) which need to be considered in identity and branding-related communication. Rather than assuming interest in all messages put forward in corporate communication discourse, important themes should be worked out together with stakeholders.

Stakeholder thinking also means the integration of stakeholders in ongoing communication processes and giving them voice. 'Full participation' is the key word (Chakravarthy 1996). The Intech case shows that participation is possible and necessary at several levels, e.g. in the form of peer group networking when it comes to transforming decisions into action during strategy implementation processes (Strand 2). On the one hand, involving stakeholders from outside and inside the company was successful in the process of negotiating the issue of work conditions in Germany (Strand 4). On the other, viewing employees as stakeholders in their communication processes with team leaders, giving employees voice in this process and increasing the focus of that communication on discussions around the business concept contribute to the construction of a much stronger identity (Strand 1).

As the analysis of Strand 3 has shown, participation does not necessarily mean following the aim of one common consensus, but also accepting a multiplicity of voices. This goes beyond participation as 'sharing' practices, and includes working together towards meanings and solutions. Involving stakeholders by giving them voice also increases the likelihood that distinctive competencies of the company are shaped in this process. This was one of the findings of the analysis of Strand 4.

Real involvement of stakeholders, including the allocation of voice, including full participation and collaboration on joint solutions cannot solely be achieved by transporting messages from the company to its target groups via mediated vehicles as suggested in orthodox corporate communication theories. Instead, a redefinition of target groups as stakeholders and implementation of stakeholder thinking are necessary.

- **Proposition 1 (Participation[40]):**
  Implementing stakeholder thinking in corporate communication theory means to acknowledge the maxim of full participation and to accept the notion of stakeholders as active participants, i.e. both contributing to and constraining communication practices.

Understanding complexities

The analysis of all Strands of interrelations provided evidence that communication practices at Intech not only occurred in a highly context-sensitive way, but also produced highly context-sensitive reactions with all participants. Conclusions of the analysis of all four Strands showed that

---

[40] The terms displayed in brackets after each proposition are the terms used to identify each proposition in the integrated framework of strategy and communication practices developed below.

this makes it necessary to understand communication – in both its symbolic and substantive forms – at a much more local and, therefore, deeper level than orthodox theories suggest (Alvesson 2002).

Again some examples: Identity at Intech (Strand 1) was formed in a communication process involving both symbolic and substantive contents. To fully contribute to such processes, communication should not only understand the symbolic world of the company – the major domain of orthodox communication – but also the business concept of the company and its local application. In the process of an issue selling approach to change (Strand 3), it first needs to be understood how managers in a local context will receive the overall issue before appropriate communication structures can be set up. When looking at Strand 4 it is crucial to understand how issue communication, branding, competitive position and distinctive competencies interrelate in a concrete company context and how individual stakeholders create meaning embedded in that context.

With these processes of meaning-making happening locally, it can be concluded that corporate communication needs not only to focus on the aggregation of simple symbols for the company, but also needs to understand as much as possible of the complexity of communication at the very local level. This means 'down-to-earth' work in continuous processes of deconstructing the company's context and its substantive elements in addition to its symbolic features. At the same time communication managers need to understand how actions and structures interrelate, a framework for which was provided, for example, by Jarzabkowski (2003).

By taking this hard road, it is possible for managed communication to appeal to what people in business consider as important and meaningful. Strong identity can be achieved when local communication becomes coherent. Decisions can be turned into actions when their local application becomes meaningful.

- **Proposition 2 (Context):**
  Communication practices occur in a highly context-sensitive fashion and, at the same time, produce highly context-sensitive reactions.

- **Proposition 3 (Understanding):**
  Due to their context-sensitivity, communication practices need to be managed from a local lens, i.e. communication managers need to get involved in an ongoing deconstruction of the company's substance and symbols in order to gain deep understanding of what stakeholders consider as important and meaningful.

Gaining legitimacy

Another principle that applied to Intech, derived from the earlier analyses, is that communication unfolds only a very limited proportion of its performative capacity if it is applied as a panacea rather than a process legitimising and enacting the company. In other words, it is not the quantity of communication that needs to be increased, but its quality (Stacey 2003). A necessary condition for improving this quality of communication is, that stakeholders, including management, accept that in communicational processes nobody can get away without some sort of legitimisation (Scott and Lane 2000; Deephouse and Carter 2005) or authorization gained from those involved in the communication process[41]. Indeed, processes of exchange with stakeholders support legitimisation 'not necessarily because [stakeholders] believe that [the company] provides specific favourable exchanges, but rather because they see it as being responsive to their larger interests' (Suchman 1995, 578).

Perhaps the most obvious example for this was the communication cascade which was expected to facilitate the implementation of the Intech management system. It stopped on its way down from top management to employees after it had reached middle management. The link of a negotiation phase was missing. Also when it comes to the link of branding and forming identity, this explains why many well-intended branding and identity campaigns fail as 'pseudo events' (Alvesson 1990; Alvesson and Berg 1992; Alvesson 1994). Without passing an authorization test involving forms of negotiation, measures of this kind run the risk of not only being neglected but even being counter-productive in, for example, leading company members to construct notions of negative identification. In this sense, artifacts and symbols, which are used in the process, become automatically part of the identity negotiation process – whether this is intended or not.

It is also argued that these legitimization processes emerge in the form of mainly political processes. In order not to leave legitimisation to chance structures borrowed from federalism (Handy 1992; Handy 1994; Dearlove 2002) may be applied which have passed the 'legitimacy test' of Euro-

---

[41] Deephouse and Carter (2005) particularly refer to the proximities and differences of the terms legitimacy and reputation. While most definitions of legitimacy focus on social acceptance resulting from adherence to norms that qualify a company to exist, most definitions of reputation focus on relative comparisons among companies depending on various attributes. Losing its legitimacy, according to Deephouse and Carter is vital, while 'consequences of lower reputation are less dire' (2005: 351).

pean[42] societies. Also federalism follows the principle of actively facilitating – instead of avoiding – legitimization.

- **Proposition 4 (Legitimising):**
  Applying communicational principles to management includes the consistent implementation of legitimisation processes in corporate communication activities. Contributing to a company's legitimacy needs to be recognized as a major performative capacity of communication.

From containers to practices

A social constructionist review of corporate communication discourse has also proposed to move away from looking singularly at the conduits used towards a full recognition of communication as a practice placed within the triangle of actors, structures and activities (Jarzabkowski 2003). The important point is that conduits in this triangle are only one element of activities or 'genres' (see Chapter 11) which are enacted in the wider context.

The Intech case leads to the suggestion that the focus of attention should move from conduits, i.e. media, towards a much wider range of concrete measures which become part of overall genres of corporate communication. In the Intech case, issue communication and branding (Strand 4) were two of these genres that had been identified.

Thinking in terms of communication practices instead of conduits, however, also helps to better understand Strands 1 to 3. Symbolic management of identity formation (Strand 1), for example, does not need to be limited to design exercises and events on corporate level. Instead, each manager is asked to act according to the symbolic values which are inherent in the company identity. The Intech management system should not only be read about in corporate media (Strand 2), but its relevance should also be discussed in team meetings, and so on.

The argument here is not about replacing or abolishing mediated forms of corporate communication. The point is, however, that the orthodox view has shifted a lot of attention to these apparently comfortable means of getting the message across. 'Fixation' (Taylor, Cooren et al. 1996) remains part of the game, but the pendulum should swing back towards a balance with more communicational forms of communication, i.e. communicational practices based on face-to-face communication, dialogue, negotia-

---

[42] It is argued here that the company structures should fit the cultural aspects of the society the company is embedded in. This is part of the local context of each company. Therefore, a 'global' proposition cannot be made with regards to this part of the research.

tion and so on. In the course of this swing, attention could move from tools to genres and practices.

- **Proposition 5 (Practicing):**
  Focusing communication on conduit instruments – the predominant orthodox view – limits the performative contribution of corporate communication. Instead, viewing corporate communication as a strategic practice enacted in specific genres – e.g. issue communication and branding – helps to understand the performative capacity of communication in both contributing to and limiting organisational advantage to a fuller extent.

In summary, the Intech case showed that all five propositions enable practitioners and researchers to gain deeper understanding of the performative capacity of corporate communication than orthodox theories have provided thus far. This suggests that an alternative corporate communication theory may be appropriate which incorporates these propositions.

This alternative view opens many new opportunities for corporate communication managers. At the same time, part of the game is to move away from the comfortable desk – where most container measures were planned – and to drill down into the daily business processes, to get involved in conversations on business, to observe communication measures under continuous scrutiny and to become dissociated from measuring communicational performance in terms of awareness and perceptions to move on to evaluating concrete achievements of communicational practices in business terms. This means acting in a newly enlightened terrain, including a much deeper understanding of its uncertainties and what can go wrong.

12.3.2 Interrelations between practices

Interdiscursivity, defined as 'the forces guiding affiliation between discourses' (Taylor 1999, 62), is not limited to recurrent practices. Another dimension of interdiscursivity can be detected when setting the four Strands of interrelations in relation to each other. It is suggested that two bridges between these four Strands are particularly relevant for integrating the results of the analysis into an overall framework for strategy and communication practices.

Bridging distinctions between purpose and genres

Scott and Lane (2000), as well as Elliott (2004), advanced the notion that processes of identity construction need to be seen in reciprocal relation with other processes and concepts. In developing a view of identity construction in a 'broader context of manager-stakeholder-relationships' (2000, 43), Scott and Lane discuss the attempts of managers to influence the company's identity through corporate and marketing communication. They propose such communication – e.g. by associating the company with 'desired organizational images' through specific themes – prompt stakeholders to elaborate on the company image and to evaluate concurrence with the company's identity (2000, 52). In this, identification with the company can be strengthened as well as diminished through these communication activities. This means that legitimisation processes (Suchman 1995) which had been explained above, are in place as well in this process.

Reviewed from the perspective of the reference framework used for this study, Scott and Lane's propositions confirm Chakravarthy, Müller-Stewens et al.'s (2003) original presumption that the various strategic processes and practices occur in interrelated modes. Transferred to the adapted framework it is argued that also the Strands of interrelation between strategy and communication processes are connected.

In the Intech case, several of these interrelations were observed. The brand charter quoted above, for example, was continuously reviewed at Intech business unit level and, when approved as legitimate and in conformity with local identities, was applied in branding activities. In this concrete example, Strand 1 (identity and identification), Strand 2 (legitimisation) and Strand 4 (branding) were involved.

For corporate communication theory and practice this means that practices related to each Strand continuously need to be monitored in the context of the other Strands – and that an integrated perspective on corporate communicating includes bridging the differences between purpose (including identity) and genres (including branding). For example, if a branding activity (Strand 4) is planned, existing identities (Strand 1) can constrain (Kogut and Zander 1996) the range of symbols that would be accepted in the legitimisation process (Strand 2). If new symbols are used, managers and employees might not understand them, and, therefore, obstruct their communication in customer relationships (Strand 3). The reviewed framework below reflects on these interrelationships.

- **Proposition 6 (Identification):**
  Processes of identification of stakeholders with the company occur primarily based on the interrelationship between Strands 1 and 4 of the reference framework, i.e. managing the purpose of the company and the

genres applied in corporate communication activities. Identification with the company can be strengthened or diminished by both purpose (i.e. business concept and identity) and genres (i.e. issue communication and branding).

Bridging modes of organizing

The notion of viewing ongoing processes as constructing a company leads back to Karl Weick (1979). He proposed 'that there are processes which create, maintain, and dissolve social collectivities, that these processes constitute the work of organizing, and that the ways in which these processes are continuously executed are organization' (1979, 1). One of the implications is that the organisation needs to be continuously reconstructed in order to maintain its existence (Chakravarthy and White 2002; Chakravarthy, Müller-Stewens et al. 2003). It has been argued in earlier Chapters of this study that strategy (Whittington and Melin 2003), communication (Varey and White 2000) and interrelations of strategy and communication practices can be viewed as performative processes in this ongoing game.

Decision and actions are commonly defined as 'core elements of the strategy process' (Chakravarthy and White 2002, 187). In the terminology of this study, decisions and actions are covered as part of Strand 2 – 'Organising by linking decisions and actions' – and Strand 3 – 'Facilitating implementation and change processes'. The performative capacity of communication in this interrelation focused on mediating the way strategy was transformed into action. As examples in the Intech case have shown, communication could both enable and constrain this transformation.

It is argued that similar to Strands 1 and 4, there is also an interrelation between Strands 2 and 3. In the Intech case this was mirrored by the focus on discourse related to the implementation of the Intech management system. Meaning creation (Strand 2) was necessary in order to transform strategy into action and change (Strand 3); as part of Strand 3, also understanding with regards to actors, structures and change activities was facilitated which influenced the legitimisation process (Strand 2). Therefore, it is suggested that Strand 2 and Strand 3 act as reciprocal modes of organising which again need to be bridged in the reviewed framework.

- **Proposition 7 (Modes of organising):**
  Processes of meaning creation and of facilitating change – represented by Strands 2 and 3 in the reference framework – are two interrelated modes of organising. Communication in these processes primarily unfolds performative capacity by putting strategy into action.

12.4 Towards an alternative theory of corporate communication

Throughout the previous Sections of this Chapter interdiscursivities in the form of recurrent practices and interrelations between practices were identified. The challenge now is to propose a revised framework for strategy and communication practices that illustrates these interdiscursivities in addition to the results of the analyses of individual Strands of interrelations.

This will, first, be achieved by having a bird's eye-view on what happened at Intech – aggregated in the above propositions. This results in a revised definition of corporate communication. Second, an integrated framework of alternative corporate communication is displayed, expressing the aggregated results which had been derived throughout this study.

Summarising the seven Propositions advanced above, the following alternative definition of corporate communication, reflecting both discourse and practice paradigms, is proposed:

- **Alternative definition of corporate communication:**
  Corporate communication is a mode of managing in which communicational principles are applied in context. Corporate communication practices, as the main way of conducting corporate communication, unleash performative capacities in ongoing interactions with stakeholders.

The key concepts highlighted in this definition are: the acknowledgement of corporate communication as a mode of managing rather than a management function; the various communicational principles that apply in corporate communication activities; a strong focus on viewing corporate communication as practices, taking place in context, and generating performative capacity in ongoing interactions with stakeholders.

In moving forward to developing an integrated framework of corporate communication, it is referred back to Eisenhardt (1989). Following this approach to building theory from case studies, in previous Chapters constructs of each Strand of interrelations between strategy and communication processes were built. As part of this, evidence for having measured the respective construct in the form of a set of discourse fragments from the original data was provided. This was an iterative process moving back and forth between primary data and extant theory (Eisenhardt 1989; Watson 1997; Weick 2003), brought together in the conclusions of each of the analysis Chapters. In the subsequent interdiscursive analyses, these conclusions were further aggregated in the above propositions.

Figure 19 summarises all these findings in a single chart. It is a further development of the adapted reference framework which was proposed in

Figure 17 – and which has been developed gradually throughout this study. All strategy and communication practices are embedded in the context of the company. The interrelations of strategy and communication practices represented by Strand 1 to 4 were confirmed during fieldwork and explained in depth. Interdiscursivity analysis led to the advancement of seven propositions (see Chapter 12) which further help to explain the interrelations between the four Strands.

The suggestion based on the Intech case is that stakeholders need to have the opportunity to fully participate in communication. This is a precondition for communication being able to reveal its performative capacity. Identification with the company emerges primarily from the interrelations of managing purpose (Strand 1) and organisational advantage (Strand 4). Communication contributes to core modes of organising (Strands 2 and 3) by facilitating processes of putting strategy into action.

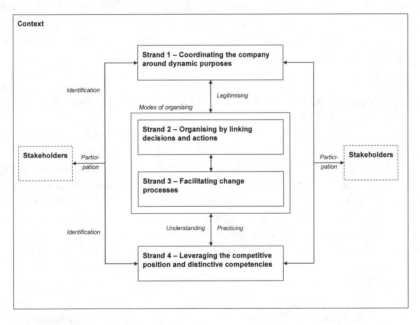

Fig. 19. Integrated framework of alternative corporate communication

These modes of organising need to involve legitimisation of the company, i.e. the authorization of the company's purpose in the eyes of the stakeholders. Evidence from the Intech case also led to the conclusion that communication unfolds its full performative capacity above all in local context and that, therefore, corporate communication should occur in an ongoing mode of practicing rather than in communication conduits.

12.5 Achievements in terms of theory-building

It is recalled at this stage of the study that the overall purpose of the study consisted of three aspects. Each of the three following sections summarises the achievements with regards to one aspect of purpose.

The first aspect of purpose is related to exploring the gap between orthodox corporate communication theory and management theories considering the linguistic and practice turns in social theory. As the individual analysis Chapters have shown, there is a clear need for such an alternative corporate communication theory, providing an integrated view of how corporate communication discourse unfolds its performative capacity.

The achievements in terms of theory-building towards an alternative corporate communication theory can be stated from three viewpoints: (1) the gaps between orthodox and alternative corporate communication theories, (2) the propositions that were developed for an integrated framework of alternative corporate communication, and (3) a contrast between key elements of orthodox and alternative corporate communication theories which can be derived from the study.

12.5.1 Review of orthodox corporate communication theory

Based on the analysis of each Strand of interrelations, individual aspects of orthodox corporate communication theory were reviewed. This review resulted in further explanations of each individual Strand, in individual gaps that were identified, and in a summarising figure for the communicational explanation of each Strand. Key conclusions with regards to an alternative corporate communication theory are: (1) a deeper understanding of the complexity of discourse focusing on business concept and identity, including the detection of a need for more substance in corporate communication and an increased focus on processes of negotiating identity (Strand 1, see Section 8.5); (2) the importance of giving decisions voice in corporate communication processes, of facilitating legitimisation processes, and of moving on from cascading to leveraging the capacity of communication (Strand 2, see Section 9.5); (3) clarity that needs to be gained in terms of understanding intention and structures before planning change processes, and full participation which needs to be ensured throughout change processes (Strand 3, see Section 10.5); (4) the recognition of stakeholders as sources of competence in branding and issue communication and of communication platforms as hubs for creating organisational advantage (Strand 4, see Section 11.5).

12.5.2 Propositions for an integrated framework of alternative corporate communication

In Chapter 12, these individual aspects of an alternative corporate communication theory have been further analysed with regards to interdiscursivities. This analysis produced seven Propositions: (1) the maxim of full participation for stakeholders, (2) an increased attention to context, (3) the requirement for local understanding, and (4) for the implementation of legitimisation processes in corporate communication activities, (5) the release of performative capacity by managing corporate communication as a strategic practice enacted in specific genres, (6) the interrelations between Strand 1 and 4 in identification processes, and (7) the interrelations between Strand 2 and 3 as modes of organising. Section 12.4 ended up by integrating these Propositions into one model and by suggesting an integrated framework of alternative corporate communication.

12.5.3 Contrasting orthodox and alternative corporate communication theory

Implications and contribution of the study can most visibly be demonstrated by summarising the key propositions underlying the alternative view of corporate communication which have been developed throughout this study in contrast to orthodox corporate communication theory as laid out in the introductory Chapters. Table 16 displays such an attempt of contrasting the alternative view of corporate communication that was identified in this study. Though remaining on a simplistic level, it points out some of the key differences between both approaches.

Table 16. Orthodox and alternative view of corporate communication

Orthodox view of corporate communication	Alternative view of corporate communication as identified in the study
Communication as container	Communication as performative process
Functional definition of corporate communication	Communicational definition of corporate communication
Context-influenced	Context-embedded
Top-down management and control	Local adaptation
Two-way communication	Participation and negotiation
Informing	Sensemaking and legitimization
Symbolic communication	Additionally substantive communication
Focus on mediated communication	Additional focus on face-to-face communication
Campaigns and programmes	Ongoing processes

Not only are the container view and the subsequent functional definition of corporate communication contrasted with a performative view leading to a communicational definition of corporate communication. Instead of viewing context as a factor influencing elements such as image and positioning, the whole system of corporate communication was reviewed as embedded in a context consisting of actors, structures and activities (Jarzabkowski 2003). Rather than integrating corporate communication top-down (Bruhn 2003), integration – achieved in both 'continuity and change' (Normann 2001) – was observed as happening primarily in local adaptation of company-wide concepts. Although processes of mere two-way communication were observed, the performative capacity of communication was increased when enacted of processes embracing open negotiation and 'full' participation (Chakravarthy 1996). Similarly, understanding at Intech was regularly not gained from purely receiving information, but in processes of sensemaking and legitimisation. With these processes primarily happening in face-to-face communication, the alternative view of corporate communication also draws some of the attention away from the symbolic and mediated forms of communication as well as the thinking in campaigns and programmes dominating in the orthodox model. Instead, rather the ongoing processes of communication, performed in direct interaction between shareholders are highlighted.

In simple terms, the resulting alternative theory of corporate communication does not completely question the relevance of aspects inherent in the orthodox view, but it provides a much richer picture of performative capacities and it helps to shed light on ongoing processes which cannot be prevented by conduit communication.

12.6 Achievements in terms of understanding

The second aspect of purpose referred to gaining a deeper understanding of how corporate communication discourse unfolds its performative capacity in the form of strategic practices. This was resolved by relating the understanding gained in the analysis of each Strand back to the original reference framework (see Chapter 4).

Based on that, a new, integrated framework was proposed which enables researchers to review corporate communication in light of the findings of this study. Additionally, it puts practitioners into the position to work towards more performative types of corporate communication practice.

Two specific aspects of the achievements gained in terms of understanding are highlighted in the following paragraphs: (1) the degree of detail gained in terms of being able to explain the performative capacity of corporate communication, and (2) the use-value that was reached by achieving a high level of detail in the explanations.

12.6.1 Performative capacity of corporate communication

Starting point for this study was a critique of orthodox corporate communication theory which views corporate communication primarily as a management function (see Chapter 2). This limited view hides the performative capacity of corporate communication away in a black box. Several aspects of this black box were cleared up throughout this study: (1) By viewing corporate communication as discourse and as a strategic practice, it was possible to focus this study on the performative capacity of corporate communication (see Chapter 2); (2) four Strands of corporate communication were identified along which the performative capacity of corporate communication unfolded in the Intech case (see Chapter 4), and themes and discourses related to each of these Strands were analysed and explained in detail (see Chapters 8 to 11); in addition, (3) interrelations between these Strands were analysed in significant detail (see Chapter 12).

This made it possible to explain the performative capacity of corporate communication at Intech on several levels: (1) a general qualification of the performative capacity, (2) an explanation of the performative capacity related to each Strand, and (3) a description of how each Strand influenced other Strands – and, in this, the other Strands' performative capacities.

12.6.2 Use-value of findings

Having achieved this degree of detail with regards to understanding the performative capacity of corporate communication also leads to a high degree of use-value of the findings.

Focusing on performative capacity revealed that corporate communication campaigns and programmes can, for example, be as well-planned and rhetorically fine-tuned as they want – these programmes and campaigns alone are not able to elude the principles stated in the alternative view. The examples given in the individual analysis Chapters are manifold. Just to repeat some: Image events may be well-intended, but processes of identification happen irrespective of the intentions in peoples' minds. An elaborated communication cascade may be in place, but middle managers often do not pass the ideas of top management on to employees if they do not consider this as relevant. On the other hand, even if processes of negotiation with stakeholders are often painful, examples demonstrated that negotiation leads to concrete results in issue communication.

A key aspect of use-value of this study, therefore, is that several phenomena were explained which would otherwise have remained locked in the black box of orthodox theory. This was achieved by viewing corporate communication as embedded in context and as an ongoing process at the same time. The former helped to understand the mutual relationship between context and corporate communication, i.e. communication shapes and is also shaped by context. The latter focused on understanding that communication never stops and continuously unfolds performative capacity – whether the corporate communication function participates or not. Practitioners need to be aware of this.

Practical use-value of the alternative theory can also be found in the Propositions which were advanced in the previous Chapter and which can be implemented gradually in ongoing corporate communication processes.

In summary, the understanding gained throughout this study leads to a conceptual device in the form of the integrated framework of corporate communication. It can be used as a template for assessing corporate communication processes and performative capacity of corporate communication in other companies. The advantages of such frameworks were outlined by Cornelissen and Lock (2005) as follows:

'Conceptual devices, as precursors of formal substantive theory, in particular, offer considerable scope for conceptual use within practitioner settings…, because they give great latitude to practitioners in selecting, redefining, altering, combining and generally reinterpreting substantive theory and the declarative knowledge that it contains to fit a wide variety of circumstances and purposes.'
(Cornelissen and Lock 2005, 175)

12.7 Achievements in terms of practical implications

This builds a direct link to the third aspect of purpose, i.e. to drawing practical lessons from both theory-building and understanding – in other words, the actual question of practical implications and contribution resulting from this research project.

According to Cornelissen and Lock (2005, 178), the strength of the link between a theory and its utilisation depends on four moderator variables:

1. 'operational quality' of a theory,
2. its 'goal relevance',
3. 'its descriptive relevance', and
4. its 'timeliness'.

Based on the degree of detail achieved in the integrated framework of alternative corporate communication, which is proposed in this study, it is argued that a high degree of operational quality was achieved. Corporate communication managers are provided with a conceptual tool against which they can benchmark their activities and which they can apply to better understand how their activities unfold performative capacity.

It is also argued that goal relevance – 'the correspondence of outcome variables in a theory to factors and issues that practitioners wish to influence' (2005, 178) – is achieved because, for example, the four Strands of interrelations between strategy and communication practices, which were detected and explained above, address issues that are crucial for the success of every communication activity. Putting strategy into action is generally a key objective of internal communication activities, and the integrated framework provides a detailed account of the possible contribution of corporate communication to this.

Descriptive relevance of the integrative framework, in the case of this study, is closely related to operational quality, and the thematic and discourse analyses conducted in Chapters 8 to 11 allow for a high degree of detail and accuracy in terms of explanation of the four Strands of interrelations.

Finally, timeliness of the subject studied, was illustrated in detail in Chapter 2, based on the recent challenges for corporate communication managers.

In conclusion, the study has highlighted some of the critical points in corporate communication practice – although the purpose of this study was not to critique corporate communication practices at Intech. On the contrary, given the extant theories of corporate communication, much of the corporate communication work done at Intech's corporate communication departments can be viewed as 'best-practice'.

It is argued, however, that existing theory only covers part of the picture and that there is much more to corporate communication than purely transporting information.

The good news, then, is that corporate communication managers can make decisions to consider and implement the propositions which were developed as constituting the alternative corporate communication theory. Even more, communication managers have to make a fundamental decision as to whether they want to manage their function in a communicational way or not. It can even be concluded that taking a decision 'pro' alternative corporate communication is a requirement for getting the opportunity to unleash the full performative capacity of corporate communication.

From a practical viewpoint, it may be argued, however, that there are some downsides associated with such a decision as well. First of all, and this has been argued before, performative capacity can generally work in more than one direction: it can support intentions of management, but it can also cause the opposite. Even when applying all principles of alternative corporate communication, members of the corporate communication department are not the only stakeholders in the process. Other stakeholders communicate likewise and unfold their performative capacities. Given the complexity of these processes, intended outcomes are not guaranteed.

While this argument holds for all communication activities, it remains that communication plays a much stronger role according to the alternative view. Increasing the importance of the communication function has been an issue in orthodox corporate communication theory for a long time (Grunig, Grunig et al. 2002). It is argued that understanding and acknowledging corporate communication as a key mode of organising helps practitioners to move forward in this effort. In other words: this will require corporate communication managers themselves to 'recognize the corporate communication managing system as central to the work of the enterprise community' (Varey and White 2000, 6).

A second alleged downside remains. The alternative view shifts the focus of communication from conduits to ongoing processes. This will involve much more down-to-earth work, in both continuously deconstructing the terms of what is 'really' happening and also shifting resources from project and campaign-based communication to ongoing, face-to-face processes of two-way communication. What Whittington had stated for strategists, then, also applies to communicators; 'Everyday continuity is not merely passive, but involves effortful achievement' (2002, 129).

In summary, it is claimed that all aspects of the purpose of this study were fulfilled – i.e. to contribute to an alternative corporate communication theory in concrete terms, to gain understanding of how corporate communication discourse unfolds its performative capacity and to draw practical lessons from both theory-building and understanding.

12.8 Methodological review

This Section of the study leads back to the methodological discussions.

Drawing on Weick (1987, 102), theory was defined as 'an inference from data that is offered as a formula to explain that abstract and general principle that lies behind them as their cause, their method of operation, or their relation to other phenomena.'

The critical term, from a methodological viewpoint, in this definition is 'inference', because it involves issues of generalization – at least if the term is followed back to its positivist roots. In this research tradition, Kaplan (1964, 91) pointed out that 'generalization must be truly universal, unrestricted as to time and space. It must formulate what is always and everywhere the case, provided only that the appropriate conditions are satisfied.' According to this definition, generalizations are both 'enduring' and 'context-free', which has been criticized as problematic with regards to qualitative research, leading to the conclusion that generalizations are not possible at all in interpretive research (Lincoln and Guba 2000).

As Williams (2002, 130) pointed out, however, 'interpretivists *do*[43] generalize' – and it is also generalized in this study, as the set of propositions derived in Chapter 12 show. It is a different concept of generalization than the positivist one, though. Williams (2002) uses the term 'moderatum generalizations' to identify such 'generalizations of everyday life'. It is this sort of rather 'propositional and experiential knowledge' (Stake 2003, 145) which is also meant by the Propositions in Chapter 12.

Williams (2002) argues further that also the sampling issue, i.e. defining the focus of investigation, which is a crucial aspect for positivist generalization, needs to be reviewed in interpretive research. He draws on Znaniecki's (1934) notion of analytic induction which 'implicitly sidesteps the sampling issue by first testing a hypothesis on a single or limited range of cases and continuing to do this until a disconforming case is found, or until the point is reached when further study will tell us nothing new' (Williams 2002, 133). According to Williams, in these inductive approaches to generalization, the problem remains inherent that only those cases are studied in which the phenomenon occurs.

Following Jäger (2001; Jäger 2004), this problem is resolved in discourse theory in which the individual is defined as a social being which constitutes and is constituted in discourse. Viewing the individual in such a way, according to Jäger, neutralizes the separation between quantity and quality which is made in positivist research. The task of generalizations is not any more one of drawing conclusions based on a sufficiently large sample, but one of closing the gap between an individual discourse fragment – representing an extract of the social world – and the social world as such. This involves the question of determining qualitative completeness rather than quantitative completeness. The task becomes to record a complete body of discourses and themes. According to Jäger (2004, 209), this is achieved when the analysis of further discourse fragments does not reveal any new aspects.

---

[43] Emphasis added.

The researcher argues that the analysis of corporate communication discourse at Intech reached this level of completeness primarily through its rigorous process of data collection, documentation and analysis: (1) The researcher had the opportunity to participate in all events and had access to all corporate communication documents at Intech which were relevant according to the situational definition of the case (Alvesson and Deetz 2000), i.e. the implementation of the Intech management system, (2) all discourse was documented in the CAQDAS software, coded and analysed along the four Strands of interrelated strategy and communication processes, and (3) discourse fragments were analysed until completeness according to Jäger's (2001; 2004) criteria was reached – both in terms of a stocktaking of themes in thematic analysis and in terms of analysing the construction of themes in the actual discourse analysis.

Williams (2002, 136), in his account of moderatum generalizations, similarly refers to interpretation as 'text centred'.

If cultural consistency between researcher and the ones researched can be assumed, he concludes:

'We are attempting to describe the reality of the people we investigate. That the accounts produced are more than a 'story' or a 'text' is verifiable by those investigated, but it is more than this. Those 'realities' as experienced are often the outcomes of processes, the evidence of structures existing beyond the individuals investigated ... If characteristics point to particular structures in one situation, then one can hypothesize that the existence of such structures in a further situation will lead to at least some similar characteristics.' (Williams 2002, 138)

The propositions made in this concluding Chapter point to interdiscursive structures which occurred in the Intech case, but which were additionally sounded in theory, i.e. in the iterative theory-building process suggested by Weick (2003).

In the sense of moderatum generalizations, the researcher advocates that the conclusions of this study do not provide a definite story (Alvesson and Kärreman 2000). They are limited in the sense that they were developed from a reference framework which had been chosen as an inductive entry point and that they have been analysed in the specific context of a large conglomerate, namely Intech. But they can serve as 'testable evidence' (Williams 2002, 139) for further research on corporate communication discourse.

12.9 Suggestions for further research

Based on a single case – Intech – important issues of an alternative corporate communication theory were pulled out in the preceding Chapters. Apart from the insights into the four Strands of interrelations gained in Chapters 8 to 11, these concentrate on the seven Propositions made in Chapter 12, leading to a new, integrated framework of alternative corporate communication (see Figure 19).

The case for an alternative theory of corporate communication was made in this study. The value of this contribution, however, will emerge and gain in its actual use and refinement.

Researchers may adopt the alternative view of corporate communication proposed in the integrated framework and test or apply it in further case studies or in more large-scale, perhaps quantitatively oriented research projects across companies or even cultural boundaries.

Each of the four Strands proposed in the integrated framework of alternative corporate communication can form the basis for such studies. These may focus on validating the importance of the themes and performative discourses proposed Chapters 8 to 11 with regards to coordinating the company around dynamic purposes (Strand 1), organising by linking decisions and action (Strand 2), facilitating change processes (Strand 3), and leveraging the competitive position and distinctive competencies (Strand 4). This way, additional themes and discourses, which were not relevant in the Intech case, can be identified, and the relative importance of the themes and discourses put forward in this study can be validated.

Additionally, the seven Propositions put forward in Chapter 12 provide a framework for validation. Recurrent practices, like implementing stakeholder thinking and gaining legitimacy, as well as interrelations between practices, e.g. bridging distinctions between purpose and genres or bridging modes of organising, can form the starting point for further studies.

Alternative approaches might be to conduct similar case studies in smaller companies in order to identify issues related to size or in other countries in order to explore cultural aspects. Other studies might focus on a quantitative validation by testing the themes and discourses put forward in this study in populations of companies representative for a certain range of size (e.g. large multinational conglomerates), specific industries (e.g. the high-tech manufacturers), or regions (e.g. Europe). Gradually, this will lead to an increased sophistication of the integrated framework of alternative corporate communication.

Appendix

Table 17. Word counts for Strand 1 – Coordinating the company around dynamic purposes: business concept theme

Words	Counts	Related generic themes as defined in taxonomy
STRATEGY	99	Strategy
CUSTOMER/CUSTOMERS	79	Strategy
EMPLOYEES/PEOPLE	68	Strategy
FOCUS/FOCUSED	40	Strategy
ACTIVITIES/ASSETS/PORTFOLIO/PRODUCTS	34	Strategy
SUCCESS/SUCCESSFUL	33	Strategy
CONCEPT	23	Strategy
ECONOMIC VALUE-ADDED (EVA)	21	Strategy
VISION	16	Strategy
RESPONSIBILITIES/RESPONSIBILITY/ RESPONSIBLE	15	Strategy
OPPORTUNITIES	14	Strategy
INNOVATION	13	Strategy
GLOBAL	12	Strategy
CAPTIVE/INTERNAL	85	Dualities
GROWTH	53	Dualities
EXTERNAL	52	Dualities
POSITION/POSITIONING	50	Dualities
PROFIT/PROFITABLE/PROFITABILITY	46	Dualities
CHANGE	29	Dualities
BALANCE	16	Dualities
HETEROGENEITY/HETEROGENEOUS	13	Dualities
CONTINUITY	9	Dualities
MARKET	39	Heterogeneity
CHALLENGE/CHALLENGES	29	Heterogeneity
FAMILY/PARENT	24	Heterogeneity
BUSINESS ENVIRONMENT	14	Heterogeneity

Table 18. Word counts for Strand 1 – Coordinating the company around dynamic purposes: identity theme

Words	Counts	Related generic themes as defined in taxonomy
CULTURAL/CULTURE	105	Culture
CHANGE	65	Culture
VALUES/PRINCIPLES	117	Values
IDENTITY	52	All
ORGANISATION	49	All
EMPLOYEES/PEOPLE	142	All
CUSTOMER/CUSTOMERS	88	All
MANAGERS/MANAGEMENT	75	All

References

Aaker DA (1996) Building strong brands. New York, The Free Press

Aberg L (1990) Theoretical model and praxis of total communications. International Public Relations Review 13(2), pp 13-16

Achtenhagen L, Melin L (2003) Managing the homogeneity-heterogeneity duality. In: Pettigrew AM, Whittington R, Melin L et al (eds) Innovative forms of organizing. London, SAGE Publications, pp 301-327

Achtenhagen L, Melin L, Müllern T, et al. (2003) Leadership: the role of interactive strategizing. In: Pettigrew AM, Whittington R, Melin L et al (eds) Innovative forms of organizing. London, SAGE Publications, pp 49-71

Ackroyd S, Thompson P (1999) Organizational *mis*behaviour. London, Sage Publications

Adler P, Adler P (1994) Observational techniques. In: Denzin NK and Lincoln YS (eds) Handbook of qualitative research. Thousand Oaks, SAGE Publications, pp 377-392

Aguinis H (1993) Action research and scientific method: presumed discrepancies and actual similarities. Journal of Applied Behavioral Science 29(4), pp 416-431

Ainsworth S, Hardy C (2004) Discourse and identity. In: Grant D, Hardy C, Oswick C and Putnam LL (eds) The SAGE handbook of organizational discourse. London, SAGE Publications, pp 153-173

Albert S, Whetten DA (1985) Organizational identity. In: Cummings LL and Staw BM (eds) Research in organizational behaviour. Greenwich, JAI Press, Vol. 7, pp 263-295

Albert S (1998) The definition and metadefinition of identity. In: Whetten DA and Godfrey PC (eds) Identity in organizations: building theory through conversations. Thousand Oaks, SAGE Publications, pp 1-13

Albert S, Ashforth BE, Dutton JE (2000) Organizational identity and identification: charting new waters and building new bridges. Academy of Management Review 25(1), pp 13-17

Allen BJ (2005) Social constructionism. In: May S and Mumby DK (eds) Engaging organizational communication: theory & research. Thousand Oaks, SAGE Publications, pp 35-53

Allen G (2000) Intertextuality: the new critical idiom. London, Routledge

Altrichter H, Kemmis S, McTaggart R, et al. (2002) The concept of action research. The Learning Organization 9(3), pp 125-132

Alvesson M (1990) Organization: from substance to image? Organization Studies 11(3), pp 373-394

Alvesson M, Berg PO (1992) Corporate culture and organizational symbolism: an overview. Berlin, Walter de Gruyter

Alvesson M (1994) Managing identity and impressions in an advertising agency. Organization Studies 15(4), pp 535-563

Alvesson M, Deetz S (2000) Doing critical management research. London, SAGE Publications

Alvesson M, Kärreman D (2000) Varieties of discourse: on the study of organizations through discourse analysis. Human Relations 53(9), pp 1125-1149

Alvesson M (2002) Understanding organizational culture. London, SAGE Publications

Andersen NA (2000) Public market - political firms. Acta Sociologica 43, pp 43-61

Antaki C, Billig M, Edwards D, et al (2003) Discourse analysis means doing analysis: a critique of six analytic shortcomings. Discourse Analysis Online 1(1)

Argenti J (1997) Stakeholders: the case against. Long Range Planning 30(3), pp 442-445

Argenti PA (1997) Corporate communication. New York, Irwin/McGraw-Hill

Argenti PA (2003) Corporate communication. New York, McGraw-Hill/Irwin

Argenti PA, Howell RA, Beck KA (2005) The strategic communication imperative. MIT Sloan Management Review 46(3), pp 82-89

Ashforth BE, Mael FA (1996) Organizational identity and strategy as context for the individual. Advances in Strategic Management 13, pp 19-64

Ashkenas RN, Jick TD (1992) From dialogue to action in GE work-out. Research in Organizational Change and Development 6, pp 267-287

Auer P (1999) Sprachliche Interaktion: eine Einführung anhand von 22 Klassikern. Tübingen, Max Niemeyer Verlag

Baecker D (2000) Mit der Hierarchie gegen die Hierarchie. In: Hejl PM and Stahl HK (eds) Management und Wirklichkeit: das Konstruieren von Unternehmen, Märkten und Zukunften. Heidelberg, Carl-Auer-Systeme, pp 235-264

Baecker D (2003) Organisation und Management. Frankfurt, Suhrkamp Verlag

Balmer JMT, Greyser SA (eds) (2003) Revealing the corporation: perspectives on identity, image, reputation, corporate branding, and corporate-level marketing. London, Routledge

Balogun J, Huff AS, Johnson P (2003) The responses to the methodological challenges of studying strategizing. Journal of Management Studies 40(1), pp 197-224

Banerjee B, Browne M, Fulop L, et al (2004) Managing strategically. In: Linstead S, Fulop L and Lilley S (eds) Management and organization: a critical text. Basingstoke, Palgrave Macmillan, pp 495-538

Barbasi A-L (2002) Linked - the new science of networks. Cambridge, MA, Perseus Publishing

Bargiela-Chiappini F (2004) Introduction: reflections on a new research paradigm. International Journal of the Sociology of Language (166), pp 1-18

Barney JB, Stewart AC (2000) Organizational identity as moral philosophy: competitive implications for diversified corporations. In: Schultz M, Hatch MJ and Larsen MH (eds) The expressive organization: linking identity, reputation and corporate brand. Oxford, Oxford University Press, pp 36-47

Barrett FJ, Thomas GF, Hocevar SP (1995) The central role of discourse in large-scale change: a social construction perspective. Journal of Applied Behavioral Science 31(3), pp 352-372

Barry D, Elmes M (1997) Strategy retold: toward a narrative view of strategy discourse. Academy of Management Review 22(2), pp 429-452

Bengtsson A (2003) Towards a critique of brand relationships. Advances in Consumer Research 30, pp 154-158

Berger PL, Luckmann T (1966) The social construction of reality. Garden City, NY, Doubleday

Blackler F (1993) Knowledge and the theory of organizations: organizations as activity systems and the reframing of management. Journal of Management Studies 30(6), pp 863-884

BOAG (2000) Wirklichkeitsprüfung: eine sozial-konstruktivistische Forschungsperspektive für die Psychologie. Bochum, Bochumer Arbeitskreis für sozialen Konstruktivismus und Wirtklichkeitsprüfung, Arbeitspapier Nr. 10: 1-39.

Boden D (1994) The business of talk. Cambridge, Polity Press

Boje DM (2001) Narrative methods for organizational and communication research. London, SAGE Publications

Boje DM, Oswick C, Ford JD (2004) Language and organization: the doing of discourse. Academy of Management Journal 29(4), pp 571-577

Brewer JD (2000) Ethnography. Buckingham, Open University Press

Broadfoot K, Deetz S, Anderson D (2004) Multi-levelled, multi-method approaches in organizational discourse. In: Grant D, Hardy C, Oswick C and Putnam LL (eds) The SAGE handbook of organizational discourse. London, SAGE Publications, pp 193-211

Broich U, Pfister M (1985) Intertextualität: Formen, Funktionen, anglistische Fallstudien. Tübingen, Niemeyer

Brown A (1998) Narrative, politics and legitimacy in an IT implementation. Journal of Management Studies 35(1), pp 35-57

Bruhn M (2003) Integrierte Unternehmens- und Markenkommunikation. Stuttgart, Schäffer-Poeschel Verlag

Brunsson N (1982) The irrationality of action and action rationality: decisions, ideologies and organizational actions. Journal of Management Studies 19(1), pp 29-44

Brunsson N (1985) The irrational organization: irrationality as a basis for organizational action and change. Chichester, John Wiley & Sons

Brunsson N (1990) Deciding for responsibility and legitimation: alternative interpretations of organizational decision-making. Accounting, Organizations and Society 15, pp 47-59

Brunsson N, Olsen JP (1998) Organization theory: thirty years of dismantling, and then? In: Brunsson N and Olsen JP (eds) Organizing organizations. Bergen-Sandviken, Fakbokforlaget, pp 13-43

Bryant M, Cox JW (2004) Conversion stories as shifting narratives of organizational change. Journal of Organizational Change 17(6), pp 578-592

Bryman A (2001) Social research methods. Oxford, Oxford University Press

Buttle FA (1995) Marketing communication theory: what do the texts teach our students? International Journal of Advertising 14, pp 297-313

Castaner X, Ketokivi M, 2004. Promoting convergent organizational priorities: tensions and complementarities among integrative mechanisms. Paper presented at EURAM Conference, May 5th-8th, 2004, St Andrews

Chakravarthy B (1996) The process of transformation: in search of Nirvana. European Management Journal 14(6), pp 529-539

Chakravarthy B, Müller-Stewens G, Lorange P, et al. (2003) Defining the contours of the strategy process field. In: Chakravarthy B, Mueller-Stewens G, Lorange P and Lechner C (eds) Strategy process: shaping the contours of the field. Oxford, Blackwell Publishing Ltd., pp 1-17

Chakravarthy BS, White RE (2002) Strategy process: forming, implementing and changing strategies. In: Pettigrew A, Thomas H and Whittington R (eds) Handbook of strategy and management. London, SAGE Publications, pp 182-205

Cheney G, Tompkins PK (1988) On the facts of the 'text' as the basis of human communication research. In: Anderson JA (ed) Communication Yearbook 11. Newbury Park, SAGE Publications, pp 455-481

Cheney G, Frenette G (1993) Persuasion and organization: values, logics and accounts in contemporary corporate public discourse. In: Conrad C (ed) Ethical nexus. Norwood, NJ, Ablex, pp 49-73

Cheney G, Mumby DK, Stohl C, et al. (1997) Communication and organizational democracy. Communication Studies 48, pp 277-278

Cheney G, Christensen LT (2001) Public relations as contested terrain: a critical response. In: Heath RL Handbook of public relations. Thousand Oaks, SAGE Publications, pp 167-182

Cheney G, Christensen LT (2001) Organizational identity: linkages between internal and external communication. In: Jablin FM and Putnam LL (eds) The new handbook of organizational communication: advances in theory, research, and methods. Thousand Oaks, SAGE Publications, Inc., pp 231-269

Cheney G, Christensen LT, Zorn TE, et al. (2004) Organizational communication in an age of globalization. Long Grove, Ill., Waveland Press, Inc.

Choo CW (2002) Sensemaking, knowledge creation, and decision making. In: Choo CW and Bontis N (eds) The strategic management of intellectual capital and organizational knowledge. Oxford, Oxford University Press

Christensen LT, Cheney G (2000) Self-absorption and self-seduction in the corporate identity game. In: Schultz M and Larsen MH (eds) The expressive organization: linking identity, reputation, and the corporate brand. Oxford, Oxford University Press, pp 246-270

Christensen LT, Askegaard S (2001) Corporate identity and corporate image revised: a semiotic perspective. European Journal of Marketing 35(3/4), pp 292-315

Christensen LT, Torp S, Firat AF (2005) Integrated marketing communication and postmodernity: an odd couple? Corporate Communications: an international journal 10(2), pp 156-167

Clark C (2000) Differences between public relations and corporate social responsibility: an analysis. Public Relations Review 26(3), pp 363-380

Coffey A (2002) Ethnography and self: reflections and representations. In: May T (eds) Qualitative research in action. London, SAGE Publications, pp 313-331

Coghlan D, Brannick T (2001) Doing action research in your own organization. London, SAGE Publications

Cool K, Costa LA, Dierickx I (2002) Constructing competitive advantage. In: Pettigrew A, Thomas H and Whittington R (eds) Handbook of strategy and management. London, SAGE Publications, pp 55-71

Cooren F (1999) The organizing property of communication. Amsterdam, John Benjamins Publishing Company

Cornelissen J, Lock AR (2000) Theoretical concept of management fashion? Examining the significance of IMC. Journal of Advertising Research (September October), pp 7-15

Cornelissen J (2001) Integrated marketing communications and the language of marketing development. International Journal of Advertising 20, pp 483-498

Cornelissen J, Harris P (2001) The corporate identity metaphor: perspectives, problems and prospects. Journal of Marketing Management 17, pp 49-71

Cornelissen J, Lock AR, Gardner H (2001) The organisation of external communication disciplines: an integrative framework of dimensions and determinants. International Journal of Advertising 20, pp 67-88

Cornelissen J, Thorpe R (2001) The organisation of external communication disciplines in UK companies: a conceptual and empirical analysis of dimensions and determinants. The Journal of Business Communication 38(4), pp 413-438

Cornelissen J (2003) Change, continuity and progress: the concept of integrated marketing communications and marketing communications practice. Journal of Strategic Marketing 11, pp 217-234

Cornelissen J (2004) Corporate communications - theory and practice. London, SAGE Publications

Cornelissen J, Lock AR (2005) The uses of marketing theory: constructs, research propositions, and managerial implications. Marketing Theory 5(2), pp 165-184

Cortazzi M (2001) Narrative analysis in ethnography. In: Atkinson P, Coffey A, Delamont S, Lofland J and Lofland L (eds) Handbook of ethnography. London, SAGE Publications, pp 384-394

Costello N (2000) Stability and change in high-tech enterprises: organisational practices and routines. London, Routledge

Cova B (1996) The postmodern explained to managers: implications for marketing. Business Horizons (November-December), pp 15-23

Crabtree BF, Miller WF (1992) A template approach to text analysis: developing and using codebooks. In: Crabtree BF and Miller WL (eds) Doing qualitative research. Newbury Park, SAGE Publications, Vol. 3, pp 93-109

Cuervo-Cazurra A (2003) Transforming the firm through the co-evolution of re-
sources and scope. In: Chakravarthy B, Müller-Stewens G, Lorange P and
Lechner C (eds) Strategy process: shaping the contours of the field. Oxford,
Blackwell Publishing, pp 18-45

Cunliffe AL (2003) Reflexive inquiry in organizational research: questions and
possibilities. Human Relations 56(8), pp 983-1003

Cutlip SM, Center AH, Broom GM (1985) Effective public relations. Englewood
Cliffs, Prentice-Hall

Czarniawska B (1997) Narrating the organization: dramas of institutional identity.
Chicago, The University of Chicago Press

D'Aprix R (1996) Communicating for change. San Francisco, Jossey-Bass

Daft RL (1983) Learning the craft of organizational research. Academy of Management Review 8, pp 539-546

Davies G, Chun R, Vinhas da Silva R, et al. (2003) Corporate reputation and competitiveness. London, Routledge

de Certeau M (1984) The practice of everyday life. Berkeley, University of California Press

Dearlove D (2002) Reflections of a reluctant capitalist - an interview with Charles
Handy. Business Strategy Review 13(4), pp 64-69

Deephouse DL, Carter SM (2005) An examination of differences between organizational legitimacy and organizational reputation. Journal of Management
Studies 42(2), pp 329-360

Deetz S (1992) Democracy in an age of corporate colonialization: developments
in communication and the politics of everyday life. Albany, State University
of New York Press

Deetz S (1995) Transforming communication, transforming business. Cresskill,
NJ, Hampton Press, Inc.

Deetz S (2001) Conceptual foundations. In: Jablin FM and Putnam LL (eds) The
new handbook of organizational communication. Thousand Oaks, SAGE Publications

Deetz S, Brown D (2004) Conceptualizing involvement, participation and workplace decision processes. In: Tourish D and Hargie O (eds) Key issues in organizational communication. London, Routledge, pp 172-187

Deetz SA (1997) Communication in the age of negotiation. Journal of Communication 47(4), pp 118-135

Deetz SA, Tracy SJ, Simpson JL (2000) Leading organizations through transition:
communication and cultural change. Thousand Oaks, California, Sage Publications, Inc.

Denzin NK (1994) The art and politics of interpretation. In: Denzin NK and Lincoln YS (eds) Handbook of qualitative research. Thousand Oaks, SAGE
Publications, pp 500-515

Diaz-Bone R, Schneider W (2003) Qualitative Datenanalysesoftware in der sozi-
alwissenschaftlichen Diskursanalyse - Zwei Praxisbeispiele. In: Keller R, Hirseland A, Schneider W and Viehöver W (eds) Handbuch Sozialwissenschaftliche Diskursanalyse. Opladen, Leske + Budrich Verlag, Band 2:
Forschungspraxis, pp 457-494

Doolin B (2003) Narratives of change: discourse, technology and organization. Organization 10(4), pp 751-770

Dozier DM, Grunig L, J. G (1995) Manager's guide to excellence in public relations and communication management. Mahwah, New Jersey, Lawrence Erlbaum Associates

Drucker PF (1974) Management. Oxford, Butterworth-Heinemann

Dunford R, Jones D (2000) Narrative in strategic change. Human Relations 53(9), pp 1207-1226

Dutton JE, Fahey L, Narayanan VK (1983) Towards understanding strategic issue diagnosis. Strategic Management Journal 4(4), pp 307-323

Dutton JE, Dukerich JM (1991) Keeping an eye on the mirror: image and identity in organizational adaptation. Academy of Management Journal 34, pp 514-554

Dutton JE, Ashford SJ, O'Neill RM, et al. (2001) Moves that matter: issue selling and organizational change. Academy of Management Journal 44(4), pp 716-736

Dyer WGJ, Wilkins AL (1991) Better stories, not better constructs, to generate better theory: a rejoinder to Eisenhardt. Academy of Management Review 16(3), pp 613-619

Easton G (2002) Marketing - a critical realist approach. Journal of Business Research 55, pp 103-109

Eberhardt S (1998) Wertorientierte Unternehmensführung: der modifizierte Stakeholder-Ansatz. Wiesbaden, Deutscher Universitäts-Verlag

Edwards JA (2003) The transcription of discourse. In: Schiffrin D, Tannen D and Hamilton H (eds) The handbook of discourse analysis. Malden, Blackwell Publishing, pp 321-348

Einwiller S, Will M (2002) Towards an integrated approach to corporate branding - an empirical study. Corporate Communications: an International Journal 7(2), pp 100-109

Einwiller S, Prykop C, Ingenhoff D (2003) Issues management and corporate branding: combining two concepts to enhance corporate reputation. Proceedings of the 8th International Conference on Corporate and Marketing Communications, London Metropolitan University, April 7th-8th

Eisenhardt KM (1989) Building theories from case study research. Academy of Management Review 14(4), pp 532-550

Eisenhardt KM (2001) Strategy as strategic decision making. In: Cusumano MA and Markides CC (eds) Strategic thinking for the next economy. San Francisco, Jossey-Bass, pp 85-102

Elliott R (2004) Making up people: consumption as a symbolic vocabulary for the construction of identity. In: Ekström KM and Brembeck H (eds) Elusive consumption. Oxford, Berg, pp 129-143

Fairclough N (1992) Discourse and social change. Cambridge, Polity Press

Fairclough N (1993) Critical discourse analysis and the marketization of public discourse: the universities. Discourse & Society 4(2), pp 133-168

Fairclough N (1997) Critical Discourse Analysis: The critical study of language. London, Longman

Fairclough N, Wodak R (1997) Critical discourse analysis. In: Mumby DK and Clair RP (eds) Discourse as social interaction. London, SAGE Publications, Vol. 2, pp 258-284

Fairclough N (2003) Analysing discourse - textual analysis for social research. London, Routledge

Fairclough N, Jessop B, Sayer A (2004) Critical realism and semiosis. In: Joseph J and Roberts JM (eds) Realism discourse and deconstruction. London, Routledge, pp 23-42

Feldman MS, March JG (1981) Information as signal and symbol. Administrative Science Quarterly 26, pp 171-186

Feldman MS (2000) Organizational routines as a source of continuous change. Organization Science 11(6), pp 611-629

Fetterman DM (1989) Ethnography step by step. SAGE Publications, London

Fielding NG (2002) Automating the ineffable: qualitative software and the meaning of qualitative software. In: May T (eds) Qualitative research in action. London, SAGE Publications, pp 161-178

Fitch KL (1998) Text and context: a problematic distinction in ethnography. Research on Language and Social Interaction 31(1), pp 91-107

Ford JD, Ford LW (1995) The role of conversations in producing intentional change in organizations. Academy of Management Review 20(3), pp 541-570

Ford JD, Ford LW, McNamara RT (2002) Resistance and the background conversations of change. Journal of Organizational Change 15(2), pp 105-121

Fournier S (1998) Consumers and their brands: developing relationship theory in consumer research. Journal of Consumer Research 24(March), pp 343-373

Freeman RE (1984) Strategic management: a stakeholder approach. Boston, Pitman Publishing

Frooman J (1999) Stakeholder influence strategies. Academy of Management Review 24, pp 191-205

Fulop L, Linstead S, Lilley S, et al. (2004) Decision making in organizations. In: Linstead S, Fulop L and Lilley S (eds) Management and organization - a critical text. Basingstoke, Palgrave Macmillan, pp 462-494

Gergen KJ (1994) Realities and relationships: soundings in social construction. Cambridge, MA, Harvard University Press

Gergen KJ (2001) Social construction in context. London, SAGE Publications

Gergen KJ, Thatchenkery T (2001) Organizational science in a postmodern context. In: Gergen KJ (eds) Social construction in context. London, SAGE Publications, pp 149-168

Gibbons PT (2002) A structuration approach to the resource and capability based view of the firm. Paper presented at the EURAM 2002 conference, May 5th-11th, Stockholm, pp 1-12

Gill J, Johnson P (2002) Research methods for managers. London, SAGE Publications

Gioia DA (1998) From individual to organizational identity. In: Whetten DA and Godfrey PC (eds) Identity in organizations: building theory through conversations. Thousand Oaks, SAGE Publications, pp 17-31

Gladwell M (2002) The tipping point. New York, Little, Brown and Company

Godin S (2003) Purple cow: transform your business by being remarkable. New York, Penguin Group

Grant D, Keenoy T, Oswick C (1998) Discourse and organization. London, SAGE Publications

Grant D, Keenoy T, Oswick C (2001) Organizational discourse: key contributions and challenges. International Studies of Management and Organization 31(3), pp 5-24

Grant D, Hardy C, Oswick C, et al. (2004) Introduction: Organizational discourse: Exploring the field. In: Grant D, Hardy C, Oswick C and Putnam LL (eds) The SAGE handbook of organizational discourse. London, SAGE Publications, pp 136

Grant RM (1995) Contemporary strategy analysis - concepts, techniques and applications. London, Blackwell

Grant RM (1996) Prospering in dynamically-competitive environments: organizational capability as knowledge integration. Organization Science 7(4), pp 375-387

Gray B (1991) Collaborating: finding common ground for multiparty problems. San Francisco, Jossey-Bass

Grunig JE, Hunt T (1984) Managing public relations. Fort Worth, Holt, Rinehart and Winston

Grunig JE (1992) Communication, public relations, and effective organizations: an overview of the book. In: Grunig JE (eds) Excellence in public relations and communication management. Hillsdale, NJ, Lawrence Earlbaum Associates, pp 1-28

Grunig JE, Dozier DM (1992) Excellence in Public Relations and Communication Management. Hillsdale, Lawrence Erlbaum Associates

Grunig LA, Grunig JE, Dozier DM (2002) Excellent public relations and effective organizations: a study of communication management in three countries. Mahwah, New Jersey, Lawrence Erlbaum Associates, Publishers

Gubrium JF, Holstein JA (2003) Analyzing interpretive practice. In: Denzin NK and Lincoln YS (eds) Strategies of qualitative inquiry. Thousand Oaks, SAGE Publications, pp 214-248

Gummesson E (2000) Qualitative methods in management research. London, Sage Publications

Halal W (2000) Corporate community: a theory of the firm uniting profitability and responsibility. Strategy & Leadership 28(2), pp 10-16

Hamel G, Prahalad CK (1992) Letter. Academy of Management Review 11, pp 164-165

Hammersley M, Atkinson P (1995) Ethnography - principles in practice. London, Routledge

Hammersley M, Gomm R, Foster P (2000) Case study and theory. In: Gomm R, Hammersley M and Foster P (eds) Case study method: key issues, key texts. London, SAGE Publications, pp 234-258

Handy C (1992) Balancing corporate power: a new federalist paper. Harvard Business Review (November-December), pp 59-72

Handy C (1994) The age of paradox. Boston, Harvard Business School Press

Hardy C, Palmer I, Phillips N (2000) Discourse as a strategic resource. Human Relations 53(9), pp 1227-1248

Hardy C (2001) Researching organizational discourse. International Studies of Management and Organization 31(3), pp 25-47

Hatch MJ, Schultz M (1997) Relations between organizational culture, identity and image. European Journal of Marketing 31(5/6), pp 356-365

Hatch MJ, Schultz M (2002) The dynamics of organizational identity. Human Relations 55(8), pp 989-1018

Hatch MJ, Schultz M (2003) Bringing the corporation into corporate branding. European Journal of Marketing 37(7/8), pp 1041-1064

Healey P (1997) Collaborative planning: shaping places in fragmented societies. London, MacMillan

Heath RL (1994) Management of corporate communication - from interpersonal contacts to external affairs. Hillsdale, Lawrence Erlbaum Associates

Heath RL (1997) Strategic issues management: organizations and public policy challenges. Thousand Oaks, SAGE Publications

Heath RL (2002) Issues management: its past, present and future. Journal of Public Affairs 2(4), pp 209-214

Heaton L, Taylor JR (2002) Knowledge management and professional work. Management Communication Quarterly 16(2), pp 210-236

Hendry J (2000) Strategic decision making, discourse, and strategy as social practice. Journal of Management Studies 37(7), pp 955-977

Heracleous L, Barrett M (2001) Organizational change as discourse: communicative actions and deep structures in the context of information technology implementation. Academy of Management Journal 44(4), pp 755-778

Heracleous L (2003) Strategy and organization: realizing strategic management. Cambridge, Cambridge University Press

Heugens P (2001) Strategic issues management: implications for corporate performance. Rotterdam, Erasmus Research Institute of Management (ERIM)

Heugens P (2003) Strategic issues management and organizational outcomes. Utrecht, Utrecht School of Economics, Tjalling C. Koopmans Research Institute, Discussion Paper Series 03-11: 1-65.

Hill JW (1992) The making of a public relations man. Lincolnwood, NTC Business Books

Hodge R, Kress G (1988) Social semiotics. Cambridge, Polity Press

Holstein JA, Gubrium JF (1995) The active interview. Thousand Oaks, SAGE Publications

Horton JL (1995) Integrating corporate communication: the cost-effective use of message and medium. London, Quorum Books

Hosking D-M, Haslam P (1997) Managing to relate: organizing as a social process. Career Development International 2(2), pp 85-89

Hosking D-M (2004) Change works: a critical construction. In: Boonstra JJ (ed) Dynamics of organizational change and learning. Chichester, John Wiley & Sons, Ltd., pp 259-276

Hough JR, White MA (2001) Using stories to create change: the object lesson of Frederick Taylor's "pig-tale". Journal of Management 27, pp 585-601

House R, Rousseau D, Thomas-Hunt M (1995) The meso paradigm: a framework for integration of micro and macro organizational behaviour. In: Cummings LL and Staw BM (eds) Research in organizational behavior. Greenwich, CT, JAI, Vol. 17, pp 71-114

Hruby GG (2001) Sociological, postmodern, and new realism perspectives in social constructionism: implications for literacy research. Reading Research Quarterly 36(1), pp 48-62

Humphreys M, Brown AD (2002) Narratives of organizational identity and identification: a case study of hegemony and resistance. Organization Studies 23(3), pp 421-447

Hunt T, Grunig JE (1994) Public relations techniques. Fort Worth, Harcourt Brace College Publishers

Iedema R, Wodak R (1999) Introduction: organizational discourses and practices. Discourse & Society 10, pp 5-19

Ind N (2003) A brand of enlightenment. In: Ind N Beyond branding. London, Kogan Page, pp 1-20

Jackall R (1988) Moral mazes: the world of corporate managers. New York, Oxford University Press

Jackson P (1987) Corporate communication for managers. London, Pitman

Jackson WA (1999) Dualism, duality and the complexity of economic institutions. International Journal of Social Economics 26(4), pp 545-558

Jäger S (2001) Diskurs und Wissen. In: Keller R, Hirseland A, Schneider W and Viehöver W (eds) Handbuch Sozialwissenschaftliche Diskursanalyse. Opladen, Leske + Budrich, Band 1: Theorie und Methoden, pp 81-102

Jäger S (2001) Discourse and knowledge: theoretical and methodological aspects of a critical discourse and dispositive analysis. In: Wodak R and Meyer M (eds) Methods of critical discourse analysis. London, SAGE Publications, pp 32-62

Jäger S (2004) Kritische Diskursanalyse - eine Einführung. Münster, UNRAST-Verlag

Janssens M, Steyaert C (1999) The world in two and a third way out? The concept of duality in organization theory and practice. Scandinavian Journal of Management 15, pp 121-139

Jarzabkowski P (2003) Strategic practices: an activity theory perspective on continuity and change. Journal of Management Studies 40(1), pp 23-55

Jarzabkowski P (2004) Strategy as practice: recursiveness, adaptation, and practices-in-use. Organization Studies 25(4), pp 529-560

Johnson G (1988) Rethinking incrementalism. Strategic Management Journal 6, pp 75-91

Johnson G, Melin L, Whittington R (2003) Micro strategy and strategizing: towards an activity-based view. Journal of Management Studies 40(1), pp 3-22

Johnson P, Duberley J (2000) Understanding management research - an introduction to epistemology. London, Sage Publications

Jones E, Watson B, Gardner J, et al. (2004) Organizational communication: challenges for the new century. Journal of Communication (December), pp 722-750

Kaplan A (1964) The conduct of inquiry. San Francisco, Chandler

Kärreman D (2002) Brand new world? - The management of meaning through branding in a knowledge-intensive firm. Paper presented at the EURAM 2002 conference, May 5th-11th, Stockholm, pp 1-20

Kärreman D, Alvesson M (2004) Cages in tandem: management control, social identity, and identification in a knowledge-intensive firm. Organization 11(1), pp 149-175

Keenoy T, Oswick C, Grant D (1997) Organizational discourse: text and context. Organization 4(2), pp 147-157

Kieser A (1998) Über die allmähliche Verfertigung der Organisation beim Reden. Organisieren als Kommunizieren. Industrielle Beziehungen 5(1), pp 45-74

Kieser A, Hegele C, Klimmer M (1998) Kommunikation im organisatorischen Wandel. Stuttgart, Schäffer-Poeschel Verlag

Kieser A (2002) Max Webers Analyse der Bürokratie. In: Kieser A Organisationstheorien. Stuttgart, W. Kohlhammer GmbH, 39-64

Kimmel AJ (1988) Ethics and values in applied social research. Newbury Park, SAGE Publications

King N (2004) Using templates in the thematic analysis of text. In: Cassell C and Symon G (eds) Essential guide to qualitative methods in organizational research. London, SAGE Publications, pp 256-270

Kirchner K (2001) Integrierte Unternehmenskommunikation - Theoretische und empirische Bestandsaufnahme und eine Analyse amerikanischer Großunternehmen. Wiesbaden, Gabler-Verlag

Kirsch W (1997) Kommunikatives Handeln, Autopoiese, Rationalität - Kritische Aneignungen im Hinblick auf eine evolutionäre Organisationstheorie. München, Verlag Barbara Kirsch

Kirsch W (1997) Wegweiser zur Konstruktion einer evolutionären Theorie der strategischen Führung. München, Kirsch Verlag

Kitchen PJ (2004) Corporate reputation. In: Oliver SM (eds) Handbook of corporate communication and public relations: pure and applied. London, Routledge, pp 265-276

Knights D, Morgan G (1990) The concept of strategy in sociology: a note of dissent. Sociology 24(3), pp 475-483

Knights D, Morgan G (1991) Corporate strategy, organizations, and subjectivity: a critique. Organisation Studies 12(2), pp 251-273

Knoblauch H (2001) Diskurs, Kommunikation und Wissensoziologie. In: Keller R, Hirseland A, Schneider W and Viehöver W (eds) Handbuch Sozialwissenschatliche Diskursanalyse. Opladen, Leske+Budrich, Band 1: Theorien und Methoden, pp 207-223

Knox S, Bickerton D (2003) The six conventions of corporate branding. European Journal of Marketing 37(7/8), pp 998-1016

Kodama M (2005) Knowledge creation through networked strategic communities: case studies on new product development in Japanese companies. Long Range Planning 38, pp 27-49

Kogut B, Zander U (1996) What firms do? Coordination, identity, and learning. Organization Science 7(5), pp 502-518

Kostova T, Roth K (2002) Adoption of an organizational practice by subsidiaries of multinational corporations: institutional and relational effects. Academy of Management Journal 45(1), pp 215-233

Kreiner GE, Ashforth BE (2004) Evidence toward an expanded model of organizational identification. Journal of Organizational Behavior 25, pp 1-27

Kreps GL (1990) Organizational communication. New York, Longman

Krippendorf K (1994) Der verschwundene Bote. In: Merten K, Schmidt SJ and Weischenberg S (eds) Einführung in die Kommunikationswissenschaft. Münster, Lit, Vol. 1: Grundlagen der Kommunikationswissenschaft, pp 79-113

Kristeva J (1967) Bachtine, le mot, le dialogue et le roman. Critique 33, pp 438-465

Kuhn T (1997) The discourse of issues management: a genre of organizational communication. Communication Quarterly 45(3), pp 188-210

Kuhn T, Nelson N (2002) Reengineering identity: a case study of multiplicity and duality in organizational identification. Management Communication Quarterly 16(1), pp 5-38

Kujala J (2005) Developing measures for managers' stakeholder orientation: a business ethics perspective. In: Seppä M, Hannula M, Järvelin A-M et al (eds) Frontiers of e-Business Research 2004. Tampere, Tampere University of Technology (TUT) and University of Tampere (UTA), Vol. II, pp 561-571

Kunda G (1992) Engineering culture: control and commitment in a high-tech corporation. Philadelphia, Temple University Press

Kvale S (1996) Interviews: an introduction to qualitative research interviewing. Thousand Oaks, SAGE Publications

Langer R (1999) Towards a constructivist communication theory? Report from Germany. Nordicom Information (1-2), pp 75-86

Larkin TJ, Larkin S (1994) Communicating change - how to win employee support for new business directions. New York, McGraw-Hill, Inc.

Larsen MH (2000) Managing the corporate story. In: Schultz M, Hatch MJ and Larsen MH (eds) The expressive organization: linking identity, reputation, and the corporate brand. Oxford, Oxford University Press

Larson GS, Pepper GL (2003) Strategies for managing multiple organizational identifications. Management Communication Quarterly 16(4), pp 528-557

Law J (2004) After method: mess in social science research. London, Routledge

Lechner C, Müller-Stewens G (2000) Strategy process research: What do we know, what should we know? In: Dahiya SB The current state of business disciplines. Rohtak, Spellbound

Lehtimäki H, Kujala J (2005) Strategising in multi-voiced business settings. In: Seppä M, Hannula M, Järvelin A-M et al (eds) Frontiers of e-Business Research 2004. Tampere, Tampere University of Technology (TUT) and University of Tampere (UTA), Vol. II, pp 534-545

Lev B (2001) Intangibles - management, measurement, and reporting. Washington, The Brookings Institution

Levin M (2004) Organizing change processes: cornerstones, methods, and strategies. In: Boonstra JJ (ed) Dynamics of organizational change and learning. Chichester, John Wiley & Sons, Ltd., pp 71-84

Lincoln YS, Guba EG (2000) The only generalization is: there is no generalization. In: Gomm R, Hammersley M and Foster P (eds) Case study method: key issues, key texts. London, SAGE Publications, pp 27-44

Lindkvist L, Llewelyn S (2003) Accountability, responsibility and organization. Scandinavian Journal of Management 19, pp 251-273

Linell P (1998) Approaching dialogue: talk, interaction and contexts in dialogical perspectives. Amsterdam, John Benjamins Publishing Company

Linstead S (2004) Managing culture. In: Linstead S, Fulop L and Lilley S (eds) Management and organization - a critical text. Basingstoke, Palgrave Macmillan, pp 93-122

Linstead S, Linstead A (2004) Managing change. In: Linstead S, Fulop L and Lilley S (eds) Management and organization: a critical text. Basingstoke, Palgrave Macmillan, pp 422-461

Louro MJ, Cunha PV (2001) Brand management paradigms. Journal of Marketing Management 17, pp 849-875

Mantovani G, Spagnolli A (2000) Imagination and culture: what is it like being in cyberspace? Mind, Culture and Activity 7(3), pp 217-226

Markides CC (1999) A dynamic view of strategy. Sloan Management Review(Spring 1999), pp 55-63

Mast C (2002) Unternehmenskommunikation - ein Leitfaden. Stuttgart, Lucius und Lucius

May T (2002) Introduction: transformation in principles and practice. In: May T Qualitative research in action. London, SAGE Publications, pp 1-14

McAuley J (2004) Hermeneutic understanding. In: Cassell C and Symon G (eds) Essential guide to qualitative methods in organizational research. London, SAGE Publications, pp 192-202

McCurdy DW, Spradley JP, Shandy DJ (2005) The cultural experience: ethnography in complex society. Long Grove, Waveland Press, Inc.

Miles MB, Huberman AM (1994) Qualitative data analysis; an expanded sourcebook. Thousand Oaks, SAGE Publications

Mintzberg H (1973) The nature of managerial work. New York, Harper & Row, Publishers

Mintzberg H (1979) The structuring of organizations: a sythesis of research. Englewood Cliffs, NJ, Prentice-Hall

Mintzberg H, Waters J, Pettigrew A, et al. (1990) Studying deciding: an exchange of views between Mintzberg and Waters, Pettigrew and Butler. Organization Studies 11(1), pp 1-16

Mintzberg H (1994) Rounding out the manager's job. Sloan Management Review 36(1), pp 11-26

Mintzberg H (1999) The structuring of organizations. In: Mintzberg H, Quinn JB and Ghoshal S (eds) The strategy process (revised European edition). Harlow, Person Education, pp 332-353

Mintzberg H (1999) The diversified organization. In: Mintzberg H, Quinn JB and Ghoshal S (eds) The strategy process (revised European edition). Harlow, Pearson Education, pp 646-661

Mintzberg H, Lampel J (1999) Reflecting on the strategy process. Sloan Management Review(Spring 1999), pp 21-30

Moore J (2003) Authenticity. In: Ind N (ed) Beyond branding. London, Kogan Page, pp 104-121

Morgan G (1980) Paradigms, metaphors, and puzzle solving in organization theory. Administrative Science Quarterly 25, pp 605-620

Morgan JM, Reynolds CM, Nelson TJ, et al. (2004) Tales from the fields: sources of employee identification in agribusiness. Management Communication Quarterly 17(3), pp 360-395

Müller-Stewens G, Lechner C (2001) Strategisches Management - Wie strategische Initiativen zum Erfolg führen. Stuttgart, Schäffer-Poeschel

Müller-Stewens G, Lechner C, Stahl H (2001) Die Gestaltung von Stakeholder-Beziehungen als Grundlage jedes Grenzmanagements. In: Hinterhuber H and Stahl H (eds) Fallen die Unternehmensgrenzen? Beiträge zur Aussenorientierung der Unternehmensführung. Renningen-Malsheim, Unknown, pp 270-291

Mumby DK, Clair RP (1997) Organizational discourse. In: van Dijk TA (ed) Discourse as social interaction. London, SAGE Publications, Vol. 2, pp 181-205

Münch U, Meerwaldt K (2002) Charakteristika des Föderalismus. Informationen zur politischen Bildung (275), pp 3-8

Mutch A (1999) Critical realism, managers and information. British Journal of Management 10, pp 323-333

Nahapiet J, Ghoshal S (1998) Social capital, intellectual capital and organizational advantage. Academy of Management Review 23, pp 242-267

Nandhakumar J, Jones M (1997) Too close for comfort? Distance and engagement in interpretive information systems research. Information Systems Journal 7, pp 109-131

Näsi J (1995) What is stakeholder thinking? A snapshot of a social theory of the firm. In: Näsi J (ed) Understanding stakeholder thinking. Helsinki, LSR-Publications, pp 19-32

Needle D (2004) Business in context: an introduction to business and its environment. London, Thomson Learning

Nightingale DJ, Cromby J (2002) Social constructionism as ontology: exposition and example. Theory & Psychology 12(5), pp 701-713

Normann R (2001) Reframing business. Chichester, John Wiley & Sons, Ltd.

Orlikowski WJ, Yates J (1994) Genre repertoire: the structuring of communicative practices in organizations. Administrative Science Quarterly 39, pp 541-574

Orlikowski WJ (2002) Knowing in practice: enacting a collective capability in distributed organizing. Organization Science 13(3), pp 249-273

Orr M (2003) Intertextuality: debates and contexts. Cambridge, Polity Press

Oswick C, Keenoy T, Grant D (1997) Managerial discourses: words speak louder than actions? Journal of Applied Management Studies 6(1), pp 5-12

Owen WF (1984) Interpretive themes in relational communication. Quarterly Journal of Speech 70, pp 274-287

Pajunen K, Näsi J (2005) Stakeholder management as play. In: Seppä M, Hannula M, Järvelin A-M et al (eds) Frontiers of e-Business Research 2004. Tampere, Tampere University of Technology (TUT) and University of Tampere (UTA), Vol. II, pp 520-533

Palmer I, King AW, Kelleher D (2004) Listening to Jack: GE's change conversations with shareholders. Journal of Organizational Change 17(6), pp 593-614

Parker I (Ed. (1998) Social constructionism, discourse and realism. London, SAGE Publications

Parker M (2000) Organizational culture and identity - unity and division at work. London, SAGE Publications

Pettigrew A (1987) Context and action in the transformation of the firm. Journal of Management Studies 24, pp 649-670

Pettigrew A (1990) Longitudinal field research on change: theory and practice. Organization Science 1(3), pp 267-348

Pettigrew A (2003) Strategy as process, power and change. In: Cummings S and Wilson D (eds) Images of strategy. Oxford, Blackwell Publishing Ltd., pp 301-330

Pettigrew A, Massini S (2003) Innovative forms of organizing: trends in Europe, Japan and the USA in the 1990s. In: Pettigrew A, Whittington R, Melin L et al (eds) Innovative forms of organizing. London, SAGE Publications, pp 1-32

Pettigrew AM (1992) The character and significance of strategy process research. Strategic Management Journal 13(Special Issue), pp 5-16

Pettigrew AM (1997) What is a processual analysis? Scandinavian Journal of Management 13(4), pp 337-348

Pettigrew AM, Woodman RM, Cameron KS (2001) Studying organizational change and development: challenges for future research. Academy of Management Journal 44(4), pp 697-713

Phillips N, Hardy C (2002) Discourse analysis: investigating processes of social construction. Thousand Oaks, SAGE Publications

Poland BD (2002) Transcription quality. In: Gubrium JF and Holstein JA (eds) Handbook of interview research. Thousand Oaks, SAGE Publications, pp 629-649

Porter ME (1980) Competitive strategy - techniques for analyzing industries and competitors. New York, Free Press

Porter ME (1985) Competitive advantage: creating and sustaining superior performance. New York, Free Press

Prahalad CK, Hamel G (1990) The core competence of the corporation. Harvard Business Review(May-June), pp 79-91

Prahalad CK, Ramaswamy V (2000) Co-opting customer competence. Harvard Business Review(January-February), pp 79-87

Quirke B (2000) Making the connections: using internal communication to turn strategy into action. Aldershot, Gower Publishing Limited

Rappaport A (1986) Creating shareholder value: the new standard for business performance. New York, Free Press

Reed M (1998) Organizational analysis as discourse analysis: a critique. In: Grant D, Keenoy T and Oswick C (eds) Discourse and organization. London, SAGE Publications

Rindova VP, Fombrun CJ (1999) Constructing competitive advantage: the role of firm-constituent interactions. Strategic Management Journal 20, pp 691-710

Robichaud D, Giroux H, Taylor JR (2004) The metaconversation: the recursive property of language as a key to organizing. Academy of Management Journal 29(4), pp 617-634

Robson C (2002) Real world research. Oxford, Blackwell Publishers

Röttger U (2001) Issues Management - Mode, Mythos oder Managementfunktion? In: Röttger U (ed) Issues Management: Theoretische Konzepte und praktische Umsetzung. Eine Bestandsaufnahme. Wiesbaden, Westdeutscher Verlag, pp 11-39

Rühli E (2000) Strategie ist tot: Es lebe das Neue Strategische Management. In: Hinterhuber HH, Friedrich SA, Al-Ani A and Handlbauer G (eds) Das Neue Strategische Management - Perspektiven und Elemente einer zeitgemäßen Unternehmensführung. Wiesbaden, Gabler, pp 73-90

Ruigrok W, Achtenhagen L, Rüegg-Stürm J, et al. (2000) Hilti AG: Shared leadership and the rise of the communicating organization. In: Pettigrew AM and Fenton EM (eds) The innovating organization. London, SAGE Publications Ltd.

Sánchez-Runde C, Pettigrew AM (2003) Managing dualities. In: Pettigrew AM, Whittington R, Melin L et al (eds) Innovative forms of organizing. London, SAGE Publications, pp 243-250

Schiffrin D (1994) Approaches to discourse. Cambridge, MA, Blackwell

Schiffrin D, Tannen D, Hamilton H Eds.) (2001) The handbook of discourse analysis. Malden, MA, Blackwell Publishing

Schmidt SJ (2004) Unternehmenskultur: die Grundlage für den wirtschaftlichen Erfolg von Unternehmen. Weilerswist, Velbrück Wissenschaft

Schramm WA (1948) Mass communication. Urbana, IL, University of Illinois Press

Schutz A (1973) Collected papers I: the problem of social reality. The Hague, Martinus Nijhoff

Schüz M (2001) Das Aushandeln von Interessen im Spannungsfeld zwischen E-thik und Kommunikation. In: Gerling R, Obermeier O-P and Schüz M (eds) Trends - Issues - Kommunikation. München, Gerling Akademie Verlag, pp 83-116

Schwandt T (1994) Constructivist, interpretivist approaches to human inquiry. In: Denzin NK and Lincoln YS (eds) Handbook of qualitative research. Thousand Oaks, SAGE Publications, pp 118-137

Schwandt TA (1999) On understanding understanding. Qualitative Inquiry 5(4), pp 451-464

Schwaninger M (2001) System theory and cybernetics - a solid basis for transdisciplinarity in management education and research. Kybernetes 30(9/10), pp 1209-1222

Scott CR (1997) Identification with multiple targets in a geographically dispersed organization. Management Communication Quarterly 10(4), pp 491-522

Scott CR, Corman SR, Cheney G (1998) Development of a structurational model of identification in the organization. Communication Theory 8(3), pp 298-336

Scott CR, Connaughton SL, Diaz-Saenz HR, et al. (1999) The impacts of communication and multiple identifications on intent to leave. Management Communication Quarterly 12(3), pp 400-435

Scott SG, Lane VR (2000) A stakeholder approach to organizational identity. Academy of Management Review 25(1), pp 43-62

Seale C (1999) The quality of qualitative research. London, Sage Publications

Seale C (2002) Computer-assisted analysis of qualitative data. In: Gubrium JF and Holstein JA (eds) Handbook of interview research. Thousand Oaks, SAGE Publications, pp 651-694

Seibold DR, Shea CB (2001) Participation and decision making. In: Jablin FM and Putnam LL (eds) The new handbook of organizational communication: advances in theory, research and methods. Thousand Oaks, SAGE Publications, pp 665-703

Shannon C, Weaver W (1949) The mathematical theory of communication. Urbana, IL, University of Illinois Press

Shotter J, Gergen KJ (1994) Social construction: knowledge, self, others, and the continuing conversation. In: Deetz S (ed) Communication yearbook 17. Thousand Oaks, SAGE Publications, pp 3-33

Silverman D (2001) Interpreting qualitative data - methods for analysing talk, text and interaction. London, SAGE Publications

Smircich L, Stubbart C (1985) Strategic management in an enacted world. Academy of Management Review 10(4), pp 724-736

Smith J (2004) A précis of a communicative theory of the firm. Business Ethics: A European Review 13(4), pp 317-331

Soderberg A, Björkman I (2003) From words to action? Socio-cultural integration initiatives in a cross-border merger. In: Soderberg A and Vaara E (eds) Merging across borders: people, cultures and politics. Copenhagen, Copenhagen Business School Press, pp 139-175

Soenen G, Moingeon B (2002) The five facets of collective identities: integrating corporate and organizational identity. In: Moingeon B and Soenen G (eds) Corporate and organizational identities: integrating strategy, marketing, communication and organizational perspectives. London, Routledge, pp 13-34

Spradley JP (1980) Participant observation. New York, Holt, Rinehart & Winston

Stacey RD (1996) Complexity and creativity in organisations. San Francisco, Berret Koehler Publishers

Stacey RD (2003) Strategic management and organisational dynamics. Harlow, Pearson Education Limited

Stake RE (1995) The art of case study research. Thousand Oaks, SAGE Publications

Stake RE (2003) Case studies. In: Denzin NK and Lincoln YS Strategies of qualitative enquiry. Thousand Oaks, Sage Publications, pp 134-164

Starkey K (2002) Andrew Pettigrew on executives and strategy: an interview by Kenneth Starkey. European Management Journal 20(1), pp 20-34

Steyn B (2003) From strategy to corporate communication strategy: a conceptualisation. Journal of Communication Management 8(2), pp 168-183

Streatfield PJ (2001) The paradox of control in organizations. London, Routledge

Suchman MC (1995) Managing legitimacy: strategic and institutional approaches. Academy of Management Journal 20, pp 571-610

Sveningsson S, Alvesson M (2003) Managing managerial identities: organizational fragmentation, discourse and identity struggle. Human Relations 56(10), pp 1163-1193

Sztompka P (1991) Society in action: the theory of social becoming. Cambridge, Polity Press

Taylor BC (1999) Browsing the culture: membership and intertextuality at a Mormon bookstore. Studies in Cultures, Organizations and Societies 5, pp 61-95

Taylor JR (1993) Rethinking the theory of organizational communication. Norwood, NJ, Ablex Publishing

Taylor JR, Cooren F, Giroux N, et al. (1996) The communication basis of organization: between the conversation and the text. Communication Theory 6(1), pp 1-39

Taylor JR (1999) The other side of rationality: socially distributed cognition. Management Communication Quarterly 13(2), pp 317-326

Taylor JR, Van Every EJ (2000) The emergent organization: communication as its site and surface. Mahwah, NJ, Lawrence Erlbaum Associates

Taylor JR (2002) Toward a theory of imbrication and organizational communication. The American Journal of Semiotics 17(2), pp 269-298

Taylor JR (2004) Dialogue as the search for sustainable organizational co-orientation. In: Anderson R, Baxter LA and Cissna KN (eds) Dialogue: theorizing difference in communication studies. Thousand Oaks, SAGE Publications, pp 125-140

Tedlock B (2003) Ethnography and ethnographic representation. In: Denzin NK and Lincoln YS (eds) Strategies of qualitative enquiry. Thousand Oaks, Sage Publications, pp 165-213

Teece DJ, Pisano G, Nelson RR (2000) Dynamic capabilities and strategic management. In: Dosi G, Nelson RR and Winter SG (eds) The nature and dynamics of organizational capabilities. Oxford, Oxford University Press, pp 334-362

Thomas P, 1999. Stakeholders and strategic management: the misappropriation of discourse. Paper presented at the Critical Management Studies Conference, July 14th - 16th, Manchester

Touraine A (1995) Critique of modernity. Oxford, Blackwell

Tsoukas H (1997) The tyranny of light - the temptations and the paradoxes of the information society. Futures 29(9), pp 827-843

Tsoukas H (2001) Re-viewing organization. Human Relations 54(1), pp 7-12

Tsoukas H, Chia R (2002) On organization becoming: rethinking organizational change. Organization Science 13(5), pp 567-582

Tuomi I (2002) Networks of innovation: change and meaning in the age of the Internet. Oxford, Oxford University Press

Urde M (1999) Brand orientation: a mindset for building brands into strategic resources. Journal of Marketing Management 15, pp 117-133

Urde M (2001) Core value-based corporate brand building. European Journal of Marketing 37(7/8), pp 1017-1040

Vaara E, Kleymann B, Seristö H (2004) Strategies as discursive constructions: the case of airline alliances. Journal of Management Studies 41(1), pp 1-35

Van de Ven AH, Poole MS (1995) Explaining development and change in organizations. Academy of Management Review 20, pp 510-540

van Maanen J (1988) Tales of the field: on writing ethnography. Chicago, The University of Chicago Press

van Maanen J (1995) Representation in ethnography. 1995, Thousand Oaks

van Riel CMB (1992) Principles of corporate communication. London, Prentice-Hall

van Riel CMB (1997) Research in corporate communications: overview of an emerging field. Management Communication Quarterly 11(2), pp 288-309

van Riel CMB (2001) Corporate branding management. Thexis 4, pp 12-16

Varey RJ, White J (2000) The corporate communication system of managing. Corporate Communications: an international journal 5(1), pp 5-11

Varey RJ (2001) Responsive and responsible communication practices: a pluralist perspective. In: Kitchen PJ Schultz, Don E (eds) Raising the corporate umbrella - corporate communications in the 21st century. Basingstoke, Palgrave, pp 62-81

Varey RJ, Karklins G (2001) The corporate brand and corporate communication: the corporate brand dialog box (CBDB). Thexis 4, pp 38-41

Varey RJ (2002) Marketing communication: principles and practice. London, Routledge

Vehkaperä M (2005) Corporate social responsibility in CSR reports. In: Seppä M, Hannula M, Järvelin A-M et al (eds) Frontiers of e-Business Research 2004. Tampere, Tampere University of Technology (TUT) and University of Tampere (UTA), Vol. II, pp 572-580

von Krogh G, Roos J (1995) Conversation management. European Management Journal 4, pp 390-394

Wartick SL, Heugens P (2003) Guest editorial: future directions for issues management. Corporate Reputation Review 6(1), pp 7-18

Watson TJ (1994) In search of management: culture, chaos and control in managerial work. London, International Thomson Business Press

Watson TJ (1997) Languages within languages: a social constructionist perspective on multiple managerial discourses. In: Bargiela-Chiappini F and Harris S (eds) The languages of business: an international perspective. Edinburgh, Edinburgh University Press, pp 211-227

Watson TJ (1997) Theorizing managerial work: a pragmatic pluralist approach to interdisciplinary research. British Journal of Management 8, pp 3-8

Weeks J (2004) Unpopular culture: the ritual of complaint in a British bank. Chicago, The University of Chicago Press

Weick K (1979) The social psychology of organizing. Reading, MA, Addison-Wesley

Weick KE (1987) Theorizing about organizational communication. In: Porter LM, Putnam LL, Roberts KH and Jablin FM (eds) Handbook of organizational communication. Beverly Hills, CA, SAGE Publications

Weick KE (1988) Enacted sensemaking in crisis situations. Journal of Management Studies 25(4), pp 203-317

Weick KE (1995) Sensemaking in organizations. Thousand Oaks, SAGE Publications

Weick KE, Quinn RE (1999) Organizational change and development. Annual Review of Psychology 50, pp 361-386

Weick KE (2003) Theory and practice in the real world. In: Tsoukas H and Knudsen C (eds) The Oxford handbook of organization theory. Oxford, Oxford University Press, pp 453-475

Weick KE (2004) A bias for conversation: acting discursively in organizations. In: Grant D, Hardy C, Oswick C and Putnam LL (eds) The SAGE handbook of organizational discourse. London, SAGE Publications, pp 405-412

Weiss RS (1994) Learning from strangers: the art and method of qualitative interview studies. New York, The Free Press

Wenger E (1998) Communities of practice: learning, meaning, and identity. Cambridge, Cambridge University Press

Westwood R, Linstead S Eds.) (2001) The language of organization. London, SAGE Publications

Whittington R (1996) Strategy as practice. Long Range Planning 29(5), pp 731-735

Whittington R, Pettigrew A, Peck S, et al. (1999) Change and complementarities in the new competitive landscape: a European panel study, 1992-1996. Organization Science 10(5), pp 583-600

Whittington R (2001) What is strategy - and does it matter? London, Thomson Learning

Whittington R (2001) Learning to strategise: problems of practice. SKOPE Research Paper 20

Whittington R (2002) Practice perspectives on strategy: unifying an developing a field. Academy of Management Proceedings, pp C1-C6

Whittington R (2002) Corporate structure: from policy to practice. In: Pettigrew A, Thomas H and Whittington R (eds) Handbook of strategy and management. London, SAGE Publications, pp 113-138

Whittington R, Melin L (2003) The challenge of organizing/strategizing. In: Pettigrew AM, Whittington R, Melin L et al (eds) Innovative forms of organizing. London, SAGE Publications, pp 35-48

Whittington R (2004) The practice of organising: negotiating the routinisation and standardisation traps. Academy of Management Best Conference Paper, pp F1-F6

Williams M (2002) Generalization in interpretive research. In: May T Qualitative research in action. London, SAGE Publications, pp 125-143

Winch P (1958) The idea of social science. Oxford, Blackwell

Wittgenstein L (1967) Philosophical investigations. Oxford, Blackwell

Wright LL (1996) Qualitative international management research. In: Punnet BJ and Shenkar O (eds) Handbook of international management research. Oxford, Blackwell

Yates J, Orlikowski WJ (1992) Genres of organizational communication: a structurational approach to studying communication and media. Academy of Management Review 17(2), pp 299-326

Yates J, Orlikowski WJ (2002) Genre systems: structuring interaction through communicative norms. The Journal of Business Communication 39(1), pp 13-35

Yin RK (1994) Case study research: design and methods. Thousand Oaks, California, SAGE Publications

Zerfaß A (1996) Unternehmensführung und Öffentlichkeitsarbeit - Grundlegung einer Theorie der Unternehmenskommunikation und Öffentlichkeitsarbeit. Opladen, Westdeutscher Verlag

Znaniecki F (1934) The method of sociology. New York, Farrar and Rinehart

Index

Printing: Krips bv, Meppel
Binding: Stürtz, Würzburg